Spago
Desserts

Spago Desserts

MARY BERGIN
& JUDY GETHERS

PHOTOGRAPHS BY BRENT LINDSTROM

RANDOM HOUSE ■ NEW YORK

Library of Congress Cataloging-in-Publication Data
Bergin, Mary.
Spago desserts / by Mary Bergin and Judy Gethers.——1st ed.
p. cm.
ISBN 0-679-42248-X
1. Desserts.   2. Spago (Restaurant)   I. Gethers, Judy.
II. Title.
TX773.B448   1994
641.8'6—dc20   94-14910

Manufactured in the United States of America
24689753
First Edition

BOOK DESIGN BY BARBARA M. MARKS

For all the Spago customers
who have enjoyed our desserts
throughout the years

Acknowledgments

When this book was just a notion, there were many people who helped make it a reality. It was Judy Gethers who first suggested that I do a Spago dessert book. After weeks of telling her I didn't have the time, she convinced me that with her help, I could do it. (She is also the kind of woman who does not take no for an answer.) So, to Judy, my partner and very dear friend, thanks for the push in the right direction.

It's difficult to put a thank-you into words for people like Barbara Lazeroff and Wolfgang Puck, because they are much more than employers. They have encouraged me to strive for higher goals and taught me a sense of family values, as well as how to keep focused on my work amid chaos.

Having a full-time career and writing a cookbook would not have been possible without the understanding of my children. So, thank you, Anthony and Jackie, for being great! And thanks to the members of my family, Kathy, John, Fran, Bobby, and Patti, who gave me a boost when I needed it most.

I would like to thank Eric Escalante for his artistic talents, as well as my entire pastry staff at Spago—Christophe Ithurritze, Manny, Ronbo, Zinna, Victor, and José. Thanks to David Robins, executive chef of Spago Las Vegas; Tom Kaplan, with whom I have worked since Spago Los Angeles first opened; Brant Holland and Stan Carroll; Patti Samuels; Kristen; Rhonda; Johnny Romaglia; Michael Dargin; Lois Guillerm; Annie and David Gingrass; and Nancy Silverton, my mentor and very good friend.

Thanks to Katherine Briefs for the many hours of baby-sitting my children so that I could work on the book. And a very special thanks to Deena. Thanks to Belle, for being there for Judy and lifting my spirits on many occasions.

Thanks to Dean Simon, owner and operator of CPT Produce, who provided the fruit for the photographs as well as the exceptional produce that we use at Spago.

To our agents, Maureen and Eric Lasher, thanks for your guidance and perseverance.

Thanks to Jason Epstein, our editor, for being so patient.

Years ago, when I first became interested in baking, I bought every Maida Heatter dessert book I could find. She was, and still is, the Queen of Desserts. Judy and I have become friends with Maida, and we continue to be inspired by her.

Mary Bergin

Contents

Preface

At Spago on any given night, you can hear the oohing and aahing at the display of pastries attractively arranged on one of the dessert tables. There might be a luscious chocolate cake, a hazelnut mousse cake, a white chocolate rum raisin cheesecake, an apple pie, a pecan pie, a plum almond tart, an assortment of cookies, not to mention all those desserts reserved in the refrigerator or freezer to be delivered upon request. After viewing these pastries, you understand why, even after the most filling meal, diners cannot resist ordering at least one or two of them.

Many of these delectable concoctions were developed from basic recipes, and once you have mastered them, you can then produce a number of the desserts served at Spago.

Building on the basic Chocolate Chiffon Cake, there is a recipe for a simple layer cake, a sumptuous Austrian Chocolate Cake, and, for that special occasion, an absolutely spectacular Opera Cake.

The Lemon Chiffon Cake, baked in a bundt pan, can be filled with fresh berries and topped with Crème Brûlée. The Buttermilk Cake can be layered with a Strawberry Bavarian Cream.

Spago's Cheesecake can be poured into an Apricot Macaroon Crust and served with a Blueberry Sauce, or into a Butter Crunch Crust and topped with Macadamia Brittle.

Brioche can be baked as bread, the significant ingredient in our Bread Pud-dings. The unbaked dough can be formed into filled rolls or buns and used as the lining for Ricotta Fig Tart.

The Puff Pastry chapter provides step-by-step directions for perfect pastry. When you have mastered the technique, you will be able to make a variety of desserts. You can spoon Crème Brûlée into a shell of puff pastry, or use it to top an Apple Pear Tarte Tatin, or layer a Berry Napoleon.

Even the basic Pâte Sucré (sweet pastry dough) and Pie Dough have variations that add to the flavor. After lining the pie plate or tart pan, you can choose your favorite fillings. We have included Fruit-filled pies, Brown Butter Tarts, Custard Tarts, and Nut Tarts, all Spago staples.

Most of the ingredients called for in the recipes are readily available. How-ever, for a few hard-to-find items, we have included a list of purveyors (see page 263) who usually stock special products.

We have tried to make the recipes simple to understand and, more important, simple to follow. Where the written word might not make the directions clear enough, there are illustrations. Throughout the book we have emphasized proper techniques, the very foundation of good baking. To that end, it is important to read through the chapters on Techniques and Cooking Terms and Ingredients and refer to them as necessary. When ready to proceed, read through the recipe of your choice, making certain that you understand the directions. Assemble all the required ingredients and equipment, set them in front of you, and then continue. You will be pleasantly surprised to find that this small amount of preparation before you start will make baking less of a chore and more of an enjoyable experience.

We are certain that with a little effort, you will be able to produce many of the same desserts that we serve at Spago with ease, with confidence, and with suc-cess.

Foreword

I can't think of two more talented, more creative, or nicer people in the cooking world than Mary Bergin and Judy Gethers. The fact that they are now culinary accomplices should prove a joy to cooks and cookbook readers everywhere.

Mary began working in Spago's pastry kitchen the day we opened the restaurant in 1982, and took over as pastry chef in 1987. She met the challenge, took risks, experimented, perfected, and achieved extraordinary results. Such desserts as her sublime Warm Chocolate Truffle Cake, her homey Peach Berry Cobbler, and her cool, refreshing fruit sorbets—not to mention her wonderful assortment of cookies, which I love even with my espresso in the morning—garnered her praise from critics and guests alike. When we began planning the opening of Spago Las Vegas in 1992, I could not think of a more capable person to help me orchestrate and design the pastry kitchen of this our largest restaurant. Luckily for me—and for our Las Vegas customers— Mary agreed and eagerly went off to make this culinary desert town a sweeter and more delectable oasis.

Judy and I have known each other for many years, and I have valued her knowledge and advice as the collaborator on each of my cookbooks. She was the director of the famous Ma Cuisine cooking school in Los Angeles and is the author of four delicious cookbooks herself. There are different kinds of cooks and cookbook writers. Some work entirely by instinct, others must be precise down to the most minute pinch of flour. Some can function in chaos, others need the most pristine surroundings imaginable. One of the things that makes Judy so special is that she seems to be able to work under any circumstance, anywhere and anytime. Her enthusiasm and love of food and cooking show up on every page of this wonderful book.

Desserts are the grand finale to a memorable meal, and we are fortunate that Mary and Judy share with us their passion, talent, imagination, and love in this collection of great recipes.

Suggested Equipment*

- ■ **APPLE CORER**
- ■ **BAKING DISH:** 8½ x 11 inches
- ■ **BAKING PANS (2):** We recommend using parchment paper for most baking, so a coated pan is not necessary. A 12 x 17 x 1-inch pan will accommodate most recipes in this book. A heavy-duty stainless pan will last longer than aluminum and will not warp when baking at high temperatures.
- ■ **BLENDER**
- ■ **BOWLS, MIXING:** Various sizes—small, medium, and large; glass, stainless, or heavy-duty plastic. The glass and plastic bowls can be used for mixing room-temperature or chilled ingredients, the stainless bowls for melting or whisking ingredients over hot water. A copper bowl for whipping egg whites is optional and not necessary.
- ■ **CAKE PANS:** 8- and/or 9-inch round, 8- or 9-inch square
- ■ **CAKE RACKS (2):** 11 x 17 inches is the most useful size because it will hold many cookies and different-sized cakes.
- ■ **CANDY THERMOMETER**
- ■ **CARDBOARD CAKE ROUNDS:** Can be purchased at cookware supply shops. Rounds are slipped under cakes before decorating or placing on serving plate.
- ■ **COFFEE FILTERS:** Large, optional. These are used to line tart and pie pans when baking blind. They are an alternative to parchment paper and can be reused.
- ■ **COOKIE CUTTERS:** 2½, 3½, and 4 inch, fluted or plain-edged.

---

* All the recipes in this book were tested on a gas stove. Cooking times may vary on an electric stovetop, so if your stove is electric, you may have to make some timing adjustments.

■ **COOKIE SHEETS:** Nonstick surface is optional, since you will be lining pan with parchment paper. We suggest having at least 2 cookie sheets. One can be cooling while the other is being used.

■ **DOUBLE BOILER:** Optional (heatproof bowl set over saucepan will do)

■ **DOUGH SCRAPER:** Optional. They come in heavy-duty plastic or stainless, with wooden handles.

■ **DREDGER:** For sifting powdered sugar or cocoa

■ **ELECTRIC MIXER:** The KitchenAid comes with paddle, whip, and dough hook. Others come with beaters and dough hook. We have specified which attachment to use with each recipe.

■ **FOOD PROCESSOR:** Useful in making purees and some of the pastries

■ **GRATER:** Preferably a box grater

■ **ICE CREAM SCOOP:** For scooping ice creams and sorbets. Invest in either a stainless-steel scoop with spring action or dippers made of cast aluminum.

■ **KNIVES:**
8- or 10-inch chef's knife
Small paring knife
Long serrated knife

■ **LADLES:** 2- and 4-ounce capacity

■ **LOAF PAN:** $8\frac{1}{2}$ x $3\frac{1}{2}$ x $2\frac{1}{2}$ inches. Pan should not be made of glass.
MINI LOAF PANS: Optional

■ **MEASURING CUPS:**

2 sets for dry ingredients: The cups come in graduated sizes, from $\frac{1}{4}$ to 1 cup. They should have smooth, flat rims to facilitate leveling the ingredient. To level, run a knife or spatula across the top of the cup.

2-cup and 4-cup measuring cups for liquids: These cups have spouts on one end for easier pouring. They come in Pyrex or heavy-duty plastic.

■ **MEASURING SPOONS:** 2 sets

■ **MUFFIN PAN:** 12- or 24-cup capacity
MINI MUFFIN PAN: Optional

■ **OVEN MITT:** This is useful for removing hot pans from oven and for working with saucepans holding ingredients that come to a rolling boil.

■ **OVEN THERMOMETER**

■ **PARCHMENT PAPER**

■ **PASTRY BAGS AND VARIOUS-SIZED TIPS:** The bags should be cloth or soft nylon, 10 or 12 inches long.

■ **PEELER**

■ **PIE PLATES:** 9 and/or 10 inch, preferably Pyrex

■ **PIE WEIGHTS:** These are tiny weights, made of metal or plastic, and can be purchased at cookware or specialty food shops. They are used when pre-baking pie shells to prevent shells from shrinking. Dried beans are equally as effective. Weights and beans can be cooled, removed from the pie plate, stored, and reused as desired.

■ **PLASTIC WRAP**

■ **PROPANE TORCH:** Optional, but extremely useful for many recipes. Follow directions carefully and you will find this tool simple and safe to operate. Torches can be purchased in hardware and/or building supply stores.

■ **ROLLING PIN:** We prefer a French rolling pin without handles, but use whatever is most comfortable for you.

■ **RULER:** Have a 12-inch ruler handy exclusively for kitchen use.

■ **SAUCEPANS:** 1-quart and 2-quart heavy, nonreactive saucepans

■ **SCALE:** A scale that holds 3 pounds of ingredients should be adequate. You may want to get one that registers grams as well as pounds, since some cookbooks list recipes in grams.

■ **SIFTER:** A large fine-mesh strainer is just as useful.

■ **SKILLETS OR SAUTÉ PANS:** 10 and 12 inches

■ **SMALL AND LARGE PASTRY BRUSHES:** The brushes should have soft natural bristles. Do not use brushes with plastic bristles, since these tend to burn or melt. Brand-new paintbrushes are perfect. Brushes can be washed in your dishwasher.

■ **SPATULAS:**
Wide metal spatula
Long, thin spatula
2 large and 2 small rubber spatulas
Offset spatula

■ **SPRINGFORM PANS:** 9 and/or 10 inch

■ **STRAINER, FINE-MESH:** We recommend one with at least a 4-cup capacity with a wooden handle. It will last a long time.

■ **TART PANS WITH REMOVABLE BOTTOMS:** 9- and/or 10-inch, heavy-duty aluminum or, when available, stainless steel

■ **TIMER**

■ **TOWELS:** Keep kitchen towels on hand when baking. Dry, they are more useful than pot holders, and wet, they can be used for cleanups and to help unmold desserts. *Never* use a wet towel to handle a hot pot. Heat is conducted through a wet towel and can burn your hand.

■ **WHIPS (2 BALLOON WHIPS):** These are very convenient when you don't want to or can't use your electric mixer to whip eggs or cream. The thinner and more flexible the wire, the better the whip; the length, 12 to 16 inches, includes the wooden or metal handles.

■ **WOODEN SPOONS:**
2 long-handled
2 short-handled

■ **ZESTER**

Techniques and Cooking Terms

- **BAKE:** To cook with dry heat. Oven should be turned on (preheated) 15 to 30 minutes before baking to allow oven to come to the proper temperature. Using an oven thermometer is a good idea. First, set the rack in the proper place in the oven.
- **BEATING EGGS:** When we say "beat until firm but not dry," it means that the whites should be light and fluffy and stand in soft peaks when the beater is lifted, with drops of moisture clinging to the peaks. A good test is to run your finger lightly through the whites, making a trench that does not run together and still feels smooth. Sugar added to the whites will keep them fluffy until they are ready to be used. Do not beat the batter after whites are folded in. When folding, use a rubber spatula, cutting down into the batter, scraping along the bottom of the bowl and then up to the surface. Repeat (working in the same direction, for maximum volume), gently but quickly, until ingredients are well combined, turning bowl while incorporating whites into the batter. (If there is a large amount of batter, a clean hand works as well as, if not better than, the spatula.)
- **BLANCH:** To place ingredient(s) in boiling water in order to remove fruit peels or to set color. Time depends upon texture of fruit.
- **BLIND BAKE:** This describes the method of partially baking a tart or pie shell before adding the filling, in order to keep the dough's shape. After the shell has been chilled, arrange parchment paper, aluminum foil, or large coffee filters in the pan, pressing down on the paper to fit snugly against the dough. Fill the paper to the top of the tart shell with pie weights (see page XVII) or dried beans and bake according to recipe directions. The paper,

beans, and pie weights can be easily removed and reused again and again. Store paper and weights separately, after cooling, in their own containers.

- **CARAMELIZE:** To cook sugar until it turns golden brown and then, as it continues to cook, a slightly deeper color. It is a technique that requires attention and care. To caramelize sugar with a propane torch, sprinkle the top of the dessert with a thin layer of granulated sugar. Turn on the torch and direct the flame onto the sugar, browning the sugar as you move it across the dessert.

- **CLARIFY BUTTER:** To clarify butter, melt over low heat, evaporating most of the water in the butter and separating the milk solids from the clear liquid. Skim the foam that forms on top and spoon the clear liquid into a clean container. Discard the residue that remains on bottom of pan. Clarified butter can be refrigerated, covered, for up to 1 month and frozen even longer.

- **COULIS:** A thick puree made from raw or cooked fruit. It is used as an accompaniment to hot as well as some cold desserts.

- **CREAMING BUTTER:** To "cream" butter, first remove butter from refrigerator, cut into small pieces, and let come to room temperature. Beat slowly with an electric mixer fitted with a paddle or beaters until the pieces come together. Continue to beat, raising the speed, until the butter is smooth and fluffy. The better the "creaming," the finer the texture of the batter.

- **CURDLE:** In cooking, this refers to a food that separates. Desserts that contain milk and eggs, like custards or ice cream bases, can curdle if cooked over heat that is too high. Curdled food resembles watery cottage cheese.

- **DREDGE:** To sift flour, sugar, or cocoa over a cake.

- **DUST:** To sprinkle with a dry ingredient in order to prevent sticking or to decorate. Baking pans, after being buttered or sprayed, are usually dusted with flour or sugar, the excess removed. Desserts are sometimes dusted with confectioners' sugar or cocoa powder.

- **GARNISH:** For additional eye appeal, desserts are decorated (garnished), sometimes with fruit, sometimes with ice cream or whipped cream or a sprig of fresh mint leaves.

- **GLAZE:** At Spago cakes are often glazed with chocolate. To glaze, warm the chocolate glaze mixture and ladle or spoon over the cake (see Opera Cake, page 15).

- **ICE BATH:** When ingredients need to be cooled down quickly, they are placed in an ice bath. For example, custards used for ice cream are placed in such a bath after being cooked. The hot custard is poured into a heatproof bowl, and the bowl is placed in a larger vessel filled with cold water and ice. As the ice melts, and the custard requires more time to cool, ice should be added to keep the "bath" as cold as possible.

■ **LINING A PASTRY PAN:** Place the pie or tart pan directly in front of you and then roll up dough loosely over rolling pin. Unroll over the pan, being careful that the dough is centered. With your knuckle, gently press dough against the sides and then down on the bottom of the pan. Roll the rolling pin around the outside edge of the pan to trim the overhang. Or use a small paring knife to trim. If there are any tears in the dough, brush lightly with water and press a small piece of the excess dough on the tear. Refrigerate at least 1 hour before baking.

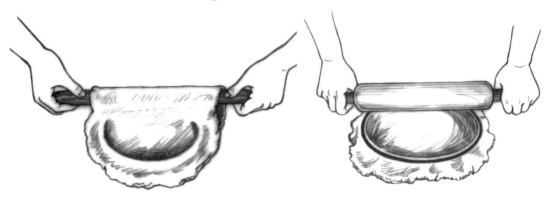

■ **MELTING CHOCOLATE:** To melt, cut chocolate into small pieces. *Do not melt over direct heat.* Melt in the top of a double boiler or heatproof bowl (size of bowl depends upon amount of chocolate used) set over a pan of gently *simmering* water. The water should not touch the bowl or the top half of the double boiler. The bowl in which the chocolate is melted must be *perfectly* dry. Drops of water in the chocolate can make the chocolate "seize up," or stiffen. If this should happen, stir 1 or 2 teaspoons of vegetable oil into the chocolate, and the original texture should be restored. However, if texture still isn't good, discard the chocolate and start over. When the chocolate has almost melted, remove the bowl from the heat and let continue to melt, stirring occasionally. (Milk and white chocolates melt faster than dark chocolate.) Keep in a warm spot until ready to use.

- **MINCE:** To chop into very fine pieces.
- **MIRROR A PLATE:** To mirror a plate, spoon about 3 tablespoons of coulis or sauce in center and tip plate on all sides so that the sauce spreads evenly around the inside of the plate. If the sauce gets on the rim of the plate, wipe away with a moistened towel.
- **PIPE:** To use a pastry bag, made of cloth or paper, to press food through the opening, usually to garnish a cake.
- **PLUMP:** To soak in liquid in order to soften and swell. Dried fruit is usually plumped before adding to a recipe, to give it a better texture and to enhance the flavor of the dried fruit.
- **PREPARING PANS:** At Spago we often use a vegetable coating to spray on pans. This is quick and almost foolproof. If brushing with butter, melt the butter and brush over pan with a pastry brush, making certain to get into all the corners. When coating with flour or sugar, spoon a good amount into pan and tilt pan around, getting it over the entire surface. Then invert pan and tap gently to remove any excess flour or sugar.
- **REDUCE:** To boil a liquid rapidly in order to decrease the volume by evaporation, thickening the consistency and intensifying the flavor in the process.
- **ROLLING OUT DOUGH:** Remove dough from refrigerator. It is best to roll out dough on a cold surface. If you don't have a piece of marble, you can chill the surface with a bag of ice cubes, then dry it thoroughly before using. Dust work surface lightly with flour and set dough on the flour. Sprinkle a little flour over dough and rolling pin and press down on dough to flatten. Start rolling from center out, first in one direction, then in another, carefully lifting and turning dough with your hands, sprinkling a little flour over and under dough as necessary to prevent sticking. Continue rolling, lifting, and turning until dough is 2 inches larger than baking pan. Slip a wide spatula under dough to loosen completely.
- **SAUTÉ:** Refers to cooking food in a skillet or sauté pan on top of the stove, first to brown, then to soften. When sautéing fruit, only a single layer of fruit should be sautéed at one time. If you pile too much into the pan, the fruit on the bottom will overcook, while the top layer will just steam. Stirring the fruit might cause it to break. Try holding the handle of the pan with

a towel and rotating the pan, moving the fruit around but keeping the pieces intact.

- **SCALD:** To bring a liquid just to a boil.
- **SIFT:** To strain through a strainer or sifter in order to remove any extraneous matter and/or to lighten the ingredients.
- **SPLITTING AND SCRAPING VANILLA BEANS:** To get the full flavor of a vanilla bean, our recipes advise you to split it lengthwise and scrape out the seeds. This is done easily with the point of a small, sharp paring knife. Place vanilla bean on a firm surface and, holding the top, carefully cut down the center of the vanilla bean, splitting it open. With the blade of the knife, scrape the seeds into the recipe as directed. (After using the bean, allow it to dry and then place it in a jar of granulated sugar to make vanilla sugar.)
- **STEEP:** To pour liquid over ingredients and let them sit in the liquid to soften or to absorb flavor or to plump.
- **TESTING A CAKE OR MUFFIN FOR DONENESS:** Insert a skewer into the center of a cake or muffin. The outer edges of a cake will cook faster, so poking the skewer into the center is a more accurate test.
- **TOASTING NUTS:** Spread nuts over an unlined baking tray. Bake in a moderate (350-degree) oven until lightly browned, turning nuts to brown as evenly as possible, 12 to 15 minutes.
- **TRIMING EDGES OF PASTRY:** The simplest way to trim excess pastry from the pie pan is to run a rolling pin around the outside rim of the pan, evenly removing the unwanted pastry.
- **WATER BATH:** A gentle way of baking. Cheesecakes, custards, and some cakes are baked in a water bath. To make a water bath, the cake pan is placed in a larger pan, and hot water is poured into the larger pan, reaching halfway up the side of the cake pan.
- **WHISK:** To beat ingredients in order to lighten and increase volume, with a wire whip or beaters, by hand, or with an electric mixer.

Ingredients

- **BUTTER:** Only *unsalted* butter is used for all the recipes.
- **CHOCOLATE:** In markets, packaged baking chocolate is divided into 1-ounce squares. The better-quality chocolates (Valrhona, Suchard, Callebaut, Lindt, Tobler, etc.) can be purchased in specialty food shops. The better the quality of the chocolate, the better the taste of the finished product. The dark chocolate used in this book is *bittersweet,* not semisweet or unsweetened. Wrapped well, chocolate can be kept in a cool spot, not refrigerated, for months. In this book, we use bittersweet, milk, and white chocolates.

  Bittersweet chocolate has a strong chocolate flavor and contains at least 35 percent chocolate liquor. Milk chocolate contains at least 12 percent milk solids and 10 percent chocolate liquor. What we call "white chocolate" is not a true chocolate; it contains no chocolate liquor. However, some of the better brands (see above) do contain cocoa butter and can be called "white chocolate." Others are "white confectionery coating." Do not use products labeled "artificial chocolate" or "chocolate-flavored." The texture and flavor are inadequate. White and milk chocolates do not keep as well because of the percentage of milk each contains.
- **CHOCOLATE CHIPS:** Available in most markets, these come in packages labeled semisweet, milk chocolate, or unsweetened. Unless otherwise specified, recipes call for semisweet chocolate chips.
- **COCOA POWDER:** There are two types of cocoa powder available in most markets—Dutch process and regular. The Dutch process cocoa, which is preferable, is richer in fat, darker in color, and milder in flavor. Cocoa used in the recipes is unsweetened.

■ **COCONUT:** We prefer to use unsweetened coconut, which can be obtained in health food stores or Asian markets.

■ **CREAM:** When recipes call for heavy cream, it is cream that can be whipped. For best results when whipping, chill bowl and beaters. Start whipping slowly so that the cream does not splatter, then increase speed as the cream thickens. Do not overbeat. The cream can always be beaten with a wire whip just before using to bring it to the desired texture.

■ **EGGS:** All the recipes in the book are based on eggs graded "large," unless otherwise specified. When adding eggs to a batter, break 1 egg at a time in a cup and then add to batter. To separate eggs, it is best to do this when they are cold, and then let the eggs come to room temperature. The egg whites should go into a perfectly clean bowl. If any of the yolk goes into the whites, remove it by dipping the eggshell half into the whites and letting the yolk particle float into the shell. If yolk is not removed, the whites cannot be beaten to the full volume.

■ **FLOURS:**

All-purpose flour is a blend of high-gluten hard and low-gluten soft wheat flours. The flour comes bleached or unbleached, and either kind can be used.

Cake flour is made from soft wheat flour. We combine cake flour with all-purpose flour to make a flakier puff pastry, since cake flour helps limit gluten development and makes the dough less springy and easier to work.

Pastry flour is softer than all-purpose flour but not as soft as cake flour. It is sold in bulk to bakeshops and restaurants, and can be purchased in specialty food shops. Some commercial distributors (Rykoff, Williams-Sonoma, etc.) have brochures available and will sell through mail order. (See Resources, page 263.)

To measure flour, scoop flour into a dry measuring cup, the exact size needed (½ cup, 1 cup). Remove excess flour by scraping the back of a knife or straight metal spatula across the top of the cup.

■ **GELATIN:** Gelatin sheets, which can be purchased in some specialty food shops, are used at Spago. However, since unflavored granulated gelatin is available in most markets, recipes in this book call for granulated gelatin.

■ **HONEY:** Nectar stored in hives by bees. Many people claim that honey is more nutritionally beneficial than sugar, but there is no solid evidence proving them correct. However, honey can give a different dimension to the flavor of a pastry.

- **LEAVENING AGENTS:** Added to flour, these lighten the mixture, distributing CO_2 gas during the baking process, causing the batter to rise. The three most common leavening agents are baking powder, baking soda, and yeast. There are two kinds of yeast, granulated and cake yeast. Both are usually marked with expiration dates and, for maximum potency, should not be used after the date. Yeast produces CO_2 relatively slowly and gives breads a characteristic flavor. Baking powder and baking soda act more rapidly, and are used for making muffins and quick breads. Baking powder consists of an alkali (sodium bicarbonate) plus an acid (cream of tartar). When a liquid is added, a chemical reaction takes place and CO_2 is produced. When baking soda, also known as sodium bicarbonate, is mixed with an acid and a liquid, CO_2 is released.

- **OILS:** When a recipe calls for vegetable oil, it can be safflower, corn or canola.

- **SALT:** With the exception of Basic Brioche (see page 140), only kosher salt is used in all the recipes. Kosher salt melts easily into batters and has a lighter taste than iodized salt.

- **SUGARS:**

  Brown sugar is a refined mixture of white sugar and molasses, with the light brown having less molasses than the dark brown. Brown sugar has a very definite flavor, color, and texture. It should be firmly packed down when measured. Brown sugar tends to harden as it stands, and there are many theories on how best to keep it. Storing in an airtight container in a cool spot is the simplest and probably most effective way.

  Confectioners' sugar, also called 10X sugar or powdered sugar, is sugar ground to a fine powdery texture and mixed with a small amount of starch to prevent caking. It should always be sifted before measuring.

  Crystal sugar, sometimes called sugar crystals, consists of large, clear crystals, larger than granulated sugar. It can be purchased in specialty food shops.

  Granulated sugar is extracted from sugar cane and beets, and is the most familiar and most used of the sugars. A simple carbohydrate, it is nearly pure sucrose. It can be ground to a finer consistency in a blender or food processor.

- **VANILLA BEAN:** The plant bearing the beans belongs to the orchid family and grows in a tropical climate. Vanilla beans can be expensive, but the flavor they impart cannot be duplicated. However, in most cake batters, vanilla extract is used, since the bean cannot be extracted from a baked cake.
- **WATER:** We recommend using filtered water for syrups and sorbets, since much too often tap water has an unpleasant taste.

I

Chocolate Cakes

Chocolate cake is one of the most popular desserts in this country, and those who love chocolate can be fanatical about what they consider to be the best chocolate cake. Our "best" chocolate cake is a chiffon cake. It is the perfect cake to build upon, rich but not too sweet, light rather than dense. This chapter is devoted to the many variations that can be created from this one cake.

To further assist you, we have included sauces and frostings that can be helpful in finishing the cake.

We start with a basic recipe for the Chiffon Cake. It can be dusted with sifted confectioners' sugar, cut into slices, each slice set on a plate mirrored with Crème Anglaise. It can be cut into layers (see page 7), filled, and frosted with a simple or rich chocolate frosting, the presentation a bit more impressive.

A fond memory of Cream-filled Chocolate Logs, popular in the northeastern part of the country, was the inspiration for our recipe for these delicate cakes, the batter spooned into éclair molds.

The Chocolate Chiffon Cake, when cut into 3 layers, filled, and frosted with a luscious Coconut Pecan Frosting, becomes our Austrian Chocolate Cake.

The construction of Mary's Cartoon Character Cake is a true labor of love. The Chocolate Chiffon Cake recipe is doubled, the cake baked in a large rectangular pan. Finally, this same chocolate cake is the foundation for the dramatic Opera Cake, filled, frosted, and glazed, with a chocolate band wrapped around the layers.

The Chocolate Truffle Cake is a recent addition to the Spago dessert menu. The Pot au Crème is new as well. Though not really variations of our chocolate cake, they both have become so popular, we would have been remiss not to include them in this book.

CHOCOLATE CHIFFON CAKE

Chocolate Chiffon Cake (Best Ever Chocolate Cake)
Crème Anglaise
How to Prepare and Frost a Layer Cake
Simple Chocolate Frosting
Rich Chocolate Frosting

CREAM-FILLED CHOCOLATE LOGS

AUSTRIAN CHOCOLATE CAKE

Assembling the Austrian Chocolate Cake
Coconut Pecan Frosting

OPERA CAKE

Assembling the Opera Cake
Chocolate Charlotte
Coffee Soaking Liquid
Coffee Buttercream
All-purpose Chocolate Glaze
Chocolate Band

MARY'S CARTOON CHARACTER CAKE

Double Recipe Chocolate Chiffon Cake
Cream Cheese Frosting for the Cartoon Character Cake
Preparing and Decorating the Cartoon Character Cake

CHOCOLATE TRUFFLE CAKE

POT DE CRÈME

EQUIPMENT

9-inch round cake pan

Sifter

Electric mixer

Rubber spatula

9-inch cardboard round

INGREDIENTS

1½ cups granulated sugar

1 cup all-purpose flour

¾ cup unsweetened cocoa

2 teaspoons baking powder

1 teaspoon baking soda

¼ teaspoon salt

4 eggs, separated

2 egg whites

¾ cup vegetable oil

½ cup water

1 teaspoon vanilla extract

Chocolate Chiffon Cake (Best Ever Chocolate Cake)

MAKES ONE 9-INCH CAKE SERVES 8 TO 10

*T*he chiffon cake is light-textured, the batter made with vegetable oil rather than butter, and cocoa rather than melted chocolate. The batter can be spooned into muffin tins to make delicate chocolate cupcakes.

1. Position rack in center of oven and preheat oven to 350 degrees. Butter, or coat with vegetable spray, a 9-inch round cake pan. Dust with flour, tapping out any excess flour. Set aside.

2. Sift together 1 cup sugar, the flour, cocoa, baking powder, baking soda, and salt. Set aside.

3. In the large bowl of an electric mixer, with paddle or beaters, beat the egg yolks at high speed. Turn speed to low and pour in the oil, water, and vanilla. Gradually add the sifted ingredients, and when almost incorporated, turn speed to medium, and beat until well combined. Remove bowl from machine.

4. In another clean large bowl, with whip or beaters, whip the 6 egg whites until soft peaks form. Start on medium speed and raise speed as peaks begin to form. Gradually pour in the remaining ½ cup sugar and whip until whites are shiny and firm but not stiff. With a rubber spatula, fold ¼ of the whites into the chocolate mixture, then scrape the chocolate mixture back into the whites, quickly folding until completely incorporated.

TO PREPARE AHEAD

THROUGH STEP 5,
CAKE CAN BE MADE
1 DAY AHEAD.

5. Scrape into the prepared pan and bake until edges of the cake pull away from the pan and a tester, gently inserted into the center of the cake, comes out clean, about 30 minutes. Cool on a rack. To remove, run a sharp knife around the inside of the pan to loosen cake. Invert onto rack. Place 9-inch cardboard round on cake and invert cake onto round. (See Cardboard Cake Rounds, page XV.)

6. To serve, the cake can be served as is, confectioners' sugar sifted over the top, and a fanned strawberry arranged on the side. Slices of cake can be arranged on plates, with vanilla- or coffee-flavored Crème Anglaise (see page 6) spooned under or over the slices. The cake also can be cut into layers with a sharp, serrated knife, and Rich Chocolate Frosting (see page 10) spread between the layers.

Crème Anglaise

MAKES ABOUT 2½ CUPS

EQUIPMENT

2 medium mixing bowls

Whip

Medium saucepan

Wooden spoon

Fine-mesh strainer

INGREDIENTS

4 egg yolks

3 tablespoons sugar

2 cups heavy cream

1½ tablespoons sour cream

1 vanilla bean, split lengthwise

TO PREPARE AHEAD

THROUGH STEP 3

*T*his is a simple sauce to prepare, and it complements many cakes, tarts, and puddings. To make Coffee Crème Anglaise, see below.

1. In a medium mixing bowl, using a whip, whisk together the egg yolks and sugar until they are very pale yellow and smooth.

2. In a medium saucepan, bring to a boil the heavy cream, sour cream, and vanilla bean with its scrapings. Whisk about half into the egg yolk mixture until well combined, then pour back into the saucepan. Over medium heat, stirring constantly with a wooden spoon, cook until the mixture heavily coats the back of the spoon. *Don't cook the eggs.*

3. Strain into a clean bowl and set the bowl over ice cubes and cold water until chilled, stirring occasionally. Refrigerate, covered, until needed.

Note: To make coffee crème Anglaise, substitute ¼ cup crushed coffee beans (with or without caffeine) for the vanilla bean. Bring to a boil and let steep in the cream mixture, covered, for about 10 minutes. When well flavored, whisk into the egg yolks. Then continue with recipe.

To crush coffee beans, place in a plastic bag, close the bag, and heavily press a rolling pin over the beans. Do not grind the beans because this will darken the Crème Anglaise.

How to Prepare and Frost a Layer Cake

EQUIPMENT

Long, serrated knife

Ruler

Toothpicks

Pastry brush

2 cardboard rounds

Small offset spatula

Long metal spatula

Pastry bag and #1 star tip

Wide metal spatula

TO PREPARE AHEAD

THROUGH STEP 7,
CAKE CAN BE MADE AND
FINISHED 1 DAY AHEAD.

Read the directions carefully, check the illustrations as you work, and you will find that cutting a cake into layers is not too difficult. Frosting the cake is the fun part, decorating even more fun.

1. To cut the cake into 3 layers, place cake on a flat, firm work surface, rounded side up. Using a long, serrated knife, starting at the outer edge of the cake, carefully trim away the rounded part of the cake so that the top is flat.

2. Using a ruler, measure the height of the cake and divide by 3. (If the cake is 3 inches high, each layer will be about 1 inch thick; if it is 2½ inches high, each layer will be about ⅝ inch thick.) (See illustration.)

3. Measure ⅓ down from the top of the cake and insert a toothpick at the exact point. Continue inserting toothpicks, spaced 1 inch apart, like spokes, around the diameter of the cake (see illustration). Place one of your hands on top of the cake and very carefully slice the cake horizontally, just above the circle of toothpicks, but not all the way through the cake.

(continued)

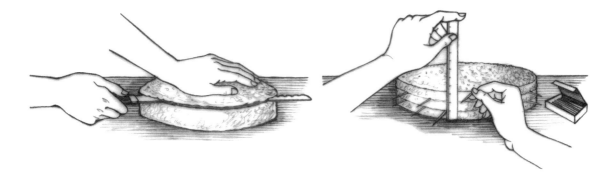

HOW TO PREPARE AND FROST A LAYER CAKE *(continued)*

Then, remove the knife, turn the cake, and continue to cut into the cake directly in front of you until the layer is cut all the way around. At this point, slide the knife from one end to the other end of the layer. You have just made the first layer. Set the layer aside and repeat the procedure, again measuring the cake, inserting the toothpicks, and cutting the cake into layers.

4. Lay all 3 layers on a flat surface and brush away excess crumbs with a soft pastry brush. Save the layer that is most level for the top of the cake.

5. Place the first layer on a cardboard round slightly larger than the cake. With a small offset spatula, coat with a thin layer of frosting. Set second layer on top, pressing down gently to secure. Frost with a thin layer of frosting and top with the third layer. Using the spatula, remove any excess frosting from the sides of the cake. Refrigerate until the frosting sets, about 30 minutes in the refrigerator or 10 minutes in the freezer.

6. When ready, brush away excess crumbs from the top. Put all but 1 cup of the remaining frosting on top of the cake and spread with the small offset spatula, covering the top and sides of the cake. With a long clean spatula, level the frosting on top, making it as smooth and even as possible. Spoon the remaining 1 cup frosting into a small pastry bag fitted with a #1 star tip. Pipe a latticework pattern on top and pipe a border all around the base of the cake.

7. Refrigerate until firm, at least 30 minutes. Run the blade of a knife under the cake, then slip a wide spatula directly under the cake and transfer to a clean plate. Refrigerate until needed. Remove from refrigerator about 30 minutes before serving.

Simple Chocolate Frosting

MAKES ABOUT 1¼ CUPS

EQUIPMENT

Heatproof bowl

Wooden spoon

Whip

INGREDIENTS

6 ounces bittersweet or semisweet chocolate, cut into small pieces

4 tablespoons (½ stick) unsalted butter, at room temperature, cut into small pieces

¼ cup light corn syrup

¼ cup brandy or liqueur of choice

TO PREPARE AHEAD

THROUGH STEP 2, FROSTING CAN BE REFRIGERATED, COVERED. REMOVE FROM REFRIGERATOR AND BRING TO ROOM TEMPERATURE BEFORE USING.

*T*his recipe can be doubled or trebled as necessary.

1. Combine chocolate and butter in a heatproof bowl and set over a pan of simmering water. With a wooden spoon, stir, over low heat, until almost melted. Turn off heat and allow to melt completely, stirring occasionally. Add corn syrup and brandy and whisk until smooth.

2. Let stand until thick enough to pour or spread over cake, stirring occasionally, about 30 minutes.

Rich Chocolate Frosting

MAKES ABOUT 2¼ CUPS, ENOUGH FROSTING
FOR ONE 8- OR 9-INCH CAKE

EQUIPMENT

Medium heatproof bowl

Electric mixer

Small saucepan

INGREDIENTS

12 ounces bittersweet chocolate,
cut into small pieces

8 ounces (2 sticks) unsalted butter,
at room temperature, cut into
small pieces

½ cup powdered sugar

¾ cup unsweetened cocoa

½ cup water or strong coffee

TO PREPARE AHEAD

THROUGH STEP 3.
REFRIGERATE, COVERED,
UNTIL NEEDED. FROSTING
CAN BE PREPARED 1
DAY AHEAD.

*T*his is a dark, fluffy, delightfully rich frosting.

1. Melt chocolate in a medium heatproof bowl placed over simmering water.

2. While chocolate is melting, in the large bowl of an electric mixer with paddle or beaters, beat butter and sugar until fluffy, stopping machine occasionally and scraping down sides of bowl and under beaters as necessary. Start on slow speed, and, when combined, turn up speed to high.

3. In a small saucepan, over low heat, dissolve cocoa in water or coffee, stirring as necessary. Remove from heat, scrape the melted chocolate into the saucepan, and stir to combine thoroughly. On low speed, pour into butter-sugar mixture, again scraping down sides of bowl and under beaters. Beat until smooth and shiny. Transfer to a medium bowl and set aside until of spreading consistency.

Cream-filled Chocolate Logs

MAKES 12 TO 14 LOGS

EQUIPMENT

Éclair pan(s)

Medium bowl

Sifter

Electric mixer

Rubber spatula

Pastry bag, optional

INGREDIENTS

¾ cup granulated sugar

½ cup all-purpose flour

⅓ cup unsweetened cocoa

1 teaspoon baking powder

½ teaspoon baking soda

⅛ teaspoon salt

2 eggs, separated

1 egg white

⅓ cup vegetable oil

¼ cup water

½ teaspoon vanilla extract

FILLING

1 cup heavy cream

2 tablespoons granulated sugar

*1 pint strawberries, hulled and
sliced, plus extra whole berries
as garnish, optional*

Sifted confectioners' sugar

Michael Dargin, maître d' at Spago, Los Angeles, is a fellow New Englander. One night, while assembling a Chocolate Cake, we reminisced about the chocolate cakes we ate as children in Massachusetts. I decided to make him my version as a surprise, and he was thrilled. The original looks like a small chocolate hot dog, sinfully delicious . . . chocolate cake on the outside and a thick layer of whipped cream in the middle. Pans that size are not readily available, but éclair pans are, so we decided to improvise. The éclair pan usually has 12 recessed molds, each 4 inches long, 1½ inches wide, and about ½ inch deep. This requires half the recipe for Chocolate Chiffon Cake (see page 4). To make 14 chocolate logs, you will need 28 cakes. (The number of cakes depends on how much batter goes into each mold.) If you have only one pan it will be necessary to refill the molds. Remember to cool the pan, recoat and refill the molds as needed.

1. Position rack in center of oven and preheat oven to 350 degrees. Coat the éclair pan(s) with vegetable spray and set aside.

2. Make the cakes: In a medium bowl sift together ½ cup sugar, the flour, cocoa, baking powder, baking soda, and salt. Set aside.

3. In the large bowl of an electric mixer, using paddle or beaters, beat the egg yolks. On low speed, pour in the vegetable oil, water, and vanilla. Raise the speed and beat until well combined. Gradually add the sifted ingredients, turn up the speed, and beat until well combined.

(continued)

CREAM-FILLED CHOCOLATE LOGS *(continued)*

TO PREPARE AHEAD

THROUGH STEP 6

4. In another clean large bowl, using whip or beaters, whip the 3 egg whites until soft peaks form. Gradually pour in remaining ¼ cup sugar and continue to beat until whites are shiny and firm but not stiff. With a rubber spatula, fold ¼ of the whites into the chocolate mixture, then scrape the chocolate mixture back into the whites, folding quickly, until completely incorporated.

5. The batter can be piped or spooned into the molds. If piping, use a #4 plain tip. Fit the tip into a large pastry bag and fill with the batter. Pipe the batter into each mold, about ¾ full. If spooning, see that the batter doesn't drip around the sides of the molds. Bake until a cake tester, gently poked into the center of a cake, comes out clean and the cake springs back when lightly pressed, about 15 minutes. Turn cakes out onto a rack and let cool completely. (If the cakes spread, you may have to ease them out of the mold with the flat side of a knife. Gently press the outer edges of the cakes toward the center and then unmold.)

6. Make the filling: In a clean chilled bowl, using a chilled whip or beaters, whip the cream and sugar until stiff peaks form. Refrigerate, covered, until needed. When ready to use, whip lightly by hand to bring back the stiff peaks.

7. Assemble the chocolate logs: Hold 2 cakes in your hand, flat sides facing each other, ready to be filled. Spoon or pipe about 2 tablespoons whipped cream into the middle, as if placing a hot dog in a bun. Arrange slices of strawberries on the cream. Repeat with the remaining cakes, cream, and berries. Sift a generous amount of confectioners' sugar over the tops of the cakes.

8. To serve, set one completed log on each of 8 dessert plates and garnish with 1 or 2 whole strawberries, if desired. Serve immediately.

Assembling the Austrian Chocolate Cake

EQUIPMENT

Two 9-inch cardboard rounds*

Long, serrated knife or slicing knife

Metal spatula

INGREDIENTS

Chocolate Chiffon Cake
(see page 4)

Coconut Pecan Frosting
(see page 14)

The classic German chocolate cake is an impressive layer cake with rich coconut frosting and big chunks of pecans. Often we get requests for a special birthday cake with a similar type of frosting using fresh cream. It has become such a favorite, it appears on the menu regularly. But it just didn't seem right to call it German chocolate cake since we work with that famous Austrian, Wolfgang Puck, so we renamed this wonderful dessert Austrian Chocolate Cake. One of the best things about it is, of course, the frosting, which is not quite as sweet as others, since we use *unsweetened* coconut and heavy cream rather than condensed milk.

Make 1 Chocolate Chiffon Cake (see page 4), using a 9-inch springform pan, and set aside to cool while preparing the frosting.

1. Place the cooled cake on a flat surface and cut into 3 even layers. (See How to Prepare and Frost a Layer Cake, page 7.)

2. Place 1 of the layers on a cardboard round and brush away any excess crumbs. Spoon 1 cup of frosting on top and spread evenly with a metal spatula. Set the second layer on top of the frosting, again brushing away excess crumbs. Press down gently but firmly with both hands, being careful not to squeeze the frosting out of the sides. Repeat the procedure with another cup of frosting and set the last layer on top. Using the spatula, remove any excess frosting from the sides of the cake. Refriger-

(continued)

*These are available at most baking supply stores, or you can make your own by placing the bottom of the springform pan on a piece of cardboard, tracing it with a pencil, and cutting out with a pair of scissors. This is not difficult, but it does require time and patience—a little practice helps, too.

ASSEMBLING THE AUSTRIAN CHOCOLATE CAKE *(continued)*

ate until the frosting sets, about 30 minutes in the refrigerator or 10 minutes in the freezer. (It is much easier to finish the cake when the frosting is firm.) When ready, brush away excess crumbs, spoon the remaining frosting on top of the cake, and spread over the top and sides, smoothing as you go.

3. At this point, the cake can be refrigerated for up to 2 days. Remove from the refrigerator 1 hour before you are ready to serve it, allowing the frosting to soften and the cake to come to room temperature.

Coconut Pecan Frosting

MAKES ENOUGH TO FILL AND FROST ONE 9-INCH LAYER CAKE

EQUIPMENT

Medium bowl

Whip

Large heavy saucepan

INGREDIENTS

1 cup heavy cream

1 cup granulated sugar

3 egg yolks, lightly beaten

4 ounces (1 stick) unsalted butter, cut into small pieces

1 vanilla bean, split lengthwise

1½ cups unsweetened shredded coconut

1 cup coarsely chopped pecans

TO PREPARE AHEAD

THROUGH STEP 3

1. In a medium mixing bowl, whisk together the cream, sugar, and egg yolks.

2. In a large heavy saucepan, melt the butter with the vanilla bean and its scrapings. Stir in the cream mixture and, over medium-high heat, bring to a boil. Continue to boil for 5 minutes.

3. Stir in the coconut and turn the heat down to low. Cook for 5 additional minutes, stirring frequently. Stir in the chopped pecans and remove from the heat. Set aside, stirring occasionally, until completely cool. Refrigerate, covered, until needed.

4. See Assembling the Austrian Chocolate Cake (above).

Assembling the Opera Cake

❧

EQUIPMENT

Long, serrated knife

Two 9-inch cardboard circles

Pastry brush

Large pastry bag and #1 and #3 plain round tips

Rack to fit into baking tray

Baking tray

Large ladle

Wide metal spatula

INGREDIENTS

Chocolate Chiffon Cake (see page 4)

Coffee Soaking Liquid (see page 18)

¹⁄₂ recipe Chocolate Charlotte (see page 17)

Coffee Buttercream (see page 19)

All-purpose Chocolate Glaze (see page 20)

Chocolate Band (see page 21)

*T*he Opera Cake, a chocolate cake with alternate layers of Chocolate Charlotte and Coffee Buttercream, is prized in France as well as in the United States. The cake can be baked in a round, square, or rectangular pan. The origin of the cake is open to some dispute, but it is considered a modern classic. At Spago, the Opera is glazed with chocolate, wrapped in a chocolate band, and bits of 24-karat gold decorate the finished cake.

When Peter Gethers had a press party for his book *The Cat Who Went to Paris,* I made a huge square Opera Cake and then cut it into 3-inch squares. Each square was decorated with milk chocolate catpaw prints, piped out of a pastry bag. It got raves, and a few chuckles, from the attendees.

1. Using a long, serrated knife, slice the Chocolate Chiffon Cake horizontally into thirds, leveling the top before dividing. (See How to Prepare and Frost a Layer Cake, page 7.) Place 1 layer on a cardboard circle and, with a pastry brush, moisten the entire surface of the cake layer with the Coffee Soaking Liquid, being careful not to soak the cake too much.

2. Fill a large pastry bag, fitted with a #3 plain round tip, with the Chocolate Charlotte. Starting in the center of the layer, make concentric circles (see illustration on page 16) covering the entire surface.

3. Place the second layer of cake on top of the charlotte and press gently into place. Again, using the pastry brush and soaking liquid, moisten the entire surface of the layer.

4. Fill a clean pastry bag, fitted with a #1 plain round tip, with the Coffee Buttercream. Since buttercream is rich, using a #1 rather than a #3 plain tip will make a thinner layer. Start-

(continued)

ASSEMBLING THE OPERA CAKE *(continued)*

TO PREPARE AHEAD

THROUGH STEP 6. THE CAKE
CAN BE MADE EARLY IN THE
DAY AND REFRIGERATED.
REMOVE FROM REFRIGERATOR
ABOUT 30 MINUTES BEFORE
SERVING.

ing at the center of the layer, make continuous concentric circles, covering the entire surface.

5. Set the last layer of cake on the buttercream and press gently into place. Again, moisten the entire surface of the cake layer with Coffee Soaking Liquid and then carefully transfer the entire cake to the refrigerator until completely set, at least 3 hours. When set, remove the cake from the refrigerator and place on a flat area. Cover the cake with a second cardboard round and flip over, making the bottom of the cake the top. (This is a professional trick, giving the cake a very flat surface that is ready to be glazed.) Remove the cardboard round from what is now the top of the cake.

6. Place the cake on a cooling rack that fits into a baking tray and place the baking tray underneath the rack. With a large ladle, spoon enough of the glaze over the cake to cover the entire top and all the sides. Then, carefully tilt the baking pan slightly so that any excess glaze will run off the top of the cake. Refrigerate the entire tray with the rack and cake until the glaze is set, about 15 minutes. Remove from the refrigerator. Slide a wide, flat spatula under the cardboard round and lift the cake off the rack, returning the cake to the refrigerator while you make the Chocolate Band.

Chocolate Charlotte

ENOUGH TO FILL ONE 9-INCH LAYER CAKE

EQUIPMENT

Medium and large heatproof bowls

Electric mixer

Small saucepan

Whip

Rubber spatula

INGREDIENTS

12 ounces bittersweet chocolate,
cut into small pieces

3 cups heavy cream

6 egg yolks

¾ cup granulated sugar

½ cup water

TO PREPARE AHEAD

THROUGH STEP 5. IF
REFRIGERATED OVERNIGHT,
REMOVE ABOUT 15 MINUTES
BEFORE NEEDED AND THEN
WHISK VIGOROUSLY FOR 1
MINUTE. IT WILL RETURN TO
ITS ORIGINAL TEXTURE.

*N*ot only does the charlotte make an excellent filling for layer cakes, it can be spooned into a champagne flute or margarita glass, atop a few fresh raspberries, and served as chocolate mousse.

1. In a medium heatproof bowl set over simmering water, melt the chocolate. When almost melted, turn off heat and let chocolate continue to melt completely, stirring occasionally. Keep the bowl over the warm water until ready to use.

2. In the large bowl of an electric mixer, using whip or beaters, whip the cream until soft peaks form. Refrigerate, covered, until needed.

3. Place the egg yolks in a large heatproof bowl and set aside.

4. In a small saucepan, combine the sugar and water and bring to a boil. Boil until the sugar dissolves, about 3 minutes, making sugar syrup. Whisking constantly, pour the boiling syrup over the egg yolks. Set the bowl over a pan of simmering water and whisk vigorously until mixture is thick and white in color. This mixture should be hot to the touch.

5. Remove the bowl from the heat and, working quickly, scrape the egg mixture into a clean large bowl of the electric mixer. On medium speed, using whip or beaters, beat until the volume has doubled and the bottom of the bowl is completely cool to the touch. Turn speed to low, scrape in the warm melted chocolate, and continue to beat until well combined. Remove the bowl from the mixer and, using a rubber spatula, fold in half the reserved whipped cream. Then fold in

(continued)

Chocolate Charlotte *(continued)*

the remaining cream. The mixture should resemble softly whipped cream. This can be used immediately or refrigerated, covered, until needed. If the mixture seems a little runny, the chocolate may have been too warm, but after refrigerating for an hour or so, it will be fine.

Coffee Soaking Liquid

MAKES ABOUT 2½ CUPS

EQUIPMENT

Medium bowl

INGREDIENTS

2 cups cold coffee

2 tablespoons instant espresso

½ cup Kahlúa or coffee liqueur

TO PREPARE AHEAD

THROUGH STEP 1. LIQUID CAN BE REFRIGERATED, COVERED, FOR UP TO 3 DAYS.

1. In a medium bowl, combine all the ingredients. Taste! You may want to add more Kahlúa or more coffee. Set aside, covered, until needed.

Coffee Buttercream

EQUIPMENT

Electric mixer

2-quart nonreactive saucepan

Rubber spatula

Wooden spoon

Fine-mesh strainer

INGREDIENTS

7 egg yolks

⅔ cup granulated sugar

½ cup milk

1 tablespoon strong coffee or espresso

1 teaspoon instant espresso

1 pound unsalted butter, at room temperature, cut into small pieces

TO PREPARE AHEAD

THROUGH STEP 4. THE BUTTERCREAM CAN BE FROZEN IN A PLASTIC BAG FOR UP TO 3 MONTHS. DEFROST IN REFRIGERATOR, RIGHT IN THE BAG. WHEN READY TO USE, SNIP A SMALL CORNER OF THE BAG AND PIPE OUT THE BUTTERCREAM AS IF IT WERE IN A PASTRY BAG.

*T*his buttercream is the one that we use on the Opera Cake (see page 15), but it can be spread on any layer of plain cake, making it more interesting and certainly more delicious.

1. In the large bowl of an electric mixer, using the paddle or beaters, beat the egg yolks with 3 tablespoons sugar until the mixture is thick and pale yellow and forms a ribbon when the beaters are lifted.

2. Meanwhile, in a 2-quart nonreactive saucepan, bring the milk just to a boil. Whisk in the remaining sugar, the strong coffee, and the instant espresso until completely dissolved.

3. With the machine running on its lowest speed, slowly pour about ⅓ of the hot milk mixture into the yolks. Turn off the machine and use a rubber spatula to scrape the mixture back into the saucepan. Cook, over medium heat, stirring constantly with a wooden spoon, until you see the first bubbles (if you stop for 1 minute, it may burn on the bottom). Stop stirring and immediately remove from the heat. Quickly strain through a fine strainer into a clean bowl of the mixer. Beat on medium-high speed until thick and doubled in volume. Set aside.

4. In a separate bowl of the mixer, using clean paddles or beaters, on medium speed, beat the butter until it begins to whiten and is very fluffy. On low speed, slowly pour the milk mixture into the butter. As you pour, you will notice that the mixture appears broken. Don't worry, it will come back together when the speed is increased. When all of the mixture has been poured, gradually increase the speed and beat until the mixture

(continued)

CHOCOLATE BUTTERCREAM *(continued)*

looks like whipped butter. At this point, the buttercream is ready and can be used immediately, if desired. If not, the buttercream can be refrigerated, covered, in a plastic container for up to 2 weeks.

All-purpose Chocolate Glaze

MAKES ABOUT 2 CUPS

EQUIPMENT
Medium heatproof bowl

Whip

Fine strainer

INGREDIENTS
8 ounces bittersweet chocolate, cut into small pieces

6 tablespoons (3 ounces) unsalted butter, cut into small pieces

⅓ cup light corn syrup

⅓ cup brandy

TO PREPARE AHEAD
THROUGH STEP 2. THE GLAZE CAN BE REFRIGERATED, COVERED, AND REMELTED BEFORE USING AS A GLAZE. REMELT OVER SIMMERING WATER UNTIL ALMOST MELTED. TURN OFF HEAT AND LET SIT OVER WATER UNTIL SMOOTH, STIRRING OCCASIONALLY.

*T*his is a very versatile chocolate glaze. It can be used to cover a cake, as a filling sandwiched between two cookies, and, when chilled slightly, can be used to make small chocolate truffles. Any leftover glaze can be wrapped in plastic and refrigerated for a few days or frozen for a few months.

1. Combine the chocolate and butter in a medium heatproof bowl and set over simmering water. Do not let the bottom of the bowl touch the water or the chocolate may burn. Let melt almost completely, turn off the heat, and let the mixture continue to melt, stirring occasionally.

2. Whisk in the corn syrup and brandy until smooth. Strain through a fine strainer. Reserve, covered, in a warm spot until needed.

Chocolate Band

EQUIPMENT

*1 sheet wax paper, about
20 inches in length*

Ruler

*Medium heatproof bowl or
double boiler*

Offset spatula

Scissors

Wide spatula

INGREDIENTS

*6 ounces bittersweet or milk
chocolate, cut into small pieces*

TO PREPARE AHEAD

THROUGH STEP 5, REMOVING
THE CAKE ABOUT 30 MINUTES
BEFORE SERVING FOR THE
FULL FLAVOR TO COME
THROUGH

A chocolate band will lend importance to any cake, especially the Opera Cake (see page 15).

1. Make the wax paper band: Measure the height of the cake with a ruler and mark it across the length of the wax paper strip. Fold over the paper as marked, across the entire length of the paper. Cut along the fold with a long, sharp knife. Set the strip aside. It will be used to wrap around the cake.

2. Place the chocolate in a medium heatproof bowl or the top of a double boiler and set over simmering water. Do not let the bottom of the bowl touch the water or the chocolate may burn. When the chocolate is almost completely melted, remove from the heat and let it continue to melt, stirring occasionally.

3. Lay the prepared length of wax paper on a flat surface. Scrape the chocolate out of the bowl onto the wax paper. With an offset spatula, spread the chocolate, as evenly as possible, over the entire surface of the paper, using long, even strokes. (Some of the chocolate may spread onto the work surface, but that's okay. This can be cleaned later.) Pick up each end of the wax paper band and transfer to a clean, smooth surface, keeping the band as straight as possible, and leaving enough room to place the cake directly in front of the band.

4. Wrap the band around the cake: Remove the cake from the refrigerator and set it directly in front of the center of the band. Pick up each end of the band and carefully wrap it around the cake, pinching the ends together and cutting off the excess "tail" with a sharp pair of scissors (see illustrations). Refrigerate the cake, picking it up with a wide spatula. Do *not* touch the sides of the cake, since the band is still soft.

(continued)

CHOCOLATE BAND *(continued)*

5. After 30 minutes, remove the cake from the refrigerator and carefully remove the wax paper from the band by gently peeling it from one end of the band to the other (see illustration). Return cake to refrigerator until needed.

6. To serve, dust the top of the cake with a little cocoa powder, if desired, cutting the cake at the table with a sharp knife. Serve with coffee ice cream or Crème Anglaise (see page 6), flavored with instant coffee.

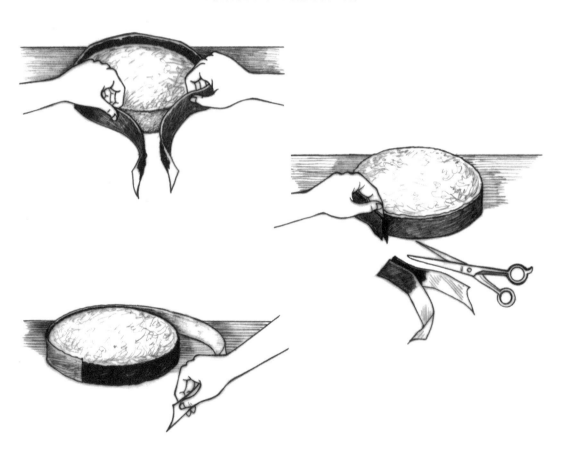

Mary's Cartoon Character Cake

For my son Anthony's eighth birthday, I told him that I would make him any kind of cake he wanted and that he could choose where he wanted to have his party. His response was immediate—a cake in the shape of his favorite cartoon character, which happened to be Bart Simpson, and dinner at Spago. Smart kid!

To make my son's cake, I decided to use the only pan in the kitchen that was oblong, and doubled the recipe for Chocolate Chiffon Cake so that the cake could be cut in half and filled with a layer of frosting. I decided on a cream cheese frosting because it is the best kind of frosting to color.

You can make the shape of just about any character or person you want to immortalize by first sketching it on parchment paper and then cutting it out to make a stencil. Place the stencil on top of the cake (the moisture of the cake will make the stencil stick) and cut out the shape with a serrated knife.

The evening was a huge success, particularly the cake. After dinner, Anthony looked at me and said, "Mom, next year will you make me a Roger Rabbit cake?"

Double Recipe Chocolate Chiffon Cake

MAKES ONE 11 x 17 x 2-INCH CAKE
SERVES UP TO 20 PEOPLE

*I*f you want to make a chocolate cake for a large group, this is a double recipe of the Chocolate Chiffon Cake (see page 4).

1. Position rack in center of oven and preheat oven to 350 degrees. Butter, or coat with vegetable spray, an 11 x 17 x 2-inch baking pan. Dust with cocoa powder, tapping out any excess. Set aside.

2. Sift together 2 cups sugar, the flour, cocoa, baking powder, baking soda, and salt. Set aside.

3. In the large bowl of an electric mixer, with paddle or beaters, beat the egg yolks at high speed. Turn the machine to low and pour in the oil, water, and vanilla. Gradually add the sifted ingredients and, when almost incorporated, turn speed to medium and beat until well combined.

4. In a separate clean large bowl, with whip or beaters, whip the 12 egg whites until soft peaks form. Start on medium speed and raise speed as peaks begin to form. Gradually pour in the remaining 1 cup sugar and continue to whip until whites are shiny and firm but not stiff. With a rubber spatula, fold ¼ of the whites into the chocolate mixture, then scrape the chocolate mixture back into the whites, quickly folding until completely incorporated.

5. Scrape into the prepared pan and spread with an offset spatula, smoothing the top. Bake until the edges of the cake pull

EQUIPMENT
11 x 17 x 2-inch baking pan

Sifter

Electric mixer

Rubber spatula

Metal offset spatula

Large cooling rack

INGREDIENTS
3 cups granulated sugar

2 cups all-purpose flour

1½ cups unsweetened cocoa

1 tablespoon plus 1 teaspoon baking powder

2 teaspoons baking soda

½ teaspoon salt

8 eggs, separated

4 egg whites

1½ cups vegetable oil

1 cup water

2 teaspoons vanilla extract

TO PREPARE AHEAD
THROUGH STEP 5

away from the pan and a tester, gently inserted into the center of the cake, comes out clean, 40 to 45 minutes. Transfer pan to a large cooling rack for 15 minutes. Then, to remove cake from pan, run a sharp knife around the inside edges of the pan, loosening the cake. Place the rack on top of the cake and invert the pan onto the rack. Carefully lift the pan off the cake and continue to cool completely while preparing the Cream Cheese Frosting (see page 26).

Cream Cheese Frosting for the Cartoon Character Cake

MAKES 2 POUNDS, 10 OUNCES

EQUIPMENT

Electric mixer

2 medium and 1 or 2 small bowls

Rubber spatula or wooden spoon

INGREDIENTS

1 pound unsalted butter, at room temperature, cut into small pieces

1 pound cream cheese, at room temperature, cut into small pieces

1 pound confectioners' sugar, sifted twice

2 teaspoons vanilla extract

Yellow food coloring

Blue food coloring

Red food coloring

TO PREPARE AHEAD

THROUGH STEP 5, THE FROSTING CAN BE MADE EARLY IN THE DAY AND REFRIGERATED, COVERED. REMOVE FROM REFRIGERATOR AND BRING TO SPREADING CONSISTENCY BEFORE USING.

The frosting in this recipe is doubled for the Cartoon Character Cake, but it can easily be cut in half, if desired. The frosting does not need to be colored; it can be kept white.

1. Using an electric mixer, fitted with paddle or beaters, cream the butter until completely smooth. Start on low speed and gradually work up to high. On medium speed, add the cream cheese and continue to beat until smooth, scraping down sides of bowl and under beaters as necessary. Turn off the machine, add sugar and vanilla, and mix for 30 seconds on low speed. Turn to high, and beat until fluffy.

2. Remove the bowl from the machine and divide the contents into 4 separate bowls in the following proportions. To make orange frosting*: In a medium bowl, place 2 cups frosting and add 15 drops of yellow, 6 drops of red, and 1 drop of green food coloring. Using a rubber spatula or wooden spoon, mix thoroughly and set aside.

3. To make blue frosting: In a medium bowl, place 1 cup frosting, add 10 drops of blue food coloring, and mix thoroughly.

4. To make red frosting: Place 1 tablespoon frosting in a small cup or bowl, add 10 drops of red food coloring, and mix thoroughly.

5. Leave the remaining frosting white.

*These colors are for a Bart Simpson cake. For other characters, adjust the amounts of food coloring to create the colors you need.

Preparing and Decorating the Cartoon Character Cake

EQUIPMENT

Cartoon character stencil

Large piece of cardboard

Sharp knife or scissors

Long, serrated knife

Sharp paring knife or steak knife

Pastry brush

Metal spatula

Parchment or wax paper

Pastry bag and #3 plain tip

Offset metal spatula

TO PREPARE AHEAD
THROUGH STEP 9. CAKE
SHOULD BE PREPARED EARLY
IN THE DAY.

1. Place the stencil on a piece of cardboard a little larger than the stencil. Trace it onto the cardboard and then cut it out with a sharp knife or pair of scissors. Set aside.

2. Slide the cake from the rack onto a flat work surface. With a long, serrated knife, cut the cake into 2 even layers, length-wise, each layer about $1\frac{1}{2}$ inches thick. Unlike other cakes, you don't have to level the top, since the frosting will do that. Do not remove the top layer.

3. Set the stencil on top of the cake, the top of the head even with the top edge of the cake. Gently smooth out the stencil.

4. Using a very sharp paring knife or steak knife, cut around the stencil, the knifepoint perpendicular to the cake, cutting through the 2 layers. Hold the stencil down with one hand while cutting. Do not discard any pieces of cake—you may need them later (an ear might fall off and need replacing). Remove the stencil.

5. Slide the cardboard cutout between the 2 cake layers, the design of the cake in line with the cardboard, separating the layers. Transfer the cardboard with the top layer to a flat work surface and cover the remaining layer with a clean towel until needed.

6. Brush away excess cake crumbs with a soft pastry brush. Spoon $1\frac{1}{2}$ cups white frosting in the center of the top layer and spread evenly with a metal spatula, covering the entire surface of the cake. Carefully set the remaining layer on the frosting and gently but firmly press into place. Refrigerate for 30 minutes.

(continued)

PREPARING AND DECORATING THE CARTOON CHARACTER CAKE *(continued)*

7. Prepare a small piping bag made with parchment paper (see illustrations). Fit a cloth pastry bag with a #3 plain tip. Set aside.

8. Remove the cake from the refrigerator and again brush away excess crumbs. Using an offset metal spatula, cover the entire cake, top and sides, with orange frosting* (see page 26).

9. Fill the cloth pastry bag with the remaining white frosting and pipe out 2 eyes and the teeth. Spoon the red frosting into the paper piping bag and pipe out the tongue. Spread the blue frosting on the bottom section of the cake for the shirt. Dot the center of the eyes with a little of the blue frosting. Refrigerate until needed.

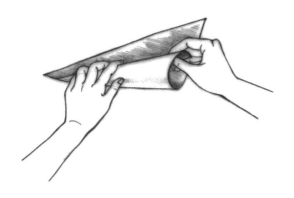

*These directions are for a Bart Simpson cake, but the procedure can be adapted for other characters and colors.

Chocolate Truffle Cake

SERVES 8

*Double boiler and/or small
heatproof bowl*

Baking tray

Wax or parchment paper

Pastry bag and #3 plain tip

*8 oversize muffin cups or
1¼-cup custard cups*

Electric mixer

Rubber spatula

INGREDIENTS

TRUFFLES

*4 ounces bittersweet or semisweet
chocolate, cut into small pieces*

3 tablespoons heavy cream

*1 tablespoon (½ ounce) unsalted
butter*

*2 tablespoons flavoring of your
choice (Grand Marnier, Amaretto,
raspberry liqueur, etc.)*

*8 fresh perfect raspberries,
optional*

CHOCOLATE CAKE

*5 ounces bittersweet chocolate, cut
into small pieces*

*5 ounces (1¼ sticks) unsalted
butter, cut into small pieces*

The truffle cake has become such a popular dessert, it is served in all of Wolfgang's restaurants. It is the most requested recipe and was featured in a *New York Times* article.

1. Make the truffles: Combine the chocolate, cream, and butter in a small heatproof bowl, set over simmering water, and let melt. When almost melted, remove from the heat and stir the mixture until smooth. Stir in flavoring of your choice and refrigerate until thick enough to mound on a spoon, stirring occasionally, about 30 minutes.

2. Line baking tray with wax or parchment paper. Scrape the chocolate mixture into pastry bag fitted with a #3 plain tip. Pipe eight 1-inch mounds onto the prepared tray. Place 1 raspberry in center of each chocolate mound and pipe a little more of the chocolate mixture to enclose completely. Refrigerate until firm, about 15 minutes.

3. Make the cake: Position rack in center of oven and preheat oven to 350 degrees. Butter, or coat with vegetable spray, 8 oversize muffin cups (4 inches wide and 2 inches deep) or 1¼-cup custard cups. Line bottoms with rounds of wax paper. (To cut out the rounds, place 1 of the cups on wax paper and trace around the bottom with a pencil. Then cut the 8 circles.) Set aside.

4. In the top of a double boiler or a small heatproof bowl set over simmering water, melt together the chocolate and butter. Cool slightly.

5. Meanwhile, in the large bowl of an electric mixer, with

(continued)

CHOCOLATE TRUFFLE CAKE *(continued)*

3 eggs, at room temperature

3 egg yolks, at room temperature

½ cup sugar

5 tablespoons plus 1 teaspoon all-purpose flour

Whipped cream, optional

Ice cream, optional

TO PREPARE AHEAD

IN STEP 5, ARRANGE FILLED CUPS ON BAKING SHEET AND REFRIGERATE UNTIL SERVING TIME. ABOUT 30 MINUTES BEFORE BAKING, PREHEAT OVEN, REMOVE BAKING TRAY FROM REFRIGERATOR, AND CONTINUE WITH RECIPE.

paddle or beaters, on high speed, beat eggs, egg yolks, and sugar until tripled in volume, about 5 minutes. Scrape in the chocolate mixture and, on low speed, beat just until combined. Remove the bowl and fold in the flour, using a rubber spatula. Spoon a little of the batter into each of the prepared cups, top with 1 truffle, and cover with the remaining batter. Arrange cups on baking tray and bake until edges of the cakes begin to pull away from the sides of the cups, 12 to 13 minutes. Let stand 10 minutes. Invert onto individual dessert plates and carefully peel off paper.

6. Serve warm. Spoon softly whipped cream or ice cream next to each cake and, if desired, garnish with a few fresh raspberries. Serve immediately.

Pot de Crème

SERVES 6

EQUIPMENT

Medium heatproof bowl

Medium saucepan

Medium bowl

Whip

Fine strainer

Ladle

Six ¾-cup ramekins

Baking pan with sides, large enough to hold ramekins

INGREDIENTS

3 ounces bittersweet chocolate, cut into small pieces

2 cups heavy cream

½ cup milk

5 egg yolks

¼ cup granulated sugar

Pinch of salt

TO PREPARE AHEAD

THROUGH STEP 7, POT AU CRÈME CAN BE PREPARED UP TO 1 DAY AHEAD.

*G*ustavo Escalante was an assistant pastry cook at Spago, Los Angeles, and now heads the pastry kitchen at Granita, Wolfgang Puck's restaurant in Malibu. This is his recipe, a deliciously smooth chocolate dessert. At Granita, when this dessert is ready to serve, granulated sugar is sprinkled over the top and the sugar is caramelized with a propane torch. We prefer a bit of whipped cream. Jason Epstein, our editor, loved this so much that he requested the recipe be put into the book.

1. Place rack in center of oven and preheat oven to 325 degrees.

2. Melt chocolate in a medium heatproof bowl set over gently simmering water. When the chocolate is almost melted, turn off the heat and let stand until completely melted.

3. Meanwhile, in a medium saucepan, scald cream and milk.

4. In a medium mixing bowl, whisk together the egg yolks, sugar, and salt until the sugar is completely dissolved. Slowly whisk the hot cream mixture into the yolks.

5. Remove the melted chocolate from the stove and pour the hot cream mixture through a fine mesh strainer into the melted chocolate. Whisk until well combined and smooth.

6. Ladle the mixture into six ¾-cup ramekins and arrange the ramekins in a baking pan. Pour in enough warm water to reach halfway up sides of ramekins, cover the entire pan with aluminum foil, and place in oven. Bake until mixture around the edges of each ramekin is firm when lightly shaken, about

(continued)

POT DE CRÈME *(continued)*

35 minutes. (Baking time will vary depending on depth and width of ramekins.) Center may still move a bit, but that's okay. It will firm up as it chills.

7. Carefully remove ramekins from baking pan, wipe dry, and let cool. Place on a baking tray and refrigerate until firm, 2 to 3 hours.

8. To serve, spoon a little whipped cream in the center of each serving and set cup on a doily-lined small plate. Accompany with fresh berries and / or cookies.

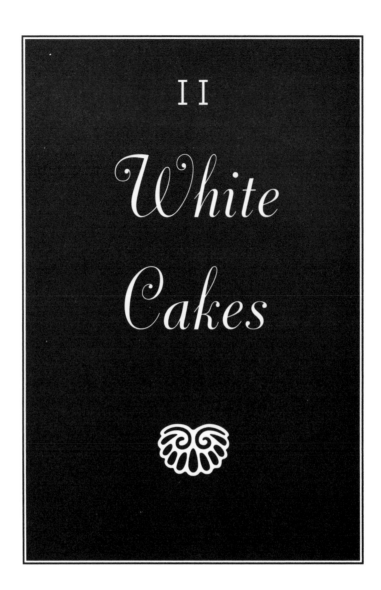

II

White
Cakes

aking a cake may take time, but often the steps can
be spread over 1 or 2 days so that the task does not
become tedious. The basic cakes in this chapter can be
baked 1 day ahead, if desired, assembled, and served the next day.

The Buttermilk and Chiffon Cakes are simple to prepare, but when transformed into cakes layered with an extravagant Bavarian Cream or a rich Lemon Buttercream, they really become works of art.

The Caramelized Lemon Chiffon Cake is another example of a plain cake that becomes an impressive creation. In a cooking class held at Spago Las Vegas, about twenty people, men and women of varied ages, made the Caramelized Lemon Chiffon Cake—under Mary's supervision, of course. Some made the cake in small and large round cake pans, others in a bundt pan. Those who used the round pans cut out a small round from the center of each of their cakes and filled the opening with berries and Crème Brûlée. All had great success, and there were many smiling faces in the kitchen that day.

The Yule Log with Meringue Mushrooms, which always has a sensational effect on its audience, can be prepared easily if the directions are carefully followed. The Meringue Mushrooms can be made a week ahead, and you will find them fun to prepare. If there are children in the house, let them help. They will love it.

Basic Buttermilk Cake

Buttermilk Layer Cake with Strawberry Bavarian Cream

Italian Meringue

Lemon Buttermilk Cake

Lemon Buttermilk Cake with Lemon Buttercream

Lemon Chiffon Cake

Caramelized Lemon Chiffon Cake with Fresh Berries and Crème Brûlée
Crème Brûlée

Yule Log with Meringue Mushrooms

Meringue Mushrooms
Hazelnut Mousse

Basic Buttermilk Cake

EQUIPMENT

9-inch round cake pan

Sifter

Electric mixer

9-inch cardboard round

INGREDIENTS

1¾ cups all-purpose flour

2 teaspoons baking powder

½ teaspoon baking soda

½ teaspoon salt

¾ cup granulated sugar

4 ounces (1 stick) unsalted butter, at room temperature, cut into small pieces

4 egg yolks

1 cup buttermilk

TO PREPARE AHEAD

THROUGH STEP 4

*T*his is a very versatile cake. It can be served plain, or just dusted with sifted powdered sugar; it can be cut into layers, filled, and frosted to make an elegant dessert; it also makes delicious cupcakes.

1. Position rack in center of oven and preheat oven to 350 degrees. Butter, or coat with vegetable spray, and flour a 9-inch round cake pan, tapping out excess flour. Set aside.

2. Sift together the flour, baking powder, baking soda, and salt. Set aside.

3. In the large bowl of electric mixer, using paddle or beaters, beat the sugar and butter. Start on low speed until slightly blended, then gradually turn to high and beat until fluffy. Add yolks, 1 at a time, beating just to combine after each addition. Turn speed to low, and alternate adding the flour mixture and buttermilk, starting and ending with the flour mixture (3 additions of flour and 2 of buttermilk).

4. Scrape batter into prepared pan and gently rap pan on work surface to level. Bake until cake tester, gently inserted into center of cake, comes out clean, about 45 minutes. Let cool in the pan for 15 minutes, then invert onto a 9-inch cardboard round and place on a rack to cool completely.

5. Use as desired.

Buttermilk Layer Cake with Strawberry Bavarian Cream

SERVES 8 TO 10

EQUIPMENT

1 or 2 small saucepans

Blender

Strainer

Electric mixer

9-inch round cake pan

Small metal spatula

INGREDIENTS

Basic Buttermilk Cake
(see page 36)

STRAWBERRY BAVARIAN CREAM

2 pints strawberries, rinsed and
stemmed

¾ cup granulated sugar

¼ cup plus 2 tablespoons cold
water

1 cup milk

4 egg yolks

2 teaspoons unflavored gelatin

Italian Meringue (see page 39)

*T*his recipe features a delicately flavored cream that can not only be used as a filling but is delicious spooned into a serving glass, alternating layers of cream with sliced strawberries.

1. Make the Basic Buttermilk Cake and set it aside.

2. Make the Strawberry Bavarian Cream: Cut 1 pint of strawberries in halves. Place in a small saucepan with ¼ cup sugar and ¼ cup water, and bring to a boil. Lower heat and cook until berries are very soft, about 15 minutes. Cool slightly, then transfer to a blender and puree. Strain and measure. If you have more than ¾ cup, return to saucepan and cook until reduced to ¾ cup. Add the milk and bring to a boil.

3. While mixture is coming to a boil, in the large bowl of an electric mixer, with paddle or beaters, on high speed, beat egg yolks with the remaining ½ cup sugar until thick and pale yellow. Lower speed to medium, slowly pour in the hot liquid, and beat just until combined. Meanwhile, in a clean small saucepan, stir the gelatin into the remaining 2 tablespoons cold water. Heat until the gelatin is completely dissolved. Scrape into the bowl and continue beating until incorporated. Strain into a clean bowl and set aside.

4. Make the Italian Meringue and fold a little into the strawberry mixture to lighten. Fold in the remaining meringue. Chill over ice cubes and cold water until thick. Then refriger-

(continued)

BUTTERMILK LAYER CAKE WITH STRAWBERRY BAVARIAN CREAM *(continued)*

TO PREPARE AHEAD

THROUGH STEP 3, CREAM CAN BE PREPARED EARLY IN THE DAY OR EVEN 1 DAY AHEAD. THROUGH STEP 6, UP TO 1 DAY AHEAD. THROUGH STEP 7, CAKE SHOULD BE FINISHED EARLY IN THE DAY AND REFRIGERATED. REMOVE FROM REFRIGERATOR ABOUT 30 MINUTES BEFORE NEEDED AND ARRANGE FANNED STRAWBERRIES ON TOP OF THE CAKE.

ate, covered, until the cream is thick enough to spread over the cake, about 2 hours.

5. When ready to use, remove 1 cup of the cream for the top of the cake and refrigerate, covered. Reserve 8 or 10 perfect berries and cut the remaining strawberries into thin slices. Fold into the large batch of cream.

6. To assemble the cake: Lightly coat a 9-inch round cake pan with vegetable spray. Level the top of the cake, cutting away the hard part of the top of the cake. Cut into 3 even layers (see page 7). Place the first layer in the prepared pan. Spread half the strawberry cream over the cake and carefully set the second layer on top. Spread the remaining cream over and top with the last cake layer. Refrigerate until firm, 2 to 3 hours, up to overnight.

7. To finish cake: Invert cake pan with cake onto a flat serving plate that is a little larger than the pan. To remove pan, wet a towel under hot water, wring dry, and wrap around outside of pan. (Or gently apply heat from a propane torch around the surface of the pan.) Carefully remove the pan. Pour the reserved 1 cup cream on the cake and, with a small metal spatula, spread over the top of the cake. Refrigerate until needed.

8. When ready to serve, partially slice the 8 or 10 reserved berries and fan (see illustration). Arrange on top of the cake, spacing them so that each serving is topped with a strawberry.

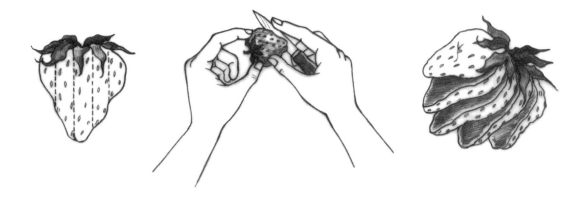

Italian Meringue

MAKES ENOUGH TO FROST AND DECORATE
ONE 8- OR 9-INCH CAKE

Italian meringue consists of beaten egg whites combined with hot sugar syrup. The addition of the hot sugar syrup stabilizes the whites, allowing the meringue to be used as a frosting for cakes.

1. Make the syrup: In a small uncoated saucepan, combine sugar and water. Cook over medium-high heat until bubbles are about dime-size, brushing down sides of pan with a moistened pastry brush as small crystals form around sides of pan. Mixture should not take on any color. Do *not* stir. While stirring, the liquid can splash around the sides of the pan and the syrup may crystallize. If that happens, you will have to start over.

2. Meanwhile, place egg whites in dry, clean large bowl of an electric mixer and, using the whip or beaters, whip whites on medium speed until frothy. Add the cream of tartar, slowly increase speed, and beat to soft peaks. If syrup isn't ready, continue beating on low speed.

3. On low speed, *very slowly* pour the sugar syrup into the beaten egg whites, avoiding the sides of the bowl and the whip if possible. When the syrup is completely incorporated, increase speed to moderate and continue to beat until egg whites are nice and shiny, forming firm peaks, and the mixing bowl is cool to the touch. Use as needed.

Lemon Buttermilk Cake

MAKES ONE 8-INCH CAKE SERVES 8 TO 10

*L*emon-flavored desserts are always a great favorite, and this is no exception. A variation of the Basic Buttermilk Cake (see page 36), the cake can be just dusted with sifted powdered sugar or cut into layers, the layers spread with Lemon Buttercream (see page 41) or Lemon Curd (see page 119).

1. Position rack in center of oven and preheat oven to 350 degrees. Butter, or coat with vegetable spray, an 8 x 2-inch round cake pan. Dust with flour, tapping to remove any excess.

2. Sift together the flour, baking powder, baking soda, and salt. Set aside. In a small bowl, combine the buttermilk and lemon juice.

3. In the large bowl of an electric mixer, on high speed, beat the butter and sugar until light and fluffy, about 5 minutes. Add the egg yolks, 1 at a time, beating just to combine after each addition.

4. On low speed, alternate adding the dry ingredients with the buttermilk mixture, starting and ending with the dry ingredients; 3 additions of the dry and 2 of the liquid. Stir in the lemon zest.

5. Scrape into the prepared pan and bake until the top is golden brown and the sides of the cake start to come away from the pan, 55 to 60 minutes. Cool on a rack. To remove from pan, run a sharp knife around the inside edges of the pan to loosen cake. Invert onto a cake round a little larger than the cake.

6. To serve, cut into slices and top each slice with a small amount of Lemon Buttercream or Lemon Curd. Or arrange a few fresh raspberries and sliced fresh peaches on the cake.

EQUIPMENT

8 x 2-inch round cake pan

Small bowl

Sifter

Electric mixer

9-inch cardboard round

INGREDIENTS

1¾ cups all-purpose flour

2 teaspoons baking powder

½ teaspoon baking soda

½ teaspoon salt

¾ cup buttermilk

¼ cup lemon juice

4 ounces (1 stick) unsalted butter, at room temperature, cut into small pieces

¾ cup granulated sugar

4 egg yolks

2 tablespoons lemon zest

TO PREPARE AHEAD

THROUGH STEP 5

Lemon Buttermilk Cake with Lemon Buttercream

Serves 8

(continued)

Equipment

Electric mixer

2-quart nonreactive saucepan

Whip

Wooden spoon

Fine-mesh strainer

Offset spatula

Long metal spatula

Pastry bag with #3 star tip

Ingredients

Lemon Buttermilk Cake
(see page 40)

LEMON BUTTERCREAM

7 egg yolks

⅔ cup granulated sugar

½ cup milk

2 tablespoons lemon juice

1 pound unsalted butter, at room temperature, cut into small pieces

1 tablespoon lemon zest

To Prepare Ahead

THROUGH STEP 5, THE BUTTERCREAM CAN BE MADE 1 DAY AHEAD. THROUGH STEP 7, THE CAKE CAN BE ASSEMBLED EARLY IN THE DAY.

The buttercream can be frozen in a plastic bag for up to 3 months. Defrost in the bag placed in the refrigerator. When ready to use, snip off a small corner of the bag and pipe out the buttercream as if it were in a pastry bag.

1. Make the Lemon Buttermilk Cake and set aside.

2. Make the buttercream: In the large bowl of an electric mixer, using paddle or beaters, on high speed, beat egg yolks with 3 tablespoons sugar until mixture is thick and pale yellow, forming a ribbon when beater is lifted, 4 to 5 minutes.

3. Meanwhile, in a 2-quart nonreactive saucepan, scald milk. Whisk in remaining sugar and lemon juice and continue whisking until sugar is completely dissolved.

4. On low speed, whisking constantly, slowly pour about ⅓ of the hot milk mixture into the yolks. Pour back into the saucepan and combine with remaining milk. Place over medium heat and, stirring constantly with a wooden spoon, cook until you see the first bubbles forming on the surface. Stop stirring and immediately remove from heat. Strain through a fine strainer into a large clean mixer bowl. Beat on medium-high speed until thick and doubled in volume. Set aside.

5. In a large clean mixer bowl, using clean paddle or beaters, on medium speed, beat butter until it begins to whiten and is very fluffy. On low speed, slowly pour milk mixture into but-

LEMON BUTTERMILK CAKE WITH LEMON BUTTERCREAM *(continued)*

ter. Mixture may appear to be broken, but don't worry, it will come back when you increase the speed of the machine. When all of the mixture has been poured and incorporated into the butter, increase the speed and beat until buttercream is smooth and shiny. Add lemon zest and beat just to combine. At this point, buttercream is ready and can be used. Refrigerate, covered, until needed.

6. To assemble the cake, cut the Lemon Buttermilk Cake into 3 layers (see page 7).

7. With an offset spatula, spread buttercream between the 2 layers and on top of the cake, smoothing the frosting on top of the cake with a long metal spatula. Using a pastry bag fitted with a #3 star tip, decorate the top of the cake with a border of rosettes (see illustration). Refrigerate, removing from refrigerator about 30 minutes before serving.

8. To serve, cut into slices and, if desired, garnish with Candied Lemon Peel (see page 188).

Lemon Chiffon Cake

MAKES ONE 9-INCH CAKE
SERVES 8 TO 10

EQUIPMENT

9-inch round cake pan

Medium bowl

Sifter

Electric mixer

Rubber spatula

9-inch cardboard round

INGREDIENTS

1½ cups granulated sugar

1 cup all-purpose flour

1 teaspoon baking powder

¼ teaspoon salt

4 eggs, separated

2 egg whites

½ cup vegetable oil (peanut,
. safflower, or corn)

½ cup fresh lemon juice

1 teaspoon vanilla extract

TO PREPARE AHEAD

THROUGH STEP 5, CAKE CAN
BE MADE 1 DAY AHEAD.

$\mathcal{T}$his is a very light-textured chiffon cake with a tang of lemon. It can be baked in a bundt pan and served with berries and Crème Brûlée (see page 46) filling the center opening. (See Caramelized Lemon Chiffon Cake, page 45.)

1. Position rack in center of oven and preheat oven to 350 degrees. Butter, or coat with vegetable spray, a 9-inch round cake pan. Dust with flour, tapping out any excess flour. Set aside.

2. In a medium bowl, sift together 1 cup sugar, the flour, baking powder, and salt. Set aside.

3. In the large bowl of an electric mixer, with paddle or beaters, beat the egg yolks at high speed. Turn the machine to low and pour in the oil, lemon juice, and vanilla. Gradually add the sifted ingredients, turn up the speed, and beat until well combined.

4. In another clean large bowl, with whip or beaters, whip the 6 egg whites until soft peaks form. Start on medium speed and raise speed as peaks begin to form. Gradually pour in the remaining ½ cup sugar and continue to whip until whites are shiny and firm but not stiff. With a rubber spatula, fold ¼ of the whites into the egg yolk mixture, then scrape the egg yolk mixture back into the whites, quickly folding until completely incorporated.

5. Scrape into the prepared pan and bake until edges of the cake pull away from the pan and a tester, gently inserted into

(continued)

Lemon Chiffon Cake *(continued)*

the center of the cake, comes out clean, 25 to 30 minutes. Cool on a rack. To remove from pan, carefully run a sharp knife around inside of pan to loosen cake. Invert cake onto rack. Place a 9-inch cardboard round on top of cake and invert onto round.

6. The cake can be served as is, confectioners' sugar sifted over the cake. Or the cake can be cut into layers, frosting spread between layers and on top (Lemon Curd, see page 119, or Crème Brûlée, see page 46), and fresh berries arranged on the frosting.

Caramelized Lemon Chiffon Cake with Fresh Berries and Crème Brûlée

SERVES 10 TO 12

EQUIPMENT

Bundt pan

Small bowl

Slotted spoon

Propane torch

INGREDIENTS

2 baskets fresh raspberries

¼ cup Chambord or liqueur of your choice

Lemon Chiffon Cake (see page 43), baked in bundt pan and cooled

Crème Brûlée (see page 46)

3 to 4 tablespoons granulated sugar

TO PREPARE AHEAD

CAKE CAN BE PREPARED 1 DAY AHEAD; CRÈME BRÛLÉE, EARLY IN THE DAY. ASSEMBLE THE CAKE SHORTLY BEFORE SERVING.

*T*he berries spooned into the center of the cake can be mixed (blackberries, blueberries, sliced strawberries, or raspberries) or you can use a single berry of your choice.

1. In a small bowl, marinate the berries in Chambord 15 to 20 minutes.

2. Place cake on serving plate. With a slotted spoon, carefully transfer berries from bowl to opening in the center of the cake. Top with Crème Brûlée, spooned over the fruit and drizzled down the sides of the cake. Sprinkle a little of the sugar over the Crème Brûlée and caramelize with the torch. Repeat with the remaining sugar, caramelizing as necessary.

3. To serve, cut cake into slices and spoon some of the brûlée and fruit over each slice.

Crème Brûlée

MAKES ABOUT 3 CUPS

Crème Brûlée can be spooned into small ramekins, over sliced or whole berries, and refrigerated, covered, until firm, about 2 hours. Or it can be used to fill baked pastry-lined individual (4-inch) tart pans. Or it can be spread between layers of cake. When ready to serve, sprinkle 1 tablespoon granulated sugar evenly over the top of each serving and caramelize with a propane torch, or set under a broiler until sugar browns. If put under a broiler, make certain that the brûlée does not soften too much. Using the propane torch is preferable.

1. In a heavy medium saucepan, combine the cream and the vanilla bean with its scrapings. Over low heat, just bring to a boil.

2. In a medium heatproof bowl, whisk together the egg yolks and sugar. Place over a pan of simmering water and continue to whisk vigorously until mixture becomes a very pale yellow and feels hot to the touch.

3. Remove from heat and whisk in the boiling cream. Transfer bowl back over saucepan, but do *not* turn on heat. Whisk mixture occasionally until it thickens, 5 to 10 minutes.

4. When mixture thickens, place bowl in a basin or larger bowl filled with cold water and ice cubes. Whisk occasionally until cool. Strain into a clean bowl and refrigerate, covered, until needed.

5. Use as needed, to make small tarts or as a filling for cakes (Lemon Chiffon Cake, see page 43).

*Crème Brûlée also can be flavored with 4 or 5 slices of fresh ginger, blanched, or the zest of 1 large orange instead of the vanilla bean.

EQUIPMENT

Heavy medium saucepan

Medium heatproof bowl

Whip

Large bowl

Strainer

Propane torch

INGREDIENTS

1½ cups heavy cream

1 vanilla bean, split lengthwise*

9 egg yolks

⅓ cup granulated sugar

TO PREPARE AHEAD

THROUGH STEP 4, CRÈME BRÛLÉE CAN BE MADE EARLY IN THE DAY.

EQUIPMENT

Half sheet pan

Parchment or wax paper

Serrated knife

Cardboard

Aluminum foil

Offset spatula

Wooden skewer or small knife

INGREDIENTS

Sponge cake, baked, as for basic
Tiramisù (see page 67)

About 4 cups Hazelnut Mousse
(see page 51)

Rich Chocolate Frosting
(see page 10)

Meringue Mushrooms
(see page 49)

TO PREPARE AHEAD

THROUGH STEP 2, 1 DAY
AHEAD; THROUGH STEP 4,
EARLY IN THE DAY

Yule Log
with Meringue Mushrooms

SERVES 10 TO 12

*T*his is usually made only at Christmas time, but I'm not sure why. It would make a lovely table decoration for any festive occasion. It isn't difficult to make, but it does take time.

1. On a firm surface, trim the edges of the sponge cake, giving you an 11½ x 15-inch cake. Line a half sheet pan with a piece of parchment or wax paper and arrange the cake on the paper, the 15-inch side directly in front of you. Spread the mousse over the surface of the cake, leaving a 1-inch space along the 15-inch side in front of you.

2. Using the paper to aid you (see illustrations), carefully roll up the cake into a thick log, enclosing the mousse. Leave the wrapped, rolled-up cake on pan and refrigerate until filling is firm, at least 2 hours, up to overnight.

3. Remove pan with cake from refrigerator and place wrapped cake on a firm surface. Carefully unwrap cake. Using a serrated knife, from one end cut a 2-inch piece of cake on the diagonal (see illustration). Set the cut piece aside.

4. Cut out a piece of cardboard the length and width of the cake. Cover the cardboard with aluminum foil and place the cake on it. Spread 1 tablespoon frosting on the bottom of the small cut piece and set on top of the cake (see photo in insert following page 68). Using an offset spatula, spread the frosting over the entire cake as well as the small piece atop the cake. Do not frost the one end of the cake that was cut. With a

(continued)

YULE LOG WITH MERINGUE MUSHROOMS *(continued)*

wooden skewer or the point of a small knife, make furrows to simulate bark along the sides and on top of the cake.

5. To serve, arrange Christmas greens on a large platter and place the foil-wrapped cardboard with the cake in the center of the greens. Decorate with Meringue Mushrooms placed on and around the "log." Fresh cranberries can be scattered for added color.

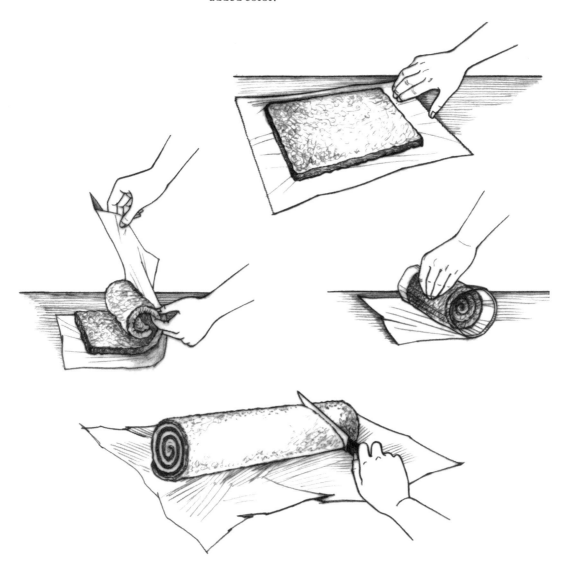

Meringue Mushrooms

MAKES 26 TO 30

EQUIPMENT

Baking trays

Parchment paper

Large pastry bag with #4 or #5 plain tip

Electric mixer

Small spatula

Small knife

Small heatproof bowl

INGREDIENTS

4 large egg whites

1 cup granulated sugar

½ teaspoon vanilla extract

About 5 ounces semisweet chocolate or chocolate chips

Sifted unsweetened cocoa

TO PREPARE AHEAD

THROUGH STEP 6, MERINGUE MUSHROOMS WILL KEEP UP TO 2 WEEKS. DO NOT STORE IN AN AIRTIGHT BAG.

Maida Heatter, our mentor and dear friend, in her very first book, introduced us to the art of making meringue mushrooms. She demystified the technique, and we are eternally grateful. The technique is the same, whether you use this recipe or the one for Italian Meringue (see page 39).

If you are placing 2 trays in the oven and they cannot fit on the center rack, bake the stems on the higher rack and the caps on the lower rack. Any meringue mushrooms that are not used to decorate the Yule Log (see page 47) can be arranged in an attractive bowl, lightly covered, and will keep for 1 or 2 weeks. (Of course, they probably will be eaten long before.)

1. Position rack in center of oven and preheat oven to 200 degrees. Line 1 or 2 baking trays with parchment paper and set aside. Fit a large pastry bag with a #4 or #5 plain tip and set aside.

2. Place egg whites in a dry, clean large bowl of an electric mixer and, using the whip or beaters, whip whites on medium speed until frothy. Turn speed to high, slowly pour in half the sugar, add vanilla, and continue to beat for 1 minute. Slowly pour in the remaining sugar and beat until the whites are very thick and shiny, about 3 to 4 minutes longer. Immediately spoon half the mixture into the prepared pastry bag. (Meringue will begin to break down if not used soon after it is ready.)

3. Make the mushroom caps: Holding the bag upright over the prepared baking trays, squeeze out 26 to 30 mushroom caps, some 1 inch and some 2 inches in diameter, placed about

(continued)

MERINGUE MUSHROOMS *(continued)*

1 inch apart. The caps can be different sizes, since real mushroom caps are never identical.

4. Make the mushroom stems: Again, holding the bag upright over the prepared baking trays, lifting the bag as you squeeze out the meringue, form 26 to 30 stems or "columns," each $\frac{1}{2}$ to 1 inch high, placed about 1 inch apart. Some will be thicker than others, some will have points, but that's okay. Use a small spatula or the tip of a small knife to separate the meringue from the pastry tip.

5. Place the trays in the oven and bake until the meringues are firm to the touch and can be lifted easily from the trays, about $1\frac{1}{2}$ hours. The meringues should be dry, but should not take on any color. Remove the trays to a cool, dry spot. When cool, with a small knife, trim any pointed tips on the caps and stems, if desired.

6. Melt the chocolate: In a small bowl set over simmering water, melt the chocolate. Cool slightly. (If the chocolate is too warm, it will be a bit more difficult for the stem to stick to the cap.)

7. Assemble the mushrooms: Hold the cap in one hand, bottom side up, and with a small spoon, spread a little of the melted chocolate on the underside of the cap. Attach the flat end of the stem to the center of the cap. Return mushroom to the tray and let remain upside down until the chocolate hardens completely. Repeat with the remaining caps, melted chocolate, and stems. When ready, turn mushrooms cap side up, and dust lightly with sifted cocoa.

8. To serve, arrange on and around the Yule Log (see page 47).

Hazelnut Mousse

MAKES ABOUT 4 CUPS

EQUIPMENT

Large bowl

Whip

Food processor

2 medium heatproof bowls

Small saucepan

Electric mixer

Baking tray

INGREDIENTS

1½ cups heavy cream

5 ounces hazelnuts, toasted*

*5 ounces milk chocolate, cut into
small chunks*

*1 tablespoon plus ½ teaspoon
hazelnut oil*

3 egg yolks

⅓ cup granulated sugar

¼ cup water

TO PREPARE AHEAD

THROUGH STEP 7, MOUSSE
CAN BE MADE 1 DAY AHEAD
AND REFRIGERATED,
COVERED.

*T*he hazelnut paste can be spread on bread or crackers, much as you would spread peanut butter. The mousse can be made 1 day ahead, but no more than that or it will lose its fluffiness and begin to break down.

1. In a large bowl, using a whip or beaters, whip heavy cream. Refrigerate, covered, until needed.

2. Place cooled hazelnuts in food processor fitted with steel blade. Process until a paste forms.

3. Melt chocolate in a medium heatproof bowl placed over simmering water. Turn off heat when almost melted and stir occasionally until completely melted. Scrape into nut paste with the hazelnut oil and continue to process until thoroughly mixed. Set aside.

4. Place the egg yolks in a clean medium heatproof bowl.

5. In a small saucepan, bring to a boil the sugar and water and boil until sugar dissolves, about 3 minutes. Whisk the boiling syrup into the egg yolks and set the bowl over simmering water. Continue to whisk until the mixture is thick, pale yellow, and hot to the touch.

6. Remove from heat and scrape into the large bowl of an electric mixer fitted with paddle or beaters. On medium-high speed, beat until mixture has doubled in volume and bottom

(continued)

*To toast hazelnuts, preheat oven to 350 degrees. Spread nuts on a small baking tray and toast in oven 10 to 12 minutes, turning nuts after 5 or 6 minutes. Enclose nuts in a clean towel and rub until as much of the skins as possible comes off. Cool before using.

HAZELNUT MOUSSE *(continued)*

of bowl is completely cool to the touch. Turn speed to low, scrape the hazelnut paste into the bowl, and continue to beat until well combined.

7. Remove bowl from mixer and fold in half the whipped cream, then the remaining half. Mixture should resemble softly whipped cream. Refrigerate, covered, until needed. Use as filling and frosting for Chocolate Chiffon Cake (see page 4) or Basic Buttermilk Cake (see page 36).

III

Cheesecakes

*C*heesecakes have such a smooth, velvety, light texture that you tend to forget that you are eating a rich dessert. However, a small portion satisfies the most demanding palate.

The cheesecakes served at Spago come in a variety of flavors, but the basic ingredients remain the same. One is spooned into a shell of Pâte

Sucrée, another has an Apricot Macaroon Crust, and another a Butter Crunch Crust. There are mini cheesecakes swirled with strawberries, Macadamia Nut Cheesecake with Macadamia Brittle, cheesecake marbled with dark chocolate, and one made with white chocolate and raisins soaked in rum.

And then there is Tiramisù, which is not really a cheesecake, but more like a pudding. It is _the_ dessert of northern Italy, made with mascarpone, an Italian cream cheese, and has become a great favorite in our country as well. We have a basic tiramisù, one made with chocolate, one with ginger, and you may be hard pressed to find a favorite among them.

SPAGO CHEESECAKE

CHEESECAKE WITH APRICOT MACAROON CRUST
AND BLUEBERRY SAUCE

MACADAMIA NUT CHEESECAKE WITH
MACADAMIA BRITTLE

CHOCOLATE MARBLED CHEESECAKE

WHITE CHOCOLATE RUM RAISIN CHEESECAKE

MINI STRAWBERRY SWIRL CHEESECAKES

TIRAMISÙ

CHOCOLATE TIRAMISÙ

GINGER TIRAMISÙ

Spago Cheesecake

MAKES ONE 9-INCH CAKE
SERVES 10

*T*his is a creamy, rich, absolutely delicious cake. The cheesecake should be baked in a *bain-marie* (water bath), created by placing one pan into a larger pan and partially filling the larger pan with hot water. When cake is baked in a springform pan, layers of aluminum foil are wrapped around the pan to prevent water from seeping into the cake.

1. Position rack in center of oven and preheat oven to 350 degrees.

2. Roll out Pâte Sucrée to a circle a little larger than the bottom of a 9-inch springform pan with 2¾-inch-high sides. Remove the bottom of the pan and use as a guide. Cut out a circle of dough and fit the dough onto the bottom of the pan. Bake until golden, about 20 minutes, turning pan halfway through. Cool and then fit bottom back into the springform pan. (Or, if using the Butter Crunch Crust, press into the bottom of the pan and continue with recipe.) Wrap heavy-duty foil (or 2 layers of regular foil) around the bottom and halfway up the sides of the pan, pleating to tighten. Set aside.

3. Make the filling: Place the cream cheese, sugar, and salt in the large bowl of an electric mixer. Using the paddle or beaters, on medium speed, beat until smooth, stopping occasionally to scrape down the sides and under the beaters with a rubber spatula. Turn the speed to high and continue to beat until nice and creamy. Stop the machine, add the sour cream, rum, lemon juice, and vanilla, then, on medium speed, continue beating until well blended. Add eggs and beat just until combined. Scrape into the prepared springform pan and set

EQUIPMENT

Rolling pin

9-inch springform pan

Aluminum foil

Electric mixer

Rubber spatula

Baking pan larger than springform pan

INGREDIENTS

¾ pound Pâte Sucrée (see page 76) or Butter Crunch Crust (see page 80)

FILLING

1½ pounds cream cheese, at room temperature, cut into small pieces

1¼ cups granulated sugar

¼ teaspoon salt

¾ cup sour cream

1 tablespoon dark rum

1 tablespoon lemon juice

2 teaspoons vanilla extract

3 eggs

TO PREPARE AHEAD

THROUGH STEP 4. THIS CAKE
CAN BE FROZEN, WRAPPED
WELL, FOR UP TO 1 MONTH.
TO DEFROST, REFRIGERATE,
STILL WRAPPED, UNTIL
READY TO SERVE.

the pan in the center of a larger baking pan. Pour enough hot water into the larger pan to reach about halfway up the sides of the springform pan, but not above the foil.

4. Carefully place both pans in the oven and bake until the top is lightly golden and slightly firm in the center, about 1 hour and 10 minutes. (Cake will become firmer as it cools.) Remove pans from the oven and *carefully* lift out the springform pan and place on a rack. Remove foil from pan to help cool the cake. When completely cool, refrigerate, covered, overnight. (The cake should not be served until it is very firm.)

5. To serve, dip a long, sharp knife into warm water and run the knife around the inside of the springform pan, loosening the cake from the pan. Remove the outer ring. To cut into slices, dip knife into warm water as necessary. Garnish each slice with berries of your choice. Or serve with Blueberry Sauce (see page 58).

Cheesecake with Apricot Macaroon Crust and Blueberry Sauce

SERVES 10 TO 12

*B*on *Appétit* magazine displayed this cheesecake on its April 1993 cover. Although the preparation may be time consuming, the results are well worth the effort.

1. Make the sauce: In a large nonreactive saucepan, combine the sauce ingredients and bring to a boil. Over medium-low heat, simmer, stirring occasionally, until mixture has a consistency of thick syrup, 20 to 30 minutes. Cool and then refrigerate, covered, until needed.

2. Make the crust: Position rack in center of oven and preheat oven to 350 degrees.

3. In a small saucepan, bring apricots and water to a boil. Remove from heat, cover, and let steep until fruit is soft, about 30 minutes. Drain apricots, pat dry, and place in food processor fitted with steel blade. Add sugar and egg whites and process until apricots are minced and mixture has a thick, fluffy consistency, scraping down sides of work bowl as necessary.

4. While apricots are softening, spread coconut on a small baking tray. Toast in oven until golden brown, about 10 minutes. Cool, transfer ½ cup to food processor with fluffy apricot mixture, and process until finely chopped. Scrape into a medium bowl and stir in remaining coconut. Freeze, covered, just until firm, about 20 minutes.

5. Spoon apricot mixture into 9-inch springform pan. Wrap

FILLING

1½ pounds cream cheese, at room temperature, cut into pieces

1¼ cups granulated sugar

¼ teaspoon salt

¾ cup sour cream

1 tablespoon dark rum

1 tablespoon fresh lemon juice

2 teaspoons vanilla extract

3 eggs

Additional blueberries, optional, as garnish

Tᴏ Pʀᴇᴘᴀʀᴇ Aʜᴇᴀᴅ

Tʜʀᴏᴜɢʜ sᴛᴇᴘ 8

plastic wrap around fingertips and press mixture evenly over bottom of pan, forming the crust. Bake until light brown, about 15 minutes. Place on rack to cool while preparing filling.

6. Make the filling: Place the cheese, sugar, and salt in the large bowl of an electric mixer. Using the paddle or beaters, on medium speed, beat until smooth, stopping occasionally to scrape down the sides of the bowl and under the beaters with a rubber spatula. Turn the speed to high and continue to beat until nice and creamy. Stop the machine, then, on medium speed, add the sour cream, rum, lemon juice, and vanilla, and continue to beat until well blended. Add the eggs and beat just until combined. Pour into the crust, tapping the pan once or twice on a firm surface to level.

7. Wrap heavy-duty foil (or 2 layers of regular foil) around the bottom and outside of the pan, pleating to tighten, and place in the center of a slightly larger baking pan. Pour enough hot water into the larger pan to reach about halfway up the sides of the springform pan, but not above the foil.

8. Carefully place both pans in the oven and bake until the top is lightly golden and slightly firm in the center, about 1 hour and 20 minutes. Remove pans from oven and carefully lift out the springform pan and place on a rack. Remove the foil from the pan to help cool the cake. When completely cool, refrigerate, covered, overnight.

9. When ready to serve, remove cake from refrigerator. Dip a long, sharp knife into warm water and carefully run the knife around the inside of the pan, loosening the cake from the pan. Remove the outer ring.

10. To serve: Dip knife into warm water and cut into slices. Spoon a little of the blueberry sauce over each slice and arrange a few whole blueberries, if desired, around the cake. Any extra sauce can be poured into a bowl and passed.

Macadamia Nut Cheesecake with Macadamia Brittle

SERVES 10 TO 12

*T*he contrasting texture of the smooth cake and the crunchy Macadamia Brittle is a winner.

1. Make the Butter Crunch Crust and press onto the bottom of a 9- or 10-inch springform pan. (If made in 10-inch pan, cake won't rise to the very top and will not brown as much.) Set aside. When ready to bake, wrap aluminum foil halfway up sides of springform pan and pleat to tighten around pan. Set in baking pan with sides, a little larger than the springform pan.

2. Position rack in center of oven and preheat oven to 350 degrees.

3. Make cheesecake and pour into prepared springform pan. Fill larger pan with enough hot water to come about halfway up sides of springform pan, but not above the foil. Carefully transfer to oven and bake until top of cake feels slightly firm to the touch and has taken on a golden color, about 1 hour 20 minutes. Remove the pans from the oven, carefully lift out the springform pan, and set on rack. Fold away the foil from the sides and discard. Let cake cool completely. When cool, refrigerate, covered, overnight.

4. When ready to serve, remove cake from refrigerator. Dip a long, sharp knife into warm water and carefully run the knife around the inside of the pan, loosening the cake from the pan. Remove the outer ring.

5. To serve, sprinkle the chopped Macadamia Brittle over the top of the cake. Dip knife into warm water and cut into slices. Garnish each plate with pieces of brittle.

Macadamia Brittle

EQUIPMENT

Medium deep saucepan

Aluminum foil

Long-handled wooden spoon

Candy thermometer

Long metal spatula

12 x 17-inch half sheet pan

INGREDIENTS

2 cups unsalted macadamia nuts

1¼ cups granulated sugar

⅓ cup light corn syrup

⅓ cup water

*8 ounces (2 sticks) unsalted butter,
cut into small pieces*

1 teaspoon salt

½ teaspoon baking soda

*B*rittle can be eaten as a candy, or it can be crushed and sprinkled over ice cream. Or it can be coarsely chopped, a little sprinkled on slices of our Basic Butter Cookies (see page 203) before baking. You can make brittle using almost any nut you like.

1. Spread the nuts on a baking tray and toast in preheated 350-degree oven 8 to 10 minutes, turning the nuts after 5 minutes. Cool and then coarsely chop. Set aside.

2. Place the sugar in a medium deep saucepan. Add the corn syrup and water and, over medium heat, bring to a boil. Boil until a layer of bubbles forms on top, 3 to 4 minutes. Cover the pan with aluminum foil and continue to boil 5 minutes longer.

3. Remove the foil, add the butter, and stir with a wooden spoon until the butter is melted. Cook over medium heat until a candy thermometer registers 300 degrees, about 30 minutes, stirring occasionally. Immediately stir in the salt, baking soda, and reserved nuts.

4. Meanwhile, coat with vegetable oil or vegetable spray a 12 x 17-inch half sheet pan. Spread the nut mixture over the prepared pan, spreading it as thin as possible with a long metal spatula. When cool, run a clean, dry towel over the top to absorb some of the oil.

5. Cut or break the brittle into desired pieces. Use as needed.

Chocolate Marbled Cheesecake

EQUIPMENT

Rolling pin

10-inch nonstick springform pan

Electric mixer

Rubber spatula

Small bowl

Small knife

Aluminum foil

Baking pan larger than springform pan

INGREDIENTS

¾ pound Pâte Sucrée (page 76)

FILLING

2¼ pounds cream cheese, at room temperature, cut into small pieces

2 cups less 2 tablespoons granulated sugar

¼ teaspoon salt

1½ cups sour cream

1½ tablespoons lemon juice

1½ tablespoons dark rum

1 tablespoon vanilla extract

5 eggs

*M*arbling is an easy way to make an elaborate decoration. By dropping spoonfuls of dark batter into the light batter and running a knife through, a beautiful and artistic effect can easily be achieved.

1. Position a rack in the center of the oven and preheat oven to 350 degrees.

2. Make the crust: On a lightly floured surface, roll out Pâte Sucrée to a circle a little larger than the 10-inch springform pan. Using the bottom of the pan as a guide, cut out a circle of dough and place on the bottom of the pan, trimming to fit. Bake until golden brown, about 20 minutes, turning pan after 10 minutes so that the crust will brown evenly. Cool, then fit bottom into the springform pan and set aside.

3. Make the filling: Place the cheese, sugar, and salt in the large bowl of an electric mixer. Using the paddle or beaters, on medium speed, beat until smooth, stopping occasionally to scrape down the sides and under the beaters with a rubber spatula. Turn the speed to high and continue to beat until nice and creamy. Stop the machine, turn speed to medium, and add the sour cream, lemon juice, rum, and vanilla, then continue to beat until well blended. Add the eggs and beat just until combined.

4. Make the chocolate mixture for marbling: Measure out 2 cups of filling and place in a small bowl. Scrape in the melted chocolate and mix well, then stir in the sifted cocoa until smooth.

CHOCOLATE FOR
MARBLING

2 ounces bittersweet chocolate, melted

¼ cup unsweetened cocoa, sifted

TO PREPARE AHEAD
THROUGH STEP 6

5. Pour the filling into the prepared pan, tapping once or twice on a firm surface to level. Add large spoonfuls of the chocolate mixture around the top of the filling and swirl through with the point of a small, sharp knife. Repeat until all the chocolate mixture is used. Wrap heavy-duty foil (or 2 layers of regular foil) around bottom and halfway up the outside of the pan, pleating to tighten, and place in the center of a slightly larger baking pan. Pour enough hot water into the larger pan to reach about halfway up the sides of the springform pan, but not above the foil.

6. Carefully place both pans in the oven and bake until the top is lightly golden and slightly firm in the center, about 1 hour and 20 minutes. Remove the pans from the oven and carefully lift out the springform pan and place on a rack. Fold away the foil from the sides to help cool the cake. Let cool completely. Refrigerate, covered, overnight.

7. When ready to serve, remove cake from refrigerator. Dip a long, sharp knife into warm water and carefully run the knife around the inside of the pan, loosening the cake from the pan. Remove the outside ring.

8. To serve, using the same knife dipped in warm water, cut cake into slices. If desired, a little shaved chocolate can be sprinkled over each slice.

White Chocolate Rum Raisin Cheesecake

MAKES ONE 9-INCH CAKE
SERVES 8 TO 10

EQUIPMENT

Rolling pin

9-inch springform pan

Aluminum foil

Small pan

Electric mixer

Rubber spatula

Baking pan with sides a little higher than springform pan

INGREDIENTS

¾ pound Pâte Sucrée (see page 76)

FILLING

½ cup dark raisins

⅓ cup dark rum

1½ pounds cream cheese, at room temperature, cut into small pieces

1 cup granulated sugar

¼ teaspoon salt

¾ cup sour cream

2 teaspoons vanilla extract

4 ounces white chocolate, melted

3 eggs

TO PREPARE AHEAD

THROUGH STEP 6

*T*he idea for this cake evolved while I was eating rum raisin ice cream. It is important to allow the raisins to marinate in the dark rum for maximum flavor.

1. Position rack in center of oven and preheat oven to 350 degrees.

2. Make the crust: On a lightly floured surface, roll out Pâte Sucrée to a circle a little larger than a 9-inch springform pan. Using the bottom of the pan as a guide, cut out a circle of dough and place on the bottom of the pan, trimming to fit. Bake until golden brown, about 20 minutes, turning pan after 10 minutes so that the crust will brown evenly. Cool on a cooling rack and then fit bottom back into the springform pan. Wrap heavy-duty foil (or 2 layers of regular foil) around bottom and halfway up the outside of the pan, pleating to tighten. Set aside.

3. Combine the raisins and rum in a small pan and heat. Remove from stove and let the raisins marinate as they cool.

4. Make the filling: Place the cheese, sugar, and salt in the large bowl of an electric mixer. Using the paddle or beaters, on medium speed, beat until smooth, stopping occasionally to scrape down the sides and under the beaters with a rubber spatula. Turn the speed to high and, on medium speed, continue to beat until nice and creamy. Stop the machine and add the sour cream and vanilla, then continue to beat until well combined. Scrape in the melted chocolate, add eggs, and beat until combined.

5. Remove bowl and fold in the rum-raisin mixture. Pour into the prepared springform pan, tapping once or twice on a firm surface to level. Set the pan in the center of a slightly larger baking pan. Pour enough hot water into the larger pan to reach halfway up the sides of the springform pan, but not above the foil.

6. Carefully place both pans in the oven and bake until the top is lightly golden and slightly firm in the center, about 1 hour and 10 minutes. (Cake will become firm as it cools.) Remove the pans from the oven and carefully lift out the springform pan and place on a rack. Fold away the foil from the sides of the pan to help cool the cake. Let cool completely. Refrigerate, covered, overnight.

7. To serve, dip a long, sharp knife into warm water and run the knife around the inside of the springform pan, loosening the cake from the pan. Remove the outer ring. To cut into slices, dip knife into warm water as necessary. This cake requires no garnish, but if you like, you can decorate each plate with berries of your choice.

EQUIPMENT

Twelve 1-cup ramekins

*Baking pan with sides, large
enough to hold ramekins*

INGREDIENTS

*About ¾ cup Strawberry Compote
(see page 225)*

*1 recipe Spago Cheesecake
(see page 56), filling only*

*Sliced fresh strawberries or
blueberries, for garnish*

TO PREPARE AHEAD

THROUGH STEP 3,
REFRIGERATING OVERNIGHT

Mini Strawberry Swirl Cheesecakes

MAKES 12 INDIVIDUAL CHEESECAKES

*I*f you don't have individual ramekins, these small cheese-cakes can be made in regular-size muffin pans. When baked, run knife around inside edge of each muffin cup and then invert onto a large baking tray. With a wide spatula, lift each cake to a serving plate, spooning the Strawberry Compote around.

1. Position rack in center of oven and preheat oven to 350 degrees. Coat with vegetable spray each of twelve 1-cup ramekins. Set aside.

2. Spoon about 1 tablespoon Strawberry Compote into the bottom of each ramekin, then fill with the cheesecake batter (scant 1 cup). Arrange the ramekins in a large baking pan with sides and fill the baking pan with hot water, reaching about halfway up the sides of the ramekins. Bake until the cheese-cakes begin to pull away from the sides of the ramekins and are almost firm to the touch, 35 to 40 minutes.

3. Remove ramekins to rack and let cool. Refrigerate, covered, overnight.

4. When ready to serve, run a sharp knife around the inside edges of each ramekin and invert the cake onto a serving plate. The compote will run down the sides of each cake. Garnish with slices of fresh strawberries or a few blueberries around the cake. Serve immediately.

Tiramisù

EQUIPMENT

12 x 17 x 1-inch half sheet pan

Parchment paper

1 or 2 large heatproof bowls

Whip

Electric mixer

Rubber spatula

Long metal offset spatula

2½-inch cookie cutter

Grater

Medium bowl

9 x 12 x 2-inch serving dish

INGREDIENTS

SPONGE CAKE

6 eggs, separated

*¼ cup plus 1 tablespoon
granulated sugar*

½ cup all-purpose flour, sifted

MASCARPONE CREAM

6 eggs, separated

2½ tablespoons granulated sugar

1 pound mascarpone cheese

About ¼ cup dark rum

About 2 tablespoons Kahlúa

4 ounces milk chocolate, grated

This is one of the most asked-for desserts served at Spago, Las Vegas. It is assembled in individual ramekins at the restaurant, but for preparation at home, it may be more practical to make it in a large dish. (See Chocolate Tiramisù, page 69, for directions on individual portions.) Leftover sponge cake makes good snacking.

1. Make the sponge cake: Butter, or coat with vegetable spray, a 12 x 17 x 1-inch half sheet pan, line with parchment paper, butter or spray paper, and sprinkle with flour, tapping to remove excess flour. Preheat oven to 350 degrees.

2. In the large bowl of an electric mixer, using paddle or beaters, combine the egg yolks with 2 tablespoons of sugar. Beat on high speed for 2 minutes. On low speed, slowly pour the flour into the egg yolk mixture, beating just until blended.

3. In a separate clean bowl, using whip or beaters, on medium speed, whip the whites to soft peaks. Gradually pour in the remaining 3 tablespoons sugar, turn up speed, and continue to beat until shiny and firm but not stiff. With a rubber spatula, fold about ¼ of the whites into the egg yolk mixture and then fold back into the whites. Do this as quickly as possible until the mixtures are thoroughly combined. Scrape into the prepared pan and even the top by running a long offset spatula across the surface. Bake until cake is golden brown and springs back when lightly touched, 12 to 15 minutes. Cool on a rack. When completely cool, using a 2½-inch cookie cutter, cut out 24 circles. Set aside.

(continued)

TIRAMISÙ *(continued)*

SOAKING LIQUID

2 cups strong hot coffee (decaf can be used)

½ cup granulated sugar

¼ cup rum

2 tablespoons Kahlúa

2 tablespoons Grand Marnier

TO PREPARE AHEAD

THROUGH STEP 3, CAKE CAN BE MADE 1 DAY AHEAD, WRAPPED WELL AND REFRIGERATED; THROUGH STEP 7, REFRIGERATE CAKE, COVERED, UNTIL NEEDED. TIRAMISÙ SHOULD ALWAYS BE ASSEMBLED 4 TO 5 HOURS AHEAD, ALLOWING IT TO SET.

4. Make the mascarpone cream: In a large, clean heatproof bowl, set over simmering water, whisk the egg yolks and 2 tablespoons sugar until sugar dissolves and mixture is hot to the touch. Remove from heat and whisk in the mascarpone.

5. In a clean bowl of the electric mixer, using whip or beaters, on medium speed, beat the egg whites to soft peaks. Add the remaining ½ tablespoon sugar, turn up speed, and beat until shiny and firm but not stiff. Fold into the mascarpone mixture. Stir in the rum, Kahlúa (adding more as necessary to taste), and 2 tablespoons grated milk chocolate. Refrigerate until needed.

6. Make the soaking liquid: In a medium bowl, combine all the ingredients for the soaking liquid. Set aside and let cool.

7. Assemble the tiramisù: Before arranging in the dish, dip each cake circle, one at a time, in the soaking liquid until saturated but still whole. If the cake circles sit in the liquid too long, they will fall apart. Arrange 8 cake circles on the bottom of a 9 x 12 x 2-inch serving dish and spread ⅓ of the mascarpone cream on top. Top with 8 more cake circles and half of the remaining mascarpone. Repeat with the remaining cake circles and remaining mascarpone. Sprinkle the remaining grated chocolate over the top. Refrigerate, covered, until needed.

8. To serve, serve directly from the dish, garnishing each plate with a few raspberries or 1 strawberry, partially sliced and fanned.

Opera Cake

Chocolate Cream-filled Logs

Mary's Cartoon Character Cake (Bart Simpson)

Caramelized Lemon Chiffon Cake with Fresh Berries and Crème Brûlée

Yule Log with Meringue Mushrooms

Mini Strawberry Swirl Cheesecake

Almond Crunch Brown Butter Tart with Chocolate Oil and Almond Toffee

Top: Fresh Berry Napoleon
Bottom: Rustic Almond Apple Tart

Chocolate Tiramisù

EQUIPMENT

12 x 17-inch half sheet pan

Parchment paper

Medium and 2 large heatproof bowls

Whip

Electric mixer

Rubber spatula

Long metal offset spatula

2-inch cookie cutter

Medium bowl

Twelve 8-ounce serving cups or ramekins

Baking tray

Grater

INGREDIENTS

CHOCOLATE CAKE

4 ounces milk chocolate, cut into small pieces

6 eggs, separated

¼ cup granulated sugar

½ cup all-purpose flour, sifted

Chocolate Tiramisù can be assembled in a baking dish (see Tiramisù, page 67, and Ginger Tiramisù, page 71), portions spooned out as desired, or in twelve 8-ounce cups, as below. At Spago, Tiramisù is served in individual cups.

1. Make the cake: Position the rack in the center of the oven and preheat oven to 350 degrees. Butter, or coat with vegetable spray, a 12 x 17-inch half sheet pan, line with parchment paper, butter or spray paper, and sprinkle with flour, tapping to remove excess flour.

2. In a medium heatproof bowl set over simmering water, melt the chocolate until almost completely melted. Turn off heat and let continue to melt until needed, stirring occasionally.

3. In the large bowl of an electric mixer, using paddle or beaters, combine the egg yolks with 2 tablespoons sugar. Beat on high speed for 2 minutes. On low speed, slowly pour the flour into the mixer and beat just until blended.

4. In a clean bowl of the mixer, on medium speed, using whip or beaters, whip the egg whites to soft peaks. Gradually add the remaining 2 tablespoons sugar, turn up speed, and continue to beat until firm but not stiff. With a rubber spatula, fold about ¼ of the whites into the egg yolk mixture, then fold back into the whites. Do this as quickly as possible until the mixtures are thoroughly combined. Fold in the melted chocolate until well mixed. Scrape into the prepared pan and even the top by running a long offset spatula across the surface. Bake until the cake springs back when lightly touched, about 15 minutes. Cool on a rack. When completely cool, using a 2-inch cookie cutter, cut out 24 circles. Set aside.

(continued)

CHOCOLATE TIRAMISÙ *(continued)*

SOAKING LIQUID

*4 cups espresso coffee,
decaffeinated or regular*

*2 cups Simple Sugar Syrup
(see page 241)*

3 tablespoons Kahlúa

3 tablespoons rum

CHOCOLATE MASCARPONE
CREAM

21 ounces mascarpone cheese

*11½ ounces milk chocolate, cut
into small pieces*

8 eggs, separated

½ cup granulated sugar

2 tablespoons Kahlúa

2 tablespoons rum

*Unsweetened cocoa, sifted, for
decoration*

*About ¼ cup coarsely grated milk
chocolate, for garnish*

TO PREPARE AHEAD

THROUGH STEP 4, CAKE CAN
BE MADE 1 DAY AHEAD,
WRAPPED WELL, AND
REFRIGERATED. THROUGH
STEP 10, TIRAMISÙ SHOULD
BE ASSEMBLED 4 TO 5 HOURS
BEFORE BEING SERVED,
ALLOWING IT TO SET.

5. Make the soaking liquid: In a medium bowl, combine all the ingredients and mix well. Set aside and let cool.

6. Make the mascarpone cream: In a large clean bowl of the electric mixer, using paddle or beaters, beat the mascarpone until fluffy, scraping down the sides of the bowl and under the beaters as necessary.

7. Meanwhile, in a medium heatproof bowl, set over simmering water, melt the chocolate until almost completely melted. Turn off the heat and let continue to melt, stirring occasionally.

8. In a large heatproof bowl, set over simmering water, whisk the egg yolks with ¼ cup sugar until sugar dissolves and mixture is hot to the touch. Remove from heat and scrape into the mascarpone. On medium speed, beat just until combined. Lower speed, add the melted chocolate, and mix well.

9. In a clean large bowl of the electric mixer, using whip or beaters, whip the egg whites to soft peaks. Add the remaining ¼ cup sugar and continue to beat until shiny and firm but not stiff. Fold into the mascarpone mixture. Stir in the Kahlúa and rum.

10. Assemble the tiramisù: Before arranging a cake circle into a cup, dip the circle in soaking liquid until saturated but still whole. For each 8-ounce serving cup, spoon about 2 ounces of mascarpone cream in the bottom of the cup and set a cake circle on the cream. Spoon about 2 more ounces of cream into the cup, top with a second cake circle, then about 2 ounces of cream. As each cup is filled, place on a large baking tray. (Each cup should have 2 cake circles and about 6 ounces of mascarpone cream.) When all the cups have been filled and placed on the tray, refrigerate, covered with a large sheet of paper or foil, until needed.

11. To serve, sift a little unsweetened cocoa over each cup and top with grated milk chocolate.

Ginger Tiramisù

EQUIPMENT

12 x 17-inch half sheet pan

Parchment paper

1 or 2 large heatproof bowls

Whip

Electric mixer

Sifter

Rubber spatula

Long metal offset spatula

2½-inch cookie cutter

Medium saucepan

Medium heatproof bowl

9 x 12 x 2-inch serving dish

Pastry bag and #4 star tip

INGREDIENTS

SPONGE CAKE

6 eggs, separated

¼ cup plus 1 tablespoon granulated sugar

½ cup all-purpose flour

2 tablespoons ground ginger

SOAKING LIQUID

3 cups water

2⅓ cups granulated sugar

10-ounce bottle ginger ale

This unconventional version of the traditional tiramisù is made with ground ginger and a very unusual ingredient, ginger ale. The better the ginger ale, the better the flavor. Do not use diet ginger ale.

1. Make the sponge cake: Position the rack in the center of the oven and preheat oven to 350 degrees. Butter, or coat with vegetable spray, a 12 x 17-inch half sheet pan, line with parchment paper, butter or spray paper, and sprinkle with flour, tapping to remove excess flour.

2. In the large bowl of an electric mixer, using paddle or beaters, combine the egg yolks with 2 tablespoons sugar. Beat on high speed for 2 minutes. Sift together the flour and ginger and, on low speed, slowly pour into the mixer and beat just until blended.

3. In a separate clean bowl, on medium speed, whisk the egg whites to soft peaks. Gradually pour in the remaining 3 tablespoons sugar, turn up speed, and continue to beat until firm but not stiff. With a rubber spatula, fold about ¼ of the whites into the egg yolk mixture, then fold back into the whites. Do this as quickly as possible until the mixtures are thoroughly combined. Scrape into the prepared pan and even the top by running a long offset spatula across the surface. Bake until the cake is golden brown and springs back when lightly touched, 12 to 15 minutes. Cool on a rack. When completely cool, using a 2½-inch cookie cutter, cut out 24 circles. Set aside.

4. Make the soaking liquid: In a medium saucepan, combine the water and sugar and bring to a boil. Over medium heat,

(continued)

GINGER TIRAMISÙ *(continued)*

MASCARPONE CREAM

1 pound mascarpone cheese

6 eggs, separated

¼ cup granulated sugar

1 tablespoon ground ginger

3 tablespoons dark rum

3 tablespoons Kahlúa

1 cup heavy cream, whipped

About ¼ cup finely chopped crystallized ginger or Candied Fresh Ginger (see page 190)

TO PREPARE AHEAD

THROUGH STEP 3, CAKE CAN BE MADE 1 DAY AHEAD, WRAPPED WELL, AND REFRIGERATED. THROUGH STEP 8, TIRAMISÙ SHOULD BE ASSEMBLED 4 TO 5 HOURS BEFORE BEING SERVED, ALLOWING IT TO SET. DECORATE ABOUT 1 HOUR BEFORE SERVING AND REFRIGERATE.

boil 1 to 2 minutes until liquid is clear. Do not let color. Stir in the ginger ale. Set aside to cool.

5. Make the mascarpone cream: In the large bowl of the electric mixer, using paddle or beaters, beat the mascarpone until fluffy, scraping down the sides of the bowl and under the beaters as necessary.

6. Meanwhile, in a medium heatproof bowl set over simmering water, whisk the egg yolks, 2 tablespoons sugar, and the ginger until sugar dissolves and mixture is hot to the touch. Remove from heat and scrape into the mascarpone. On medium speed, beat just until combined.

7. In a clean large bowl, using whip or beaters, whip the egg whites to soft peaks. Add the remaining 2 tablespoons sugar and continue to beat until shiny and firm but not stiff. Fold into the mascarpone mixture. Stir in the rum and Kahlúa.

8. Assemble the tiramisù: Steep each circle of sponge cake in the soaking liquid until saturated but still whole. Arrange 8 cake circles on the bottom of a 9 x 12 x 2-inch serving dish and spread ⅓ of the mascarpone cream over. Top with 8 more cake circles and half the remaining mascarpone. Repeat with the remaining cake circles and remaining mascarpone cream. Refrigerate, covered, until needed.

9. To serve, using a pastry bag and #4 star tip, decorate the tiramisù with piped mounds of whipped cream. Sprinkle the chopped candied ginger over. Serve directly from the dish, using a large serving spoon.

IV

Perfect Pastry Shells

Sweet pastry (Pâte Sucrée) is the most widely used pastry for pies and tarts. However, adding spices, chopped nuts, or chocolate to the pastry can increase the overall flavor of a pie or tart. Therefore, we have included a number of pastry doughs, many interchangeable with recipes in the chapter on Perfect Pies and Tarts. The less you work with the dough, the flakier the crust. After making the dough, refrigerate, well wrapped, so that the gluten in the flour can relax. When rolling out pastry, do it on a cool, preferably chilled, firm surface and work as quickly as you can so that the dough doesn't soften too much. In our Techniques section, we have described and illustrated how best to roll out dough and line a pan with it (see page xxi). Since it is important to roll out the dough properly, it seems worthwhile to repeat some of the techniques in this chapter.

To roll out dough, dust work surface lightly with flour and set dough on the flour. Sprinkle flour over dough and rolling pin and press down on dough to flatten. Start rolling from the center out, first in one direction, then in another, carefully lifting and turning dough, lightly sprinkling work surface and dough as necessary. Continue rolling, lifting, and turning until dough is about 2 inches larger than the baking pan. Slip a wide spatula under dough to loosen completely.

To line the pan, place the pie or tart pan directly in front of you and then roll up dough loosely over rolling pin. Unroll over the pan, being careful that the dough is centered. With your knuckle, gently press dough against the sides and then down on the bottom of the pan. Roll the rolling pin around the outside edge of the pan to trim the overhang, or use a small paring knife to trim. If there are any tears in the dough, brush lightly with water and press a small piece of the excess dough on the tear. Refrigerate at least 1 hour before baking to help keep the dough from shrinking down the sides of the pan while the pastry is baking.

PÂTE SUCRÉE

ALMOND PÂTE SUCRÉE

CHOCOLATE PÂTE SUCRÉE

SPICED PÂTE SUCRÉE

BUTTER CRUNCH CRUST

BASIC PIE DOUGH

SPICED PIE DOUGH

Pâte Sucrée

EQUIPMENT

Food processor

Small bowl

Whip

Plastic wrap

INGREDIENTS

2¹/₃ cups all-purpose flour

¹/₃ cup granulated sugar

*8 ounces (2 sticks) unsalted butter,
chilled, cut into small pieces*

2 egg yolks

1 to 2 tablespoons heavy cream

TO PREPARE AHEAD

THROUGH STEP 2. THE PÂTE
SUCRÉE CAN BE CUT INTO
PORTIONS, WRAPPED WELL,
AND FROZEN.

*T*his basic pâte sucrée can be used for any and all tarts. However, once you have overcome any concerns you might have about making and rolling out pastry shells, try experimenting with the different ones offered in this chapter, substituting as you see fit.

1. In a food processor fitted with the steel blade, combine the flour and sugar with 1 or 2 on/off turns. Add the butter and process until the texture resembles fine meal.

2. In a small bowl, whisk together the egg yolks and 1 tablespoon cream. Scrape into the machine and process until a ball begins to form, using the additional cream as necessary. Remove the dough from the machine and wrap in plastic wrap. Refrigerate for at least 3 hours, up to 24 hours.

3. Use as needed.

Almond Pâte Sucrée

MAKES ABOUT 2¼ POUNDS,
ENOUGH FOR THREE 9-INCH PASTRY SHELLS

EQUIPMENT

Baking tray

Food processor

Medium bowl

Electric mixer

Plastic wrap

INGREDIENTS

¾ cup (about 4 ounces) whole unblanched almonds

3⅓ cups all-purpose flour, sifted

12 ounces (3 sticks) unsalted butter, chilled, cut into small pieces

1 cup granulated sugar

1 egg

½ teaspoon lemon zest

TO PREPARE AHEAD

THROUGH STEP 4, THE DOUGH CAN BE REFRIGERATED OR FROZEN. IF FREEZING, DEFROST DOUGH, STILL WRAPPED, IN THE REFRIGERATOR.

We use this dough for the Rustic Almond Apple Tart (see page 96), the Plum Almond Tart (see page 108), and the Almond Crunch Brown Butter Tart (see page 87).

1. Position rack in center of oven and preheat oven to 375 degrees.

2. Spread the nuts on a baking tray and toast until golden, 12 to 15 minutes, turning nuts after 6 or 7 minutes. Cool completely. Place in a food processor fitted with a steel blade and grind coarsely with on/off turns. Transfer to a medium bowl and combine with the flour. Set aside.

3. In the large bowl of an electric mixer, using the paddle or beaters, combine the butter and sugar. Start on medium speed and, when fully combined, turn speed to high and continue to beat until light and fluffy, scraping down sides of bowl as necessary. Add the egg and lemon zest. Stop the machine, pour the flour-nut mixture into the bowl, and mix, starting on low speed, then raising the speed just until flour is incorporated.

4. Turn out on a lightly floured surface and knead into a ball. Flatten the ball, making a small round, and wrap in plastic wrap. Refrigerate for at least 2 hours.

Chocolate Pâte Sucrée

*T*he first major undertaking of many young bakers is a chocolate icebox cake, a combination of chocolate cookies and pudding. While thinking about that one day, I decided to experiment with the pâte sucrée. Why couldn't a chocolate pâte sucrée serve as a shell for one of our tarts? I tried it first with the Macadamia Tart (see page 114) and met with great success. I also use it with the Coconut Cream Pie (see page 120). It makes great cookies, too (see Note).

1. In a food processor fitted with the steel blade, combine the flour, cocoa, and sugar with a few on/off turns. Arrange the pieces of butter around the blade and process just until combined.

2. In a small cup, whisk together the egg yolks and cream. With the processor running, pour through the feed tube, making certain you scrape out all the liquid from the cup. Let the machine run until the dough begins to come together, about 1 minute.

3. Scrape out of the processor onto plastic wrap and flatten into a round. Wrap securely and refrigerate for at least 2 to 3 hours. Use as needed.

Note: Cookies can be made from leftover dough. Using a lightly floured rolling pin on a lightly floured surface, roll out dough to ⅛-inch thickness. Using a 2½-inch cookie cutter, cut out cookies, folding and rerolling dough as necessary. Arrange on parchment-paper-lined baking tray and bake 10 minutes in a preheated 350-degree oven.

Spiced Pâte Sucrée

MAKES 1 POUND, 11 OUNCES,
ENOUGH FOR TWO 9-INCH PASTRY SHELLS

EQUIPMENT

Food processor

Small bowl or cup

Whip

Plastic wrap

INGREDIENTS

2¼ cups all-purpose flour

½ cup granulated sugar

2 tablespoons ground ginger

1 tablespoon ground cinnamon

½ teaspoon ground nutmeg

*8 ounces (2 sticks) unsalted butter,
chilled, cut into small pieces*

2 egg yolks

2 tablespoons heavy cream

TO PREPARE AHEAD

THROUGH STEP 3. DOUGH CAN
BE REFRIGERATED UP TO 3
DAYS. DOUGH ALSO CAN BE
DIVIDED IN HALF, WRAPPED
WELL, AND FROZEN FOR UP
TO 2 MONTHS.

I use this recipe with the Strawberry Linzer Torte (see page 110), but it also goes well with Rustic Almond Apple Tart or Pecan Pie (see pages 96 and 116).

1. In a food processor fitted with the steel blade, combine the flour, sugar, ginger, cinnamon, and nutmeg with 2 or 3 on/off turns. Place pieces of butter around the blade and process until texture resembles fine meal.

2. In a small bowl or cup, whisk together the egg yolks and cream. With machine running, pour through feed tube and process until dough begins to come together.

3. Wrap in plastic wrap and refrigerate until firm, at least 2 to 3 hours. Use as needed.

Butter Crunch Crust

EQUIPMENT

Food processor

Small baking tray

*8- or 9-inch Pyrex pie plate or
9-inch springform pan*

INGREDIENTS

*4 tablespoons (½ stick) unsalted
butter, chilled, cut into 4 pieces*

2 tablespoons brown sugar, packed

½ cup sifted all-purpose flour

¼ cup pecans or walnuts

TO PREPARE AHEAD

THROUGH STEP 3

MAKES ONE 8- OR 9-INCH CRUST

*T*his butter crunch crust complements many cheese-
cakes. It is particularly delicious with the Spago Cheesecake (see page 56).

1. Position rack in center of oven and preheat oven to 400
degrees.

2. In a food processor fitted with the steel blade, combine the
butter, brown sugar, and flour with a few on/off turns. Add
the nuts and process 2 to 3 seconds longer.

3. Spread mixture in a thin layer on the baking tray and bake
about 10 minutes, watching carefully to prevent burning.
Immediately remove from oven and stir. Cool slightly and
press into an 8- or 9-inch pie plate or 9-inch springform pan.
Refrigerate until needed.

Basic Pie Dough

EQUIPMENT

Food processor

Small bowl

Whip

Plastic wrap

INGREDIENTS

3½ cups (1 pound) all-purpose flour, sifted

1 tablespoon granulated sugar

1 tablespoon orange zest

½ teaspoon salt

¾ pound (3 sticks) unsalted butter, chilled, cut into small pieces

4 egg yolks

¼ cup heavy cream

TO PREPARE AHEAD

THROUGH STEP 3, THE DOUGH CAN BE DIVIDED IN HALF OR IN THIRDS, WRAPPED WELL, AND FROZEN. DEFROST, WHILE STILL WRAPPED, OVERNIGHT IN REFRIGERATOR.

*T*his is our version of an old-fashioned pie dough, using butter rather than a solid vegetable shortening or lard. It is not as delicate as Pâte Sucrée (see page 76). It can be used with Spago's Old-fashioned Apple Pie (see page 98) or Pecan Pie (see page 116).

1. In a food processor fitted with the steel blade, combine the flour, sugar, orange zest, and salt with a few on/off turns. Arrange the butter around the bowl and process until the mixture resembles fine meal.

2. In a small bowl, whisk together the egg yolks and cream. With the machine running, pour through the feed tube and process until the dough just comes together.

3. Remove dough from machine, wrap in plastic wrap, and refrigerate until firm, at least 3 hours. Use as needed.

Spiced Pie Dough

MAKES 2¼ POUNDS,
ENOUGH FOR THREE 9-INCH PASTRY SHELLS

❀

EQUIPMENT

Food processor

Small bowl

Whip

Plastic wrap

INGREDIENTS

3½ cups all-purpose flour

2 tablespoons granulated sugar

1 tablespoon ground cinnamon

1 tablespoon ground ginger

1 teaspoon ground nutmeg

½ teaspoon salt

¼ teaspoon ground cloves

¾ pound (3 sticks) unsalted butter, chilled, cut into 1-ounce pieces

4 egg yolks

¼ cup heavy cream

TO PREPARE AHEAD

THROUGH STEP 2. DOUGH CAN BE REFRIGERATED FOR UP TO 2 DAYS AND FROZEN FOR UP TO 1 MONTH. TO DEFROST, REFRIGERATE, WRAPPED, OVERNIGHT.

*T*his pie dough will add extra zest to Spago's Old-fashioned Apple Pie (see page 98). We use it as the crust for the Fresh Cherry Lattice Tart (see page 104) and for the latticework on top of the tart. Even though the ingredients suggest a highly spiced dough, when baked the flavor is very pleasing.

1. In a food processor fitted with the steel blade, combine the flour, sugar, cinnamon, ginger, nutmeg, salt, and cloves. Process with a few on/off turns. Stop the machine and arrange the butter pieces around the flour mixture. Process until the texture resembles coarse meal.

2. In a small bowl, whisk together the egg yolks and cream. With the machine running, pour through the feed tube and process until the dough comes together.

3. Remove dough from processor and wrap in plastic wrap. Refrigerate for at least 2 hours.

4. When ready to roll out the dough, remove from refrigerator and let sit at room temperature for about 30 to 40 minutes. Use as needed.

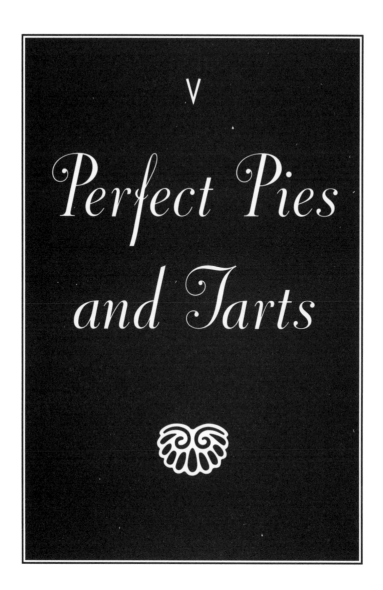

V

Perfect Pies and Tarts

A tart or pie can be made in a Pyrex pie plate or in a tart pan with a removable bottom, the ring lifted off and the bottom forming a firm base for the tart. It can also be made in individual or large pans.

At Spago the fruit tarts are designed seasonally, when particular fruits are available and at their peak. Before making a fruit pie or tart, the first step should be to take a trip to the market to determine which fruits are in season and what looks and tastes good. Befriending the person behind the fruit display may be to your advantage, as he or she can help you in the selection of the ripest and best fruits.

There are tarts for special occasions, tarts that are particularly appropriate around the holidays, and old-fashioned homey tarts, all favorites at the restaurant. You will find Apple Tarts, Cherry Tarts, Pecan Pie, Pumpkin Pie, Plum Almond Tart, Macadamia Tart, and many more.

We have provided illustrations where we deemed necessary, and photographs of many of the finished products, making it "easy as pie" for anyone attempting these recipes.

ALMOND CRUNCH BROWN BUTTER TART

Almond Toffee
Chocolate Oil

AUTUMN APPLE BROWN BUTTER TART

RASPBERRY BROWN BUTTER TART

RUSTIC APRICOT TART

RUSTIC ALMOND APPLE TART

SPAGO'S OLD-FASHIONED APPLE PIE

APPLE AND DRIED CHERRY TURNOVERS

CHERRY CLAFOUTI WITH CHERRY COMPOTE

FRESH CHERRY LATTICE TART

PEAR HAZELNUT SOUR CREAM PIE

PLUM ALMOND TART WITH PLUM COMPOTE

STRAWBERRY LINZER TORTE

PUMPKIN PIE WITH CRANBERRY MARMALADE

MACADAMIA TART WITH CHOCOLATE PÂTE SUCRÉE

PECAN PIE

LEMON TART

Lemon Curd

COCONUT CREAM PIE

EQUIPMENT

9-inch Pyrex pie plate

Rolling pin

INGREDIENTS

12 ounces (1/3 recipe) Almond Pâte Sucrée (see page 77) or Spiced Pie Dough (see page 82)

8 ounces (about 1/4 block) Almond Toffee (see page 88)

Brown Butter Filling (see page 92)

Chocolate Oil (see page 90)

TO PREPARE AHEAD

THROUGH STEP 3. TART SHOULD BE MADE EARLY IN THE DAY SO THAT FILLING SETS.

Almond Crunch Brown Butter Tart

MAKES ONE 9-INCH TART SERVES 8

1993 was the first year that Spago, Las Vegas, participated in Meals on Wheels, a major event that Wolfgang hosts every year. I wanted to come up with something special, something that had never been served before. This was it! I made 1,100 small tarts, and every single tart was eaten well before the evening ended.

1. Position rack in center of oven and preheat oven to 350 degrees. Coat a 9-inch Pyrex pie plate with butter or vegetable spray.

2. Roll out pastry: Roll out pastry to an 11-inch circle, about 1/8 inch thick. Fit into prepared pie plate and trim edges. (If you want to make a simple decorative design on top, see page 92.) Refrigerate until needed.

3. Assemble the tart: Cut toffee into 1-inch pieces and arrange on the tart shell. Pour Brown Butter Filling over the toffee. Bake until crust is golden, about 40 minutes. Lift up pie plate to make sure the bottom of the crust is golden brown. Cool on a rack.

4. To serve, mirror each of 8 plates with Chocolate Oil and set 1 slice of the tart in the center of each plate.

Almond Toffee

MAKES A 2-POUND BLOCK, 10 X 13 INCHES

EQUIPMENT

1 or 2 baking trays, 11 x 15 inches

Offset spatula

Small deep saucepan

Candy thermometer

Long-handled wooden spoon

Medium heatproof bowl

Aluminum foil

INGREDIENTS

10 ounces whole unblanched almonds

1¼ cups granulated sugar

⅓ cup light corn syrup

⅓ cup water or rum

8 ounces (2 sticks) unsalted butter, cut into small pieces

1 teaspoon salt

½ teaspoon baking soda

8 ounces bittersweet chocolate, cut into small pieces

TO PREPARE AHEAD

THROUGH STEP 8, STORING IN A COVERED CONTAINER PLACED IN A COOL SPOT

Almond Toffee is a major component of the filling for the Almond Crunch Brown Butter Tart (see page 87). It can also be broken into large pieces to make a delectable bit of candy. Arrange on a small plate and serve with coffee or tea at the end of a meal.

1. Position rack in center of oven and preheat oven to 375 degrees.

2. Spread nuts on a baking tray and bake until toasted, 10 to 15 minutes, turning nuts after 7 to 8 minutes to ensure even toasting. Cool and then finely chop. You should have about 2 cups. Set aside. Clean baking tray and coat with vegetable oil or vegetable spray. Spray both sides of the offset spatula with vegetable spray. Set aside.

3. Make the toffee: Place sugar in a small deep saucepan. Add the corn syrup and water or rum and, over medium heat, bring to a boil. Let boil until large bubbles form on the surface, 3 to 4 minutes. Cover with foil and boil 5 minutes longer.

4. Add the pieces of butter and continue cooking, uncovered, over medium heat until temperature reaches 300 degrees on a candy thermometer, about 30 minutes. (The candy thermometer has a clip on the side that can be slid up or down. If desired, you can fit the thermometer on the side of the pan, making sure that it rests in the mixture, not on the bottom of the pan, so that the reading is accurate.) Remove from heat and immediately add the salt, baking soda, and 1 cup of the chopped nuts. Stir with a wooden spoon until well combined.

5. Pour the toffee mixture on the oiled baking tray and, using the offset spatula, spread the mixture out, making a block about 10 x 13 inches. The toffee will thicken very quickly, so work as fast as you can. When cool, blot some of the oil or vegetable spray with a clean towel.

6. While the toffee mixture is cooling, melt the chocolate in a medium heatproof bowl placed over simmering water. When almost melted, turn off heat and let the chocolate continue to melt, stirring occasionally. Keep warm.

7. When you can lift up the block of toffee, transfer it to a flat work surface or to a clean baking tray. Pour the melted chocolate over the toffee, spreading to cover the entire surface and, before the chocolate cools, sprinkle with the remaining chopped nuts. If the chocolate takes a long time to harden, refrigerate for about 10 minutes to set the chocolate.

8. Return the block of toffee to the work surface and break up into pieces approximately 1 to 1½ inches wide. Then cut into smaller pieces, as desired. Use as needed.

Chocolate Oil

EQUIPMENT

Blender

Strainer

INGREDIENTS

*2 cups Simple Sugar Syrup
(see page 241)*

½ cup plus 2 tablespoons water

½ cup unsweetened cocoa

1 tablespoon walnut oil

1 teaspoon vanilla extract

TO PREPARE AHEAD

THROUGH STEP 1

*P*lates are mirrored with this sauce and then slices of Almond Crunch Brown Butter Tart (see page 87) placed on the sauce, which has a nutty, chocolate flavor that will go well with many pastries.

1. In a blender, combine all ingredients and mix until well combined. Strain into a container and refrigerate, covered. When ready to use, bring to room temperature.

Autumn Apple Brown Butter Tart

MAKES ONE 9-INCH TART
SERVES 8

EQUIPMENT

Rolling pin

9-inch Pyrex pie plate

Large and medium bowls

INGREDIENTS

12 ounces ($\frac{1}{3}$ recipe) Spiced Pie Dough (see page 82)

FILLING

1 pound (3 medium) Granny Smith apples, peeled and cored

1 cup (about 5$\frac{1}{2}$ ounces) coarsely chopped walnuts

$\frac{1}{2}$ cup (about 2 ounces) dried cranberries

1 tablespoon lemon juice

1 teaspoon ground cinnamon

Brown Butter Filling (see page 92)

1 cup Streusel (see page 171)

TO PREPARE AHEAD
THROUGH STEP 6. TART SHOULD BE PREPARED EARLY IN DAY SO THAT FILLING SETS.

*A*nother Brown Butter Tart variation, this has as its principal ingredients apples, walnuts, and dried cranberries.

1. Position rack in center of oven and preheat oven to 350 degrees.

2. Line the pie plate: On a lightly floured work surface, roll out pastry to an 11-inch round, about $\frac{1}{8}$ inch thick. Roll onto rolling pin and unroll over pie plate, pressing down to fit into plate. Trim edges and refrigerate until needed.

3. Make the filling: Cut each apple into eighths, and then cut each eighth into 4 small chunks. In a medium bowl, combine the apples, walnuts, cranberries, lemon juice, and cinnamon. Toss well and set aside.

4. Make the Brown Butter Filling.

5. Assemble the tart: Remove tart shell from refrigerator. Arrange apple mixture in shell and pour Brown Butter Filling evenly over the mixture. Sprinkle top with Streusel.

6. Bake until apples are tender and shell is golden brown, about 1 hour. Lift up the pie plate and check that bottom of tart is golden. Cool on rack and then refrigerate so that filling sets.

7. To serve, remove tart from refrigerator about 40 minutes before serving. Cut tart into portions and arrange 1 slice in the center of each plate. Serve with a dollop of whipped cream or a small scoop of vanilla ice cream. Serve immediately.

Raspberry Brown Butter Tart

MAKES ONE 9-INCH TART
SERVES 8

EQUIPMENT

9-inch Pyrex pie plate

Rolling pin

Large mixing bowl

Whip

*10-inch skillet, preferably
uncoated*

INGREDIENTS

*½ recipe (12 ounces) Pâte Sucrée
(see page 76)*

BROWN BUTTER FILLING

3 eggs

1 cup granulated sugar

½ cup all-purpose flour, sifted

*6 ounces (1½ sticks) unsalted
butter, cut into pieces*

1 vanilla bean, split lengthwise

*2 baskets fresh raspberries, gently
patted clean*

Confectioners' sugar

TO PREPARE AHEAD

THROUGH STEP 6. TART
SHOULD BE BAKED EARLY IN
THE DAY SO THAT THE
FILLING SETS.

𝒪ne basket of blueberries or 2 baskets of blackberries can be substituted for the raspberries. Or you can combine berries, making a mixed berry tart. It is important to use a Pyrex pie plate because then you can actually see when the bottom of the crust is golden brown.

1. Line pie plate: On a lightly floured work surface, roll out Pâte Sucrée to an 11-inch round, about ⅛ inch thick. Roll up on rolling pin and unroll over pie plate, gently pressing down into plate. Trim edges and refrigerate until needed. If desired, make a simple decorative design on top: Roll out the excess dough to a piece ⅛ inch thick. Cut into 1-inch squares (more or less), set on a small tray as cut, and refrigerate.

2. Position rack in center of oven and preheat oven to 350 degrees.

3. Make the Brown Butter Filling: In a large mixing bowl, whisk together the eggs and sugar until well combined.

4. In a 10-inch skillet, over medium-high heat, melt the butter with the vanilla bean and its scrapings. Continue cooking until the butter browns and begins to give off a nutty aroma. As it cooks, swirl the pan so that you can see the butter in the pan below the surface of bubbles. When the butter is brown, you will hear the vanilla bean "pop." Immediately whisk into the egg-sugar mixture and combine thoroughly.

5. Assemble the tart: Remove the pie plate from the refrigerator and arrange the berries in the pie plate. Pour the Brown Butter Filling over the fruit. Place the cut squares of dough

along the outside rim of the plate, pressing the top end against the edge of the crust. Arrange them at equal intervals around the filling, the spacing dependent on how many pieces you have.

6. Place the pie plate directly on a rack in the oven (not on a baking tray) and bake until the shell is golden brown, about 50 minutes. Lift up the pie plate and check the bottom of the shell. If not brown enough, return to oven for a few minutes longer. Cool completely on a rack, then refrigerate until filling is set, 3 to 4 hours.

7. To serve, remove from refrigerator 40 minutes to 1 hour before needed. Sift confectioners' sugar over top of tart. For each portion, mirror the plate (see page XXII) with a berry compote and set 1 slice of the tart in the center of the plate.

Rustic Apricot Tart

MAKES ONE 10-INCH TART   SERVES 8 TO 10

EQUIPMENT

Small saucepan

10-inch tart pan with removable bottom

Rolling pin

Cardboard

Baking tray

Small bowl

Strainer

Electric mixer

10- or 12-inch skillet

Pastry brush

Wide metal spatula

Plastic wrap

Sharp knife or pastry cutter

INGREDIENTS

FILLING

8 ounces dried apricots

1 cup water

⅓ cup Grand Marnier

¼ cup orange juice

½ recipe Pâte Sucrée (see page 76)

4 tablespoons (½ stick) unsalted butter, at room temperature

1 tablespoon finely chopped orange zest

*T*his tart is made with dried apricots, making it an all-year-round dessert. The lattice pattern on top is not as difficult to make as it may seem at first appearance. If the dough is chilled slightly, it will be easier to weave the pattern. But if you prefer, you can use the lattice pattern on the Strawberry Linzer Torte (see page 110).

1. Make the filling: In a small saucepan, combine the apricots, water, Grand Marnier, and orange juice and bring to a boil. Remove the pan from the heat and let the apricots soak for 1 hour.

2. While the apricots are soaking, line the tart pan: On a lightly floured surface, roll out half of the pastry to a 12-inch round, about ⅛ inch thick. Fit into the pan, gently pressing down into the bottom of the pan and around the sides. Trim the edges and add the trimmings to the remaining pastry. Refrigerate the lined pan until the pastry is firm to the touch.

3. On a lightly floured surface, roll out the remaining half of the pastry to a 10-inch square, evening the sides with the rolling pin. From a piece of cardboard, cut out a strip ½-inch wide and about 10 inches long. Wrap the strip in plastic wrap and use as a guide. With a sharp knife or pastry cutter, cut out sixteen ½-inch strips. Lay 8 strips vertically on the underside of a baking tray, about ½ inch apart. Weave a lattice pattern by placing each of the remaining strips horizontally over and under the vertical strips. To weave, turn back every other vertical strip of dough (1, 3, 5, 7), lay a horizontal strip across, and return the turned-back strips to the original length. For the next row, turn back strips 2, 4, 6, 8 and again lay a horizontal strip across. (Strips do not have to be placed close together.)

1½ cups (9 ounces) pine nuts

⅓ cup granulated sugar

2 tablespoons apricot jam

TO PREPARE AHEAD

THROUGH STEP 8.
REFRIGERATE UNTIL
NEEDED. REMOVE FROM
REFRIGERATOR ABOUT 30
MINUTES BEFORE SERVING
AND WARM SLIGHTLY, IF
DESIRED.

Repeat this procedure until all the strips are used. Refrigerate just until slightly firm. Place a 9-inch round plate, pot cover, or cardboard on top of the chilled lattices and cut out a circle. Refrigerate, on the tray, until needed. Excess pastry can be wrapped well and refrigerated or frozen for future use.

4. Reserving the apricots in a small bowl, strain the liquid and return to the saucepan. Reduce until 3 tablespoons remain. Cool.

5. With an electric mixer, using paddle or beaters, beat the butter until light and fluffy. Add the cooled liquid and the chopped orange zest and mix until just combined.

6. In a 10- or 12-inch skillet, over medium heat, lightly toast the pine nuts, stirring constantly and watching carefully to prevent burning, about 2 minutes. Cool. Add ½ cup pine nuts and the sugar to the apricots and stir to combine.

7. Position rack in center of oven and preheat oven to 375 degrees.

8. Assemble the tart: Using a pastry brush, coat the pastry shell with the jam. Arrange the apricot mixture on top, spreading as evenly as possible. Sprinkle the remaining 1 cup of pine nuts over the apricots and dot with bits of the butter mixture. Using a wide metal spatula, transfer the latticework circle from the baking tray and place over the filling. Bake until the top crust is golden brown, about 35 minutes. Cool on a rack. When cool, set the tart pan on a wide-mouthed jar (the top of the jar smaller than the pan) and slip the outer ring down. If the ring sticks, run the propane torch around the sides to loosen.

9. To serve, warm slightly and serve with vanilla ice cream. Or mirror each plate with Crème Anglaise (see page 6), flavored with apricot brandy. Place a slice of the tart on the Crème Anglaise and serve immediately.

Rustic Almond Apple Tart

MAKES ONE 10-INCH TART
SERVES 8

Rolling pin

9-inch pie plate or tart pan with 1½-inch sides

Cookie sheet or baking tray

Food processor

10-inch skillet or sauté pan

Large mixing bowl

Whip

½ recipe Almond Pâte Sucrée (see page 76)

FILLING

1½ cups (about 8 ounces) almonds with skins

¾ pound (2 medium) Granny Smith apples, peeled and cored

2 tablespoons (¼ stick) unsalted butter

3 eggs

⅔ cup pure maple syrup or golden syrup*

½ cup heavy cream

Juice of 1 large lemon

1 tablespoon grated lemon peel

½ teaspoon ground cinnamon

¼ teaspoon ground ginger

About 10 scrapings of fresh nutmeg

*T*his tart has a wonderful almond crust and a crunchy almond filling.

1. Make the pastry shell: On a lightly floured surface, flouring the rolling pin as necessary, roll out the Almond Pâte Sucrée to about a 10-inch round. Coat a 9-inch pie plate or tart pan with vegetable spray. Roll the pastry around the rolling pin and lay it into the pan (if it breaks, that's okay—just press pieces together in the pan). Press down on the pastry, fitting it into the pan (see page XXI). Trim edges and refrigerate while preparing the filling.

2. Make the filling: Position rack in center of oven and pre-heat oven to 350 degrees. Arrange the almonds on a cookie sheet or baking tray and toast in oven, about 15 minutes, turning nuts with a spatula after 7 to 8 minutes. Cool completely, then place in food processor fitted with steel blade. Chop with on/off turns until coarsely ground. Set aside.

3. Cut apples into quarters and cut each quarter into 6 or 7 thin slices. In a 10-inch skillet, melt butter. Over medium-high heat, sauté the apples just until they take on some color, about 10 minutes. Set aside.

4. In a large mixing bowl, whisk the eggs with the syrup and cream. Add the lemon juice and peel, the cinnamon, ginger, nutmeg, and the reserved ground nuts, and whisk until well combined.

*Golden syrup is available in most markets.

TO PREPARE AHEAD

THROUGH STEP 5, WARMING
SLIGHTLY IN A LOW OVEN
JUST BEFORE SERVING

5. Remove the pastry shell from the refrigerator and arrange the apple slices in the shell in 1 layer. Pour the egg mixture over the apples. Bake until tart is firm to the touch and the pastry shell is lightly browned, 45 to 50 minutes. Cool on a rack.

6. Warm tart in low oven when ready to serve. Serve with Vanilla Ice Cream (see page 253) or Crème Anglaise (see page 6), flavored with Calvados to taste.

Spago's Old-fashioned Apple Pie

MAKES ONE 9-INCH PIE
SERVES 8

EQUIPMENT

Rolling pin

9-inch pie plate

2 baking trays

12-inch skillet or sauté pan

Small bowl

Pastry brush

INGREDIENTS

*1 recipe Pâte Sucrée (see page 76)
or Basic Pie Dough (see page 81)*

FILLING

*5 pounds (13 to 14 medium)
Granny Smith apples, peeled and
cored, each apple cut into quarters*

*9 tablespoons (1 stick plus
1 tablespoon) unsalted butter*

1½ vanilla beans, split lengthwise

1½ cups granulated sugar

*6 tablespoons Calvados or brandy
of your choice*

*¾ cup heavy cream plus a little
extra for brushing over pastry*

CINNAMON SUGAR

1 tablespoon granulated sugar

⅛ teaspoon ground cinnamon

This apple pie has been on the Spago menu since the restaurant opened in 1982. Because of the demand, we never take it off the menu and the recipe has never been changed. Pâte Sucrée or Basic Pie Dough can be used to make the crust.

1. Roll out the pastry: Butter, or coat with vegetable spray, a 9-inch pie plate. Divide the pastry into 2 pieces, one a little larger than the other. On a lightly floured surface, flouring the rolling pin as necessary, roll out the smaller piece to an 11-inch round and fit into the pie plate, pressing down with your knuckle to conform to the shape of the pan. Trim the edges and add scraps to the remaining piece of dough. Roll out the second piece to a 12-inch circle and place on a lightly floured baking tray. Refrigerate until needed.

2. Make the filling: Cut each apple quarter into slices, about ½ inch thick. You will be sautéing the apples in three batches. Melt 3 tablespoons butter in a 12-inch skillet. Arrange ⅓ of the apples in the skillet. Add ½ vanilla bean with its scrapings and sprinkle ½ cup sugar over the apples. Over medium-high heat, sauté apples until lightly caramelized and tender, about 15 minutes, turning often so that the apples cook as evenly as possible. Pour in 2 tablespoons Calvados and cook just until the alcohol burns off. (If the brandy ignites, remove pan from heat or place a cover over pan for a few seconds.) Pour in ¼ cup cream, stir through, and cook 1 minute longer. Spread contents of skillet onto large baking tray to cool while sautéing remaining apples. Wash and dry skillet. Repeat pro-

TO PREPARE AHEAD

THROUGH STEP 2. THE
PASTRY CAN BE MADE,
ROLLED OUT, AND
REFRIGERATED, COVERED, 1
DAY AHEAD. THE APPLES CAN
BE SAUTÉED 1 OR 2 DAYS
AHEAD, SPREAD ON A BAKING
TRAY, AND REFRIGERATED.

cedure 2 more times with remaining butter, apples, vanilla bean, sugar, cream, and brandy.

3. Position rack in center of oven and preheat oven to 400 degrees.

4. Make the cinnamon sugar: In a small bowl or cup, combine the sugar and cinnamon and mix well. Set aside.

5. Remove lined pie plate and circle of pastry from refrigerator. Pile the cooled apples in the pie plate, mounding apples slightly in the middle. Roll circle of pastry over rolling pin and unroll over apples. With a sharp knife, cut away excess dough and gently pinch together the edges of the pastry. Cut 3 or 4 slits in the top of the pastry, brush with cream, and sprinkle with cinnamon sugar.

6. Bake 15 minutes, turn oven down to 350 degrees, and bake until crust is golden brown, 30 to 35 minutes longer. Cool on rack.

7. To serve, serve warm or at room temperature with a scoop of Cinnamon Ice Cream (see page 249) or a dollop of whipped cream.

Apple and Dried Cherry Turnovers

MAKES 16 TURNOVERS

*W*hen I promised my children that I would bring a cherry pie home from the restaurant, I didn't count on cherries being unavailable. Dried cherries saved the day. Wolfgang tasted the turnovers and liked them so well, he decided to prepare them on *Good Morning America*.

1. Make the filling: In a 2-quart saucepan, combine the cherries, walnuts, water, sugar, cranberries, cinnamon stick, vanilla bean with its scrapings, orange zest, and nutmeg. Over medium heat, cook until the cherries are plump and tender, 10 to 15 minutes, stirring occasionally. Most of the water will evaporate, so watch carefully to avoid burning.

2. Meanwhile, in a medium skillet, melt the butter. Sauté the apples until lightly caramelized and tender, turning as necessary. Remove from heat and then scrape into the cherry mixture during the last 2 or 3 minutes of cooking. Remove the cinnamon stick and vanilla bean and transfer the contents to a food processor fitted with the steel blade. Process with on/off turns until coarsely chopped and transfer to a clean bowl.

3. Roll out the pastry: Cut the Pâte Sucrée in half. Keeping the unused half covered, on a lightly floured surface, roll out 1 piece to a 12-inch square, about ¼ inch thick. Using a 4½-inch cookie cutter, cut out 6 circles. Press the scraps together and reroll to an 8-inch square. Cut out 2 more circles. Repeat with the reserved pastry. (To prevent sticking, dip the cookie cutter in flour occasionally.)

EQUIPMENT

2-quart saucepan

Medium skillet

Food processor

Medium bowl

Rolling pin

4½-inch cookie cutter

Pastry brush

1 or 2 baking trays

Parchment paper

Fluted pastry cutter

Nutmeg grater

INGREDIENTS

FILLING

2 cups (about ½ pound) dried cherries

1 cup (¼ pound) walnuts

¾ cup water

¼ cup granulated sugar

¼ cup whole fresh cranberries

1 cinnamon stick

1 vanilla bean, split lengthwise

Zest of 1 medium orange

Freshly grated nutmeg, to taste

1 tablespoon unsalted butter

¾ *pound (2 medium) apples,*
peeled, cored, and cut into thin
slices

1½ pounds Pâte Sucrée
(see page 76)

1 egg, lightly beaten

Crystal sugar

TO PREPARE AHEAD

THROUGH STEP 6, REHEATING
IN OVEN WHEN NEEDED

4. Divide the filling into 16 equal portions, a little more than 1 ounce each. To make the turnovers, place a portion of the filling in the center of one of the circles of dough and brush egg wash around the edges of the circle. Fold the dough over the filling, making a semicircle, and gently pinch the edges together. Repeat with the remaining circles of dough, filling, and egg wash. Arrange on 1 or 2 baking trays lined with parchment paper.

5. Position rack in center of oven and preheat oven to 350 degrees.

6. Trim the edges of each turnover with a fluted pastry cutter and brush with egg wash. With the point of a sharp knife, make 2 or 3 slits in the top of each turnover and sprinkle with crystal sugar. Refrigerate at least 30 minutes, up to overnight. Bake until the pastry is golden, 30 to 35 minutes. Cool on a rack.

7. To serve, warm in oven, if desired. You can serve with a small scoop of ice cream of your choice.

Cherry Clafouti with Cherry Compote

MAKES ONE 9-INCH TART
SERVES 8

$\mathcal{C}$hristophe, Mary's assistant pastry chef at Spago, Las Vegas, drew on his French background to create this magnificent dessert.

1. In a large bowl, soak 3½ pounds cherries in kirsch for 2 hours, up to overnight. (The longer the cherries are soaked, the stronger the kirsch flavor.)

2. Make the tart shell: On a lightly floured surface, roll out the Pâte Sucrée to an 11-inch circle. Line the bottom and sides of a 9-inch tart pan, trimming to fit. Refrigerate until needed.

3. Position a rack in the center of the oven and preheat oven to 350 degrees.

4. Make the filling: In a food processor fitted with a steel blade, process the almond meal and confectioners' sugar to a fine texture. In a medium bowl, whisk the eggs. Add the almond-meal mixture all at once, and whisk until thoroughly combined. Set aside.

5. In a 10-inch sauté pan, melt the butter with the vanilla bean and its scrapings. Turn up the heat and let the butter

---

*Almond meal is finely ground blanched almonds, available in many markets. To blanch almonds, drop unpeeled almonds into boiling water for about 30 seconds. Drain and remove the skins. Dry well before grinding.

To make 2 cups almond meal, in a food processor fitted with the steel blade, grind about 1⅓ cups blanched almonds with 2 teaspoons granulated sugar. Start with on/off turns and then grind until fluffy. Do not grind to a paste. The almonds can also be ground in a nut grinder.

CHERRY COMPOTE

2¼ pounds (about 4 heaping cups) Bing cherries, pitted and stemmed

Reserved liquid from soaked cherries

½ cup granulated sugar

1 medium cinnamon stick

1 vanilla bean, split lengthwise

TO PREPARE AHEAD

THROUGH STEP 6, TART CAN BE MADE EARLY IN THE DAY. PREPARE THROUGH STEP 7, WARMING BEFORE SERVING.

brown. Shake pan gently and often to check the color. When the vanilla bean begins to "pop" and the butter gives off a nutty aroma and is a deep golden brown, it should be ready. Gradually whisk into the egg mixture.

6. Drain the soaked cherries, reserving the liquid, and arrange the cherries in the tart shell. Pour filling over cherries and bake until top is golden brown, about 30 minutes. Cool on a rack.

7. Make the cherry compote: In a medium saucepan, over high heat, combine all the ingredients with the scrapings of the vanilla bean and bring to a boil. Turn heat down and simmer until the cherries are tender, about 15 minutes. Remove pan from heat and discard vanilla bean and cinnamon stick. Set the compote aside.

8. To serve, serve at room temperature. With a sharp knife, cut the clafouti into slices. Arrange 1 slice on each plate and spoon a little of the warm cherry compote over. Serve with vanilla ice cream, if desired.

Fresh Cherry Lattice Tart

EQUIPMENT

Rolling pin

9-inch tart pan with removable
bottom

Ruler

Parchment paper

Baking tray

Small knife or cherry pitter

Large heavy-bottomed saucepan

Small cup

Whip

Pastry brush

INGREDIENTS

1½ pounds Spiced Pie Dough
(see page 82)

FILLING

2 pounds fresh cherries

1¼ cups granulated sugar

¼ cup all-purpose flour

2 tablespoons kirsch

Zest of 1 medium orange

1 whole cinnamon stick

6 to 8 scrapings of fresh nutmeg or
⅛ teaspoon ground nutmeg

1 egg, lightly beaten

1 tablespoon heavy cream

1½ tablespoons crystal sugar

*T*his beautiful tart is filled with a generous amount of pitted fresh cherries. During the short season when cherries are available, we can't make enough tarts to keep from
selling out nightly.

1. Roll out the dough: Divide dough in half. Keeping one half
covered, on a lightly floured surface, roll out 1 piece of dough
to an 11-inch circle. Roll up dough on rolling pin and fit into
9-inch tart pan with removable bottom. Trim edges. Refrigerate until needed. Add pastry scraps to remaining half of
dough.

2. On a lightly floured surface, roll out second half of dough
to a 9-inch square. Cut out eighteen ½-inch strips and arrange
on parchment-paper-lined baking tray. Refrigerate until
needed. (Chilling will make the strips easier to handle when
forming the latticework on top of the tart.)

3. Make the filling: With a small knife or cherry pitter,
remove pits from cherries, leaving each cherry as whole as
possible. In a large heavy-bottomed saucepan, combine the
cherries, sugar, flour, kirsch, orange zest, cinnamon stick, and
nutmeg. Start on low heat, and when the juices begin to
appear, turn heat up a little and cook, stirring occasionally,
until the cherries begin to soften and the juices thicken, about
10 minutes. Set aside to cool.

4. Position rack in center of oven and preheat oven to 350
degrees.

5. Assemble the tart: Scrape the cooled filling into the pre-

TO PREPARE AHEAD

THROUGH STEP 3, SHELL AND
STRIPS CAN BE CUT OUT AND
FILLING CAN BE
REFRIGERATED, COVERED,
1 DAY AHEAD. IN STEP 5,
TART CAN BE COMPLETELY
ASSEMBLED, REFRIGERATED,
AND THEN BRUSHED WITH EGG
WASH AND BAKED AS IN STEP
6. OR, THROUGH STEP 6,
TART CAN BE PREPARED
EARLY IN THE DAY,
REFRIGERATED, AND
REMOVED FROM
REFRIGERATOR ABOUT
1 HOUR BEFORE SERVING.

pared shell and level. Arrange 9 strips of dough across the top of the filling in one direction, spacing them as evenly as possible. Lay the remaining 9 strips across in the opposite direction, again spacing them evenly, creating a latticework pattern. Press each strip down at the edge of the pan to secure, and trim off the ends. In a small cup, whisk together the egg and cream. Brush over the strips of dough and sprinkle with crystal sugar.

6. Place pan on baking tray and bake until crust is golden brown and filling begins to bubble up out of the pan, about 50 minutes. Remove from oven and set on a rack to cool for about 20 minutes. Gently tap the outer ring of the pan with the back of a large spoon or knife. Set pan on a wide-mouthed jar that is narrower than the pan. Carefully release the ring and let slip down the side of the jar. Return to rack to cool completely.

7. To serve, place tart on serving plate and, with a sharp knife, cut into portions. Serve with vanilla ice cream or a dollop of soft whipped cream.

Pear Hazelnut Sour Cream Pie

EQUIPMENT

Rolling pin

9-inch pie plate

Parchment or wax paper

Pie weights or dried beans

Small baking sheet

10- or 12-inch skillet

Sifter

Large mixing bowl

Whip

INGREDIENTS

¾ pound Pâte Sucrée (see page 76)

FILLING

1 cup hazelnuts

2 tablespoons (¼ stick) unsalted butter

2½ pounds (about 5 medium) Bosc or Anjou pears, peeled, cored, and cut into eighths

½ vanilla bean, split lengthwise

½ cup granulated sugar

¼ cup all-purpose flour

½ teaspoon ground cinnamon

½ teaspoon freshly ground nutmeg

Pinch of salt

1 egg

1 cup sour cream

*J*annis Swerman, whose smiling face greets customers at Granita, in Malibu, gave us this recipe. It has been in her family for years, originally with a layer of apples. We chose to substitute pears, and it is superb with either fruit.

1. Preheat oven to 350 degrees.

2. Roll out the Pâte Sucrée to a round slightly larger than the pie plate. Fit into the plate and trim. Refrigerate for 20 minutes. Line with parchment or wax paper and fill with pie weights or dried beans up to the very top of the shell. Bake 12 minutes. Cool and remove weights and paper. Set aside.

3. Make the filling: Spread the hazelnuts in a single layer on a small baking sheet. Bake until toasted, 10 to 12 minutes, turning nuts after 5 or 6 minutes. Cool slightly, then place in clean tea towel, fold towel to enclose nuts, and rub between your hands to remove as much of the nut skins as possible. (Some of the skins may not come off, but that's okay.) Chop coarsely and set aside.

4. In a heavy 10- or 12-inch skillet, melt the butter. Add the pears and the vanilla bean with its scrapings. Pour the granulated sugar on top of the pears and sauté over medium heat until tender and lightly caramelized, carefully turning to sauté all sides of the pears. Remove vanilla bean and let the fruit cool. When cool, arrange the pears in the pie shell, spreading them as evenly as possible.

5. Sift together the flour, cinnamon, nutmeg, and salt. Set aside.

½ cup brown sugar, packed

1 teaspoon vanilla extract

Zest of 1 medium lemon

TO PREPARE AHEAD

THROUGH STEP 6.
REFRIGERATE UNTIL
NEEDED. REMOVE ABOUT 30
MINUTES BEFORE SERVING.

6. In a large mixing bowl, whisk the egg, sour cream, brown sugar, vanilla extract, and lemon zest until well combined. Whisk in the flour mixture until smooth and pour over the pears. Bake 40 minutes, remove pie, and sprinkle the reserved hazelnuts over the top. Return to the oven and bake until a small knife inserted in the center of the filling comes out clean, about 20 minutes longer. Cool on a rack.

7. To serve, serve directly from the pie plate using a long, sharp knife to cut into slices. Serve with Caramel Sauce (see page 136) or Crème Anglaise (see page 6), flavored with Poire Williams to taste.

Plum Almond Tart with Plum Compote

MAKES EIGHT 5-INCH TARTS

*T*his plum almond tart is served at Spago at the end of the summer and during the early fall, when plums are at their peak.

1. Position rack in the center of oven and preheat oven to 350 degrees. Line 1 or 2 baking trays with parchment paper.

2. Make the pastry shells: Cut the dough into 8 pieces, each a little more than 2 ounces. On a lightly floured surface, lightly flouring your rolling pin, roll out 1 piece of dough to a 5½-inch circle. (The dough breaks easily, but can be pushed together just as easily.) Using a 5-inch round (cup, plate, cardboard) cut out a circle of dough and, with a wide spatula, carefully place on the prepared baking trays. Repeat with the remaining balls of dough and arrange on the trays, about 2 inches apart. Refrigerate about 30 minutes. Remove from refrigerator and bake until lightly golden, 10 to 12 minutes. Set aside to cool.

3. Make the filling: In a medium bowl, combine the almond meal, sugar, eggs, and lemon zest with a wooden spoon. Set aside.

4. Cut each plum in half and remove the pit. Cut each half into 5 or 6 thin wedges, the number of wedges depending upon the size of the plums.

*To make 1 cup loosely packed almond meal, in a food processor fitted with the steel blade, grind about 4 ounces blanched almonds with 1 teaspoon granulated sugar. Start with on/off turns and then grind until fluffy. Do not grind to a paste. The almonds can also be ground in a nut grinder.

TO PREPARE AHEAD

THROUGH STEP 6. WHEN
READY TO SERVE, WARM THE
TART IN A MEDIUM OVEN AND
SET THE SAUCEPAN WITH
COMPOTE OVER A LOW FLAME.

5. Divide the filling evenly and spread over each cooled pastry shell, leaving a small border around the outside edges. Arrange the reserved plums in a circular pattern on the filling, sprinkle about ½ teaspoon crystal sugar over the plums, and place a few sliced almonds in the center. Return to the oven and bake until the plums are lightly caramelized, about 20 minutes.

6. While the tarts are baking, make the compote: In a small saucepan, combine the plums, sugar, and vanilla bean with its scrapings. Cook over a low flame, stirring often to prevent scorching, until the compote thickens. Set aside in a warm spot. Remove vanilla bean.

7. To serve, place a warm tart on each of 8 dessert plates. Surround the tart with the warm compote and top with a scoop of Cinnamon Ice Cream (see page 249), if desired.

Strawberry Linzer Torte

EQUIPMENT

Rolling pin

9-inch tart pan with removable bottom

Parchment paper

Baking tray

Large heavy saucepan

Wooden spoon

Medium bowl

Food processor

Small cup

Whip

Pastry brush

Wide spatula

INGREDIENTS

1½ pounds Spiced Pâte Sucrée (see page 79)

FILLING

1½ medium oranges

1 medium lemon

3 pints strawberries, hulled, wiped clean, and cut in half

1¾ cups granulated sugar

3 tablespoons chopped, peeled fresh gingerroot

⅛ teaspoon ground black pepper

1 egg yolk

*C*itrus fruit and fresh ginger liven the flavor of the berry filling. Leftover Pâte Sucrée can be formed into 1-inch balls, rolled in sugar, and arranged on a parchment-lined baking tray. Bake in a preheated 350-degree oven for 15 minutes, and you will have delicious cookies.

1. Roll out the dough: Divide Pâte Sucrée in half. On a lightly floured work surface, roll out first half of dough to an 11-inch round, keeping the remaining half covered. Transfer to a 9-inch tart pan with removable bottom and press dough gently into the pan. Trim by rolling the rolling pin around the edges of the pan and removing excess dough. (Add the scraps of dough to the remaining half of dough.) Refrigerate until needed.

2. Roll out the second half of dough to a 10-inch square. Cut into sixteen ½-inch-wide strips and place strips on a parchment-paper-lined baking tray. Refrigerate until needed. (If strips are too difficult to transfer, use a long spatula.)

3. Make the filling: Using a small, sharp knife, remove the peel and white pith from the oranges and lemon. Cut into quarters, discarding seeds, and place in a large heavy saucepan. Add the strawberries, sugar, ginger, and pepper. Over medium heat, bring to a boil, stirring constantly with a wooden spoon, until the fruits begin to make their own juices. Cook until mixture is very thick, stirring often, about 35 minutes. Transfer to a medium bowl and cool. Then scrape into a food processor fitted with a steel blade, and process for 2 to 3 minutes to puree. Set aside.

4. Position rack in center of oven and preheat oven to 350 degrees.

1 tablespoon heavy cream

Crystal sugar

TO PREPARE AHEAD

THROUGH STEPS 1, 2, AND 3, CRUST AND FILLING CAN BE MADE THE DAY BEFORE AND REFRIGERATED, LIGHTLY COVERED. THROUGH STEP 6, THE TORTE CAN BE MADE EARLY IN THE DAY.

5. Assemble the torte: Spoon the filling into the chilled tart shell. Arrange 8 strips of dough across top of filling, spacing as evenly as possible. Arrange the remaining 8 strips in the opposite direction, across the first strips of dough, making a lattice pattern. Press each strip at edge of pan to secure as well as trim. In a small cup, whisk together the egg yolk and cream, and brush over the strips of dough. Sprinkle with crystal sugar.

6. Place pan on baking tray and bake until crust is golden brown and filling begins to bubble up and out of pan (thus the tray under the tart), about 50 minutes. Remove from oven and set on a rack for about 20 minutes. Gently tap the outer ring of the pan with the back of a large spoon or knife. Place the entire pan on a wide-mouthed jar that is smaller than the pan, and carefully slide the outer ring off. Using a wide spatula, return the torte to the rack to cool completely.

7. To serve, cut torte into wedges and serve with a dollop of whipped cream or Strawberry Ice Cream (see page 255). Garnish each serving with a whole, fanned strawberry. (See illustration on page 38.)

Pumpkin Pie
with Cranberry Marmalade

MAKES ONE 10-INCH PIE
SERVES 12

EQUIPMENT

*10 x 1-inch flan ring or 10-inch
shallow pie dish*

Rolling pin

*Parchment paper or large coffee
filter papers*

Pie weights or dried beans

Nonreactive medium saucepan

Large bowl

Whip

INGREDIENTS

*12 ounces Pâte Sucrée
(see page 76) or Basic Pie Dough
(see page 81)*

CRANBERRY MARMALADE

*4 tablespoons Simple Sugar Syrup
(see page 241)*

1 tablespoon orange zest

2 tablespoons Grand Marnier

*1 cinnamon stick or a pinch of
ground cinnamon*

6 to 8 scrapes of whole nutmeg

*8 ounces fresh cranberries, picked
over and rinsed*

When I first made this American classic for Wolfgang, he wasn't impressed. He wanted the filling to include a cranberry marmalade, and he insisted that the pumpkin puree be made from fresh pumpkin rather than canned. I protested, but I made the pie as he requested. He was right and the pie was a huge success.

1. Position rack in center of oven and preheat oven to 375 degrees.

2. Line pie dish: Coat a 10 x 1-inch flan ring or a 10-inch pie dish with vegetable spray. On a lightly floured surface, roll out dough to a 12-inch circle. Fit into prepared pan and trim the edges. Refrigerate for 30 minutes. Line with parchment paper or large coffee filter papers and fill with pie weights or beans (see page XVII). Bake 15 minutes, remove the paper and beans, and bake 10 minutes longer.

3. Meanwhile, make the cranberry marmalade: In a nonreactive medium saucepan, combine the sugar syrup, orange zest, Grand Marnier, cinnamon stick, and nutmeg. Bring to a boil, reduce heat, add the cranberries, and simmer until the berries have softened, 4 to 5 minutes. Cool and remove the vanilla bean and cinnamon stick. Spread in a thin layer over the bottom of the prebaked tart shell.

4. Make the filling: In a large bowl, combine the pumpkin puree, sugar, ginger, cinnamon, nutmeg, cloves, salt, and pepper. Whisk in the eggs, cream, and bourbon and mix well.

FILLING

*2 cups pumpkin puree, preferably
made from fresh pumpkin**

1 cup dark brown sugar

1 teaspoon ground ginger

$\frac{1}{2}$ teaspoon ground cinnamon

$\frac{1}{2}$ teaspoon ground nutmeg

$\frac{1}{2}$ teaspoon ground cloves

Pinch of salt

Pinch of ground white pepper

4 eggs, lightly beaten

$1\frac{1}{2}$ cups heavy cream

3 tablespoons bourbon

TO PREPARE AHEAD

THROUGH STEP 2, PASTRY
CAN BE PREPARED A DAY
AHEAD AND BLIND-BAKED
EARLY ON DAY NEEDED.
THROUGH STEP 4, PIE CAN
BE MADE EARLY IN DAY AND
WARMED JUST BEFORE
SERVING.

Pour into the pastry shell. Bake until the filling is firm to the touch, 35 to 40 minutes. Cool on a rack.

5. To serve, warm pie in low oven and serve with Cinnamon Ice Cream (see page 249). Pass warm Caramel Sauce (see page 136), flavored with bourbon.

---

*To make fresh pumpkin puree, cut the pumpkin into about 4-inch chunks, remove the seeds and strands of fiber, and arrange the pieces on a baking tray. Bake in a preheated 325 degree oven until dry, $2\frac{1}{2}$ to 3 hours. Cool and complete the drying-out process for another 3 hours. Scoop out the inside of the pumpkin and puree through a food mill.

Macadamia Tart
with Chocolate Pâte Sucrée

MAKES ONE 9-INCH TART
SERVES 8

EQUIPMENT

9-inch tart pan with removable
bottom

Rolling pin

Baking tray

Small skillet

Medium mixing bowl

Whip

Ladle

Wooden spoon or spatula

INGREDIENTS

1 pound Chocolate Pâte Sucrée
(see page 78)

FILLING

1 pound (3 heaping cups)
macadamia nuts

3 tablespoons unsalted butter, cut
into small pieces

1 vanilla bean, split lengthwise

1⅓ cups light corn syrup

⅔ cup packed brown sugar

1 whole egg

3 egg yolks

1 tablespoon Frangelico

4 ounces shredded coconut,
preferably unsweetened

Since whole macadamia nuts are very expensive, halves or pieces can be used for this tart. The tart can also be made with walnuts or a combination of different nuts. It is important to remove the tart from the pan while still warm so that the ring can be taken off easily.

1. Preheat oven to 375 degrees. Lightly butter, or coat with vegetable spray, a 9-inch tart pan.

2. Line the tart pan: On a lightly floured surface, roll out Chocolate Pâte Sucrée to an 11-inch circle, about ¼ inch thick. Roll up on rolling pin and fit into prepared tart pan. Dough may break, but that's okay. Press pieces into pan and smooth to even. Trim edges (see illustration on page XXI). Refrigerate at least 30 minutes, or until needed.

3. Make the filling: Spread nuts on a baking tray and toast in oven until golden brown, not too dark, about 10 minutes, turning after 5 minutes. Set aside to cool.

4. Place the butter and the vanilla bean with its scrapings in a small skillet. Over medium heat, melt butter and then continue to cook until butter turns golden brown and has a nutty aroma, about 5 minutes. Watch carefully to prevent burning. Scrape into a medium mixing bowl. Add the corn syrup, sugar, whole egg, egg yolks, and Frangelico, and whisk until well combined. Refrigerate, covered, until needed.

TO PREPARE AHEAD

THROUGH STEP 4,
COMPONENTS CAN BE MADE 1
DAY AHEAD. THROUGH STEP
6, TART CAN BE BAKED
EARLY IN THE DAY.

5. Assemble the tart: Set the prepared tart shell on a baking tray and fill with the nuts. Ladle the filling over and level. (The filling should reach the top of the tart shell.)

6. Bake until filling feels firm to the touch, 50 to 55 minutes. Remove from oven and cover top with the coconut. Return to oven and continue to bake until coconut turns golden, about 10 minutes longer. Cool on rack for 20 minutes. Then, tap around sides of pan with a knife or spoon and set pan on wide-mouthed jar a little narrower than the pan. Gently release outer rim and let slip down the side of the jar. Return tart to rack to cool completely.

7. To serve, place tart on serving plate and, with a sharp knife, cut into slices. Serve with Caramel Sauce (see page 136) or a spoonful of soft whipped cream.

Pecan Pie

MAKES ONE 9-INCH PIE
SERVES 8

EQUIPMENT

9-inch tart pan with removable
bottom

Rolling pin

Small skillet

Medium bowl

Whip

Baking tray

Ladle

INGREDIENTS

1 pound Pâte Sucrée (see page 76)

FILLING

3 tablespoons unsalted butter, cut
into small pieces

1 vanilla bean, split lengthwise

1⅓ cups light corn syrup

⅔ cup light brown sugar, packed

1 whole egg

3 egg yolks

1 tablespoon Frangelico or brandy

¼ pound chopped pecans

¾ pound pecan halves

*W*e like the crisp texture of a pâte sucrée to line the pan for pecan pie. As with so many of our pies at Spago, this is baked in individual tartlet pans. If you want to make single servings, line 8 tartlet pans with pastry, divide the filling among the pans and arrange on a baking tray. Bake until filling is firm to the touch, 30 to 35 minutes.

1. Position rack in center of oven and preheat oven to 375 degrees. Lightly butter, or coat with vegetable spray, a 9-inch tart pan.

2. Line tart pan: On a lightly floured surface, roll out the Pâte Sucrée to an 11-inch circle. Roll up on rolling pin and fit into prepared tart pan. If dough breaks, press pieces into pan and smooth to even. Trim edges. Refrigerate for 30 minutes or until needed.

3. Make the filling: Place the butter and the vanilla bean with its scrapings in a small skillet. Over medium heat, melt butter and then continue to cook until butter turns golden brown and has a nutty aroma, about 5 minutes. Watch carefully to prevent burning. Scrape into a medium mixing bowl. Add the corn syrup, sugar, whole egg, egg yolks, and liqueur, and whisk until well combined. Refrigerate, covered, until needed.

4. Assemble the tart: Set the prepared shell on a baking tray. Spread the chopped pecans over the bottom of the shell. Then arrange the pecan halves in circles, rounded side up, starting at the outside edge of the pan, placing the pecans as close together as possible, until the entire surface of the tart is cov-

TO PREPARE AHEAD

THROUGH STEP 5, WARMING
JUST BEFORE YOU ARE READY
TO SERVE

ered with circles of pecans. Carefully ladle the filling over and level. (The filling should reach the top of the tart shell.)

5. Place the baking tray with the tart pan in the oven and bake until filling feels firm to the touch, 55 to 60 minutes. Cool on rack for 20 minutes. Then, tap around sides of pan with the back of a spoon or knife and set pan on a wide-mouthed jar that is narrower than the pan. Gently release outer ring and let slip down the side of the jar. (If you find it difficult to remove, heat the outside of the ring with a propane torch.) Return tart pan to rack to cool completely.

6. To serve, warm tart in oven. Cut into slices with sharp knife and serve with Caramel Sauce (see page 136) or ice cream of your choice.

Lemon Tart

*T*he filling for this tart is Lemon Curd. The topping can be either caramelized sugar or circles of fresh raspberries.

1. Preheat oven to 350 degrees.

2. Roll out the Pâte Sucrée to an 11-inch circle, about ¼ inch thick. Fit the dough into a 9-inch tart pan or Pyrex pie plate and trim the edges. Line the bottom and sides of the shell with parchment paper (or large coffee filter papers) and fill with pie weights or dried beans (see page XVII) up to the very top of the tart shell. Bake 20 minutes, take from oven, cool, and carefully remove the weights and paper. Return the shell to the oven and bake until golden, 5 to 10 minutes longer.

3. Make the Lemon Curd and scrape into the pie shell, smoothing with a metal spatula. Cool and refrigerate until firm, 3 to 4 hours, up to overnight.

4. Sprinkle the 2 tablespoons of sugar evenly over the top of the filling. With the propane torch, caramelize the sugar, starting at the edge closest to you and working out to the opposite end of the tart. Or, if desired, eliminate the sugar and arrange circles of raspberries on top of the filling. Just before serving, sift a little powdered sugar over the berries.

EQUIPMENT

Rolling pin

9-inch tart pan or Pyrex pie plate

Parchment paper or large coffee filter papers

Pie weights or dried beans

Metal spatula

Propane torch

INGREDIENTS

½ recipe Pâte Sucrée (see page 76)

1 recipe Lemon Curd (see page 119)

2 tablespoons granulated sugar, optional

TO PREPARE AHEAD

THROUGH STEP 4.
REFRIGERATE UNTIL
NEEDED. REMOVE FROM
REFRIGERATOR ABOUT 30
MINUTES BEFORE SERVING.

Lemon Curd

MAKES FILLING FOR ONE 9-INCH TART

*T*his is delicious as a filling for a tart or it can be used as a preserve and served on toasted Basic Brioche (see page 140).

EQUIPMENT

Large heatproof bowl

Whip

Strainer

Medium bowl

Plastic wrap

INGREDIENTS

4 whole eggs

4 egg yolks

¾ cup granulated sugar

1 cup lemon juice

5½ ounces (1 stick plus 3 tablespoons) unsalted butter, at room temperature, cut into small pieces

TO PREPARE AHEAD

THROUGH STEP 2

1. In a large heatproof bowl, whisk together the whole eggs, egg yolks, sugar, and lemon juice. Set over a pan of simmering water and continue to whisk until mixture thickens, about 10 minutes.

2. Remove the bowl from the heat and add the pieces of butter. Let the butter melt a little into the mixture, then whisk, as quickly as possible, before the mixture cools down. Strain into a clean medium bowl and use as needed. If not using immediately, press a piece of plastic wrap directly on top of the lemon curd to prevent a film forming.

Coconut Cream Pie

EQUIPMENT

Rolling pin

9-inch Pyrex pie plate

Parchment or wax paper

Pie weights or dried beans

Large saucepan

Strainer

Baking tray

Large, medium, and small bowls

Whip

Plastic wrap

Pastry bag with #4 star tip

Offset spatula

INGREDIENTS

12 ounces (½ recipe) Pâte Sucrée (see page 76) or Chocolate Pâte Sucrée (see page 78)

COCONUT PASTRY CREAM

2 cups unsweetened coconut milk*

1 cup shredded unsweetened coconut

6 egg yolks

½ cup granulated sugar

3 tablespoons all-purpose flour, sifted

S ometimes we make this with Pâte Sucrée and sometimes with Chocolate Pâte Sucrée. Serve this pie family style, cutting slices at the table and spooning any excess filling on the plate.

1. On a lightly floured surface, roll out pastry to an 11-inch circle. Fit into a 9-inch Pyrex pie plate and trim by running the sharp blade of a small knife around the edges. Chill for about 30 minutes.

2. Position rack in center of oven and preheat oven to 350 degrees.

3. Line pie plate with parchment or wax paper. Fill, to the very top of the plate, with pie weights or dried beans, making certain the weights are pressed into the corners of the shell. Bake 20 minutes, cool slightly, remove paper and weights (see page XVII), and return to oven until shell is nicely browned, about 10 minutes longer. Set aside.

4. Meanwhile, make the coconut pastry cream: In a large saucepan, scald the coconut milk. Remove from the heat and steep the shredded coconut in the milk until the milk has a strong coconut flavor, 40 to 45 minutes. Strain into a clean bowl, reserving the coconut. Spread coconut out on a baking tray to dry, about 30 minutes. Then toast in oven until golden, about 10 minutes.

5. In a large bowl, whisk together the egg yolks and sugar until sugar is dissolved and mixture is pale yellow. Whisk in

*Unsweetened shredded coconut can be purchased in most health food stores or Asian markets, and unsweetened coconut milk can also be found in Asian markets.

3 tablespoons dark rum, heated

1 tablespoon unflavored gelatin

1 cup heavy cream

1 ripe banana

TO PREPARE AHEAD

THROUGH STEP 3, SHELL CAN
BE BAKED 1 DAY AHEAD AND
REFRIGERATED, COVERED.
IN STEP 7, PIE CAN BE
COMPLETED EARLY IN THE
DAY AND REFRIGERATED
UNTIL NEEDED. WHIPPED
CREAM SHOULD BE PIPED
JUST BEFORE SERVING.

the flour. Whisk in the strained coconut milk and return to the saucepan. Cook, over medium heat, stirring constantly, until mixture thickens and bubbles begin to appear on the surface. Strain into a clean bowl and place plastic wrap directly on the surface of the pastry cream. Refrigerate until needed.

6. When ready to assemble the pie, heat the rum and dissolve the gelatin in it. Cool slightly and stir into the pastry cream.

7. Assemble the pie: Whip 1 cup cream and fold ¾ of it into the chilled pastry cream. Spoon the remaining whipped cream into a pastry bag fitted with a #4 star tip. Peel the banana, cut into thin slices, and arrange on the pie shell. Spoon the pastry cream on top of the bananas and smooth with offset spatula. Pipe small mounds of whipped cream around the outer edges of the pie and sprinkle toasted coconut over the top, reserving a small amount to decorate the plates. Refrigerate until needed.

8. To serve, decorate each plate with a sprinkling of toasted coconut and place 1 slice of pie in the center. Serve immediately.

VI

Puff Pastry and Phyllo

*P*uff pastry is most versatile, well worth the time it takes to roll out all the "turns." It can be used for savory dishes as well as for the desserts in this book. We have tried to simplify the directions as much as possible.

When we prepare puff pastry at Spago, we use half pastry flour and half all-purpose flour. However, if a good pastry flour is not available, just follow the recipe using only all-purpose flour.

Read through the recipe before starting to work. You will notice that the butter is wrapped in a clean white napkin. This allows the napkin to absorb the moisture found in butter. That excess moisture acts upon the flour, forming gluten, which would make your puff pastry tough and elastic and more difficult to roll out.

When rolling out the pastry, lightly flour the work surface and the dough, brushing away any excess flour before folding the dough for the "turns."

Phyllo leaves can be purchased in most food markets, sometimes in the frozen food section. If frozen, remove the sheets needed, one day ahead, and defrost, wrapped well, in the refrigerator.

PUFF PASTRY

APPLE PEAR TARTE TATIN

INDIVIDUAL PEAR TARTS WITH PHYLLO LAYERS

PEAR CHERRY NAPOLEON WITH PHYLLO NESTS

FRESH BERRY NAPOLEON WITH CARAMEL SAUCE

Vanilla Pastry Cream
Caramel Sauce

Puff Pastry

MAKES 3 POUNDS

EQUIPMENT

Food processor

White linen napkin

Heavy rolling pin

Large pastry brush

Plastic wrap

INGREDIENTS

DÉTREMPE

2 pounds (6¾ cups) all-purpose flour

1½ pounds (5¼ cups) pastry flour

½ teaspoon salt

2 sticks plus 5 tablespoons unsalted butter, chilled and cut into small pieces

1 to 1¼ cups chilled water

BUTTER BLOCK

3 sticks plus 5 tablespoons unsalted butter

*D*étrempe is the French technical name given to a mixture of flour and water. Puff pastry is not very difficult to make, and with a little practice, you will find it a very handy item to have in your freezer. It does freeze well and can be wrapped in ½- or 1-pound packages.

1. Make the détrempe: In a food processor fitted with the steel blade, combine the two flours and salt with 1 or 2 on/off turns. Arrange the pieces of butter evenly around the blade and process until the texture resembles fine meal. (Turn off the machine while checking texture.)

2. With the machine running, pour the well-chilled water through the feed tube just until a ball begins to form. The amount of water needed depends upon the water content of the butter. Start with 1 cup and if the dough still looks dry in some spots, add the remaining ¼ cup as necessary. Turn out onto a lightly floured board, shape into a round ball, and cut an X with the point of a sharp knife. Wrap securely in plastic wrap and refrigerate overnight.

3. Make the butter block: Arrange the butter into as much of a square as possible. Wrap in a clean white linen napkin to absorb excess moisture found in the butter. With a heavy rolling pin, pound the butter to form an 8-inch square, about 1 inch thick. Even the sides as necessary with the rolling pin. Refrigerate overnight.

4. The next day, remove the détrempe and butter block from the refrigerator and bring to room temperature before using. This should take about ½ hour in warm weather or in a warm kitchen; 1½ hours in cold weather. Both détrempe and butter

block should have the same texture before rolling. (Your thumb pressed into each one will leave an indentation.)

5. Lightly flour your work surface and rolling pin. Roll out the détrempe to an 18-inch square. Remove the butter from the napkin and set in the middle of the détrempe. Fold 2 opposite sides of détrempe over to meet in the center of the butter. If the overlapping ends become too thick, level by lightly moving the rolling pin over the ends. Fold the 2 remaining opposite ends to meet in the center, stretching as necessary until the seams come together.

6. Roll out the pastry to a rectangle, about 12 x 18 inches. Starting with the 12-inch side nearest you, fold the dough into thirds. Turn the dough so that the seam is on your right and again roll out to the same-size rectangle, dusting the work surface and dough with flour as necessary to prevent sticking and tearing. Using a large, dry pastry brush, brush away excess flour before and after folding. Use the rolling pin to even the sides of the pastry as it is being rolled. Press 2 indentations in the dough with your knuckles, to remind you of the number of "turns" you have made, and wrap securely in plastic wrap. (You have just completed 2 turns.) Refrigerate for at least 4 hours, up to overnight.

7. Remove the pastry from the refrigerator and let soften slightly before rolling. With the seam on your right, again complete 2 turns. Press 4 indentations in the dough, rewrap well, and refrigerate for 2 hours. Again, let the dough soften slightly and roll one more time to complete 5 turns. At this point, your pastry can be cut, wrapped, and frozen for future use.

Apple Pear Tarte Tatin

SERVES 8

🦪🦪

*T*his is a variation of the classic tarte Tatin, made with apples and pears. Try to buy fruit of the same size, medium or large. It is a great company dessert because it can be made early in the day, reheated, and finished just before serving.

1. Cut the apples and pears in half, through the stem. Core, peel, and sprinkle with lemon juice. Set aside.

2. Wrap the outside of a 10-inch skillet in 2 layers of aluminum foil. (The fruit is very juicy and the foil will catch much of the overflow.) Melt the butter in the skillet. Add ¾ cup sugar and when it just begins to caramelize, remove pan from heat. Arrange the fruit in the pan, rounded side out: first, a row of apples placed around the sides of the skillet, then a row of pears, a second row of apples, and 2 or 3 pear halves in the center. (If there are 1 or 2 pieces that don't fit, place them on top of the fruit. As the apples and pears soften, you will be able to fit the extra fruit into the pan.) Return the pan to medium-high heat and cook until the liquid in the pan turns lightly golden and the fruit begins to soften. (Be patient . . . this may take about 45 minutes, depending on the texture and size of the fruit.)

3. Meanwhile, on a lightly floured surface, roll out the puff pastry to a 13-inch circle or square. Using a round plate or pot cover, cut out an 11-inch circle. With the tines of a fork, lightly prick the entire surface of the pastry. Refrigerate until needed.

4. Preheat oven to 400 degrees.

EQUIPMENT

10-inch skillet, with rounded sides

Aluminum foil

Rolling pin

Propane torch

INGREDIENTS

2½ pounds (6 to 7 medium) Golden Delicious apples

2½ pounds (4 to 5 medium) pears

Juice of 1 large lemon

6 tablespoons (¾ stick) unsalted butter, cut into pieces

1 cup granulated sugar

¾ pound Puff Pastry (see page 126)

Candied Fresh Ginger (see page 190)

TO PREPARE AHEAD

THROUGH STEP 5, THE TARTE CAN BE PREPARED EARLY IN THE DAY.

5. When the fruit has reached the proper consistency, arrange the circle of pastry on top of the fruit and set the skillet in the oven, with the foil still surrounding the pan. (If the handle of the skillet is made of wood, wrap well in aluminum foil.) Bake until the pastry is golden brown, about 30 minutes. Remove from oven and place skillet on rack to cool.

6. When ready to serve, return the pan to a preheated 400-degree oven to warm, about 10 minutes. Remove from the oven and place a large platter over the skillet. (If there is too much liquid in the pan, you may want to pour a little of it out.) Invert the tarte onto the platter and if the apples have separated from each other, gently press them back together (see illustration). The tarte can be served at this point, if desired.

7. To serve, sprinkle 2 tablespoons of the remaining sugar over the fruit and, with a propane torch, caramelize the sugar. Repeat with the remaining 2 tablespoons of sugar, and continue to caramelize until the top of the tarte is a rich golden brown. Arrange a slice of the tarte on a dessert plate and serve with a spoonful of lightly whipped cream or a scoop of vanilla ice cream. Garnish with a few pieces of julienned Candied Fresh Ginger.

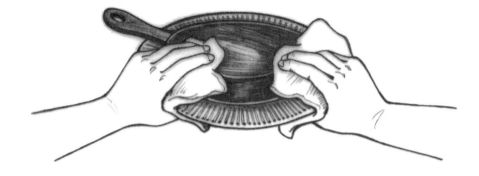

EQUIPMENT

Food processor

2 small bowls

1 or 2 baking trays

Parchment paper

Pastry brush

4-inch cookie cutter

Large heavy skillet or sauté pan

Slotted spoon

INGREDIENTS

ALMOND TOPPING

*¼ cup (1 ounce) almonds, toasted
(see page XXIII)*

Scant ½ cup almond paste

*4 tablespoons (½ stick) unsalted
butter, at room temperature, cut
into small pieces*

2 eggs

*¼ cup plus 2 tablespoons
all-purpose flour*

*¼ cup pear brandy, pear liqueur,
or brandy*

PHYLLO LAYERS

½ cup granulated sugar

1 teaspoon ground cinnamon

*8 phyllo pastry sheets, fresh or
frozen, thawed*

Individual Pear Tarts with Phyllo Layers

SERVES 8

*T*he pastry for these tarts is layers of phyllo leaves. The leaves usually come in two sizes, 12 x 17 inches or 14 x 18 inches. Either size will work. Remove the number of leaves you need for the recipe, returning the remainder to the box. As you work, keep the unused leaves covered with plastic wrap or wax paper and place a moistened towel on top of the plastic to prevent drying.

1. Make the topping: In a food processor fitted with the steel blade, finely grind the toasted almonds, starting with on/off turns. Stop the machine, add the almond paste and butter, and process until smooth, scraping down sides of work bowl as necessary. Add the remaining ingredients and process until well blended. Transfer to a small bowl and set aside.

2. Make the phyllo layers: Preheat oven to 350 degrees. Line baking trays with parchment paper and set aside.

3. In a small bowl, combine sugar and cinnamon. Spread out 1 phyllo sheet on a flat work surface, brush lightly with melted butter, and sprinkle with 1 tablespoon cinnamon sugar. Repeat with a second and third layer of phyllo, melted butter, and cinnamon sugar. Top with a fourth sheet of phyllo. Using a 4-inch cookie cutter, cut out 8 circles and arrange on the prepared baking trays. Repeat with the remaining 4 phyllo sheets, melted butter, and cinnamon sugar, and again cut out 8 circles. (You now have 16 phyllo circles.) Spread 1 tablespoon almond topping over the top of each circle, covering completely.

4 ounces (1 stick) unsalted butter, melted

PEARS

1 ounce (2 tablespoons) unsalted butter

4 pounds (about 8 medium) pears, Anjou or Bosc, peeled, halved, cored, and cut into thin slices

1 vanilla bean, split lengthwise

1 cup granulated sugar

Vanilla Ice Cream (see page 253)

Confectioners' sugar

TO PREPARE AHEAD

THROUGH STEP 1, TOPPING CAN BE MADE 1 DAY AHEAD AND REFRIGERATED, COVERED. BRING TO ROOM TEMPERATURE WHEN READY TO USE. THROUGH STEP 2, PHYLLO CIRCLES CAN BE MADE EARLY IN THE DAY AND KEPT AT ROOM TEMPERATURE. IN STEP 5, PEARS CAN BE COOKED UNTIL JUST TENDER EARLY IN DAY AND TRANSFERRED TO LARGE BOWL. AT SERVING TIME, CONTINUE WITH RECIPE.

4. Bake until tops brown and are firm to the touch, about 15 minutes. Transfer baking trays to cooling rack. Let cool.

5. Caramelize the pears: In large heavy skillet or sauté pan, melt the butter. Arrange the pears in the pan, add the vanilla bean with its scrapings and the sugar and cook, over medium heat, until the pears are just tender, 5 to 10 minutes, occasionally stirring or shaking pan to make certain the pears do not burn. *Do not overcook.* Using a slotted spoon, transfer the pears to a large bowl. Reduce juices in pan until thick and syrupy, stirring frequently, 10 to 13 minutes. Return pears to pan and cook until caramelized, about 6 minutes. Cool slightly.

6. To serve, place 1 phyllo circle, almond-coated side up, on each of 8 dessert plates. Divide pears and arrange in a circular pattern on the phyllo. Place a scoop of Vanilla Ice Cream in the center and top with a second phyllo circle, almond-coated side down. Sift confectioners' sugar over the circles and around the perimeter of the plates and serve immediately.

EQUIPMENT

Parchment paper

1 or 2 baking trays

Small cup

Large sauté pan

Large bowl

6-inch stainless steel bowl

Wooden spoon

Heavy-bottomed small saucepan

2 stainless steel dinner forks

INGREDIENTS

PHYLLO NESTS

1/4 cup granulated sugar

1 teaspoon ground cinnamon

8 ounces (1/2 package) phyllo
dough

Vegetable spray

PEAR CHERRY FILLING

8 medium (about 4 pounds) pears,
Bosc or Bartlett, peeled, cored, and
cut into 1/2-inch slices

2 cups whole cherries, pitted

1 cup granulated sugar

1 tablespoon fresh lemon juice

2 medium cinnamon sticks

Pear Cherry Napoleon
with Phyllo Nests

SERVES 6 TO 8

*Y*ou will find the phyllo crust simple to prepare. Fresh cherries are preferable, but if not available, you can use frozen. The sugar dome is a decorative addition and will break when the napoleon is sliced, but it makes a spectacular presentation.

1. Set racks in center of oven and preheat to 325 degrees. Line 1 or 2 baking trays with parchment paper and set aside.

2. Make the nests: In a small cup, combine the sugar and cinnamon and set aside.

3. Phyllo pastry comes in a thick roll: For this recipe, do not unroll. Place the roll of phyllo dough on a firm work surface and cut strips, about 1/2 inch wide. Toss the strips together, as if tossing fettuccini. You should have about 8 cups.

4. Divide the pile of cut dough in half and place each half on prepared baking trays. Arrange each into a neat circle, about 8 or 9 inches in diameter. Lightly coat each circle with vegetable spray and sprinkle with the cinnamon sugar. Bake until golden brown and crisp, 15 to 20 minutes. Set on rack to cool.

5. While nests are browning, make the filling: In a large sauté pan, arrange half the pears, 1 cup cherries, 1/2 cup sugar, 1 1/2 teaspoons lemon juice, and 1 cinnamon stick. Cook over medium-high heat until the pears are tender, about 15 minutes (time depends on ripeness of pears), stirring occasionally with a wooden spoon to ensure even cooking. Transfer to a large bowl. Repeat procedure with remaining pears, cherries,

SPUN SUGAR DOME

1 cup granulated sugar

TO PREPARE AHEAD

THROUGH STEP 7. WHEN
NAPOLEON IS ASSEMBLED,
SERVE IMMEDIATELY.

sugar, lemon juice, and cinnamon stick. Set aside to cool and remove the 2 cinnamon sticks.

6. Make the spun sugar dome: Set a baking tray on a flat surface and coat lightly with vegetable spray. Place the 6-inch bowl, upside down, on the tray and coat well with vegetable spray. (The baking tray will catch the excess sugar and cleanup will be easier.)

7. Pour the sugar into a heavy-bottomed small saucepan and cook over medium-high heat until the sugar is a dark golden color (caramel). (Watch carefully once the sugar starts to color to avoid burning.) Immediately remove the pan from the heat and place next to the bowl. Holding two stainless steel dinner forks in the same hand, stir the caramel until it begins to thicken. When you can actually hold enough caramel on the forks to drizzle, start drizzling the caramel, back and forth, side to side, over the bowl. Return the forks to the pan as necessary to gather up more caramel and continue to drizzle over the bowl until you have created a dome, covering the bowl completely. Do not remove the dome until it is cool.

8. To assemble the napoleon, place one phyllo nest on a flat serving plate. Arrange the pear cherry filling on the nest and top with the remaining phyllo nest. Set the spun sugar dome in the center of the nest (see photo in insert following page 196). Serve immediately.

Fresh Berry Napoleon with Caramel Sauce

SERVES 6

EQUIPMENT

Rolling pin

1 or 2 baking trays

Parchment paper

4-inch round cookie cutter

Small cup

Whip

Pastry brush

Serrated knife

INGREDIENTS

*1 recipe Vanilla Pastry Cream
(see page 135)*

*½ pound Puff Pastry
(see page 126)*

1 egg

1 tablespoon heavy cream

Crystal sugar

*2 pints assorted berries (sliced
strawberries, blueberries, or
raspberries)*

Caramel Sauce (see page 136)

TO PREPARE AHEAD

THROUGH STEP 4. PASTRIES
CAN BE BAKED 2 TO 3 HOURS
BEFORE NEEDED, CUT, AND
ASSEMBLED WHEN READY TO
SERVE. CARAMEL SAUCE CAN
BE SERVED AT ROOM
TEMPERATURE OR WARM.

*T*his is one of the recipes featured in *Bon Appétit* magazine, April 1993, using only strawberries. We decided that assorted berries would make the recipe more interesting and infinitely more delicious.

1. Make the pastry cream and refrigerate, covered, until needed.

2. Roll out the pastry: Position rack in center of oven and preheat oven to 400 degrees. Line 1 or 2 baking trays with parchment paper.

3. On a lightly floured surface, roll out the pastry to a 12-inch square. Using a 4-inch round cookie cutter, cut out 9 rounds, dipping the cutter in flour as necessary to make a clean cut. Arrange the rounds on prepared trays and, with the tines of a fork, prick each round several times. Refrigerate 20 minutes.

4. In a small cup, whisk together egg and cream. Using a pastry brush, brush over the surface of 6 rounds and sprinkle lightly with crystal sugar. Bake all 9 rounds until nicely puffed and golden, about 18 minutes. Cool on a rack.

5. Assemble the napoleons: Using a serrated knife, cut each pastry in half, *horizontally.* Set aside the 6 sugar-coated tops. Place 1 plain round on each of 6 dessert plates and spoon a heaping tablespoon of pastry cream over. Top with some of the berries, cover with a second plain round, and layer with pastry cream and remaining berries. Set the reserved 6 rounds on each of the napoleons and spoon Caramel Sauce around. Serve immediately.

Vanilla Pastry Cream

MAKES ABOUT 3 CUPS

Medium noncorrosive saucepan

Electric mixer or whip

Wooden spoon

Strainer

Medium bowl

Plastic wrap

2 cups milk

½ vanilla bean, split lengthwise

6 egg yolks

½ cup granulated sugar

3 tablespoons all-purpose flour, sifted

THROUGH STEP 3, THE PASTRY CREAM CAN KEEP, REFRIGERATED, UP TO 3 DAYS.

*P*astry cream has the consistency of a pudding, very delicate and very creamy. It is used as a filling for a layer cake or it can be spooned over fresh fruit. To make Coffee Pastry Cream, dissolve 1 tablespoon instant espresso and ¼ cup crushed coffee beans in 2 cups scalded milk (see page 6). Let steep for 15 minutes, strain, and then continue step 2 of recipe.

1. In a medium saucepan, scald the milk with the vanilla bean and its scrapings.

2. While the milk is being scalded, in the large bowl of an electric mixer, using the paddle or beaters, whisk together the egg yolks and sugar on high speed until mixture is pale yellow and forms a ribbon when beaters are lifted from the bowl. (This also can be done with a whip and large mixing bowl, if desired.) Whisk in the flour.

3. Turn speed to low and pour about half the hot milk into the egg yolk mixture. Turn off the machine, pour contents back into the saucepan, and cook over medium heat, stirring constantly with a wooden spoon, until the mixture thickens and bubbles *begin* to appear on the surface. Strain into a clean medium bowl and cover with plastic wrap placed directly on the surface of the cream to prevent a skin forming. Refrigerate and use as desired.

Caramel Sauce

MAKES 1¹/₂ CUPS

*T*his delicious, smooth sauce has the consistency of a thin custard. Spooned over ice cream or used to mirror a dessert plate, it changes a plain dessert into something memorable.

1. In a small saucepan, combine 1 cup cream with butter and heat until butter melts and cream is hot. Keep warm.

2. Spoon the corn syrup into a medium deep saucepan and top with the sugar. On medium heat, cook until mixture turns a deep amber color and temperature reaches 225 degrees on a candy thermometer, stirring often with a wooden spoon. As mixture turns golden, check thermometer often until correct temperature is reached. (A candy thermometer usually has a clip on the side, so that you can clip it to the side of the pan, making certain that it rests in the mixture, but does not touch the bottom of the pan.) Immediately remove pan from heat and pour cream mixture into the sugar, stirring to combine well. Mixture will bubble up as you pour, so be careful not to burn yourself.

3. Stir in remaining ¹/₄ cup cream. Strain through a fine-mesh strainer into a heatproof bowl. If not using the sauce immediately, let cool and refrigerate, covered, until needed.

4. To serve, warm sauce over low heat, stirring occasionally. If sauce has thickened too much, add cream, a small amount at a time, to thin to desired consistency.

EQUIPMENT

Small saucepan

Medium deep saucepan

Candy thermometer

Long-handled wooden spoon

Fine-mesh strainer

Small heatproof bowl

INGREDIENTS

1¹/₄ cups heavy cream

4 tablespoons (¹/₂ stick) unsalted butter, cut into small pieces

2 tablespoons light corn syrup

1¹/₂ cups granulated sugar

TO PREPARE AHEAD

THROUGH STEP 3, SAUCE WILL KEEP, REFRIGERATED, UP TO 3 WEEKS.

VII

Brioche

*B*rioche is an egg-enriched bread, the texture light and soft.
It is extremely versatile, used to make many types of
desserts as well as savory dishes. At one time,
breadmaking was an all-day chore, kneading a tiring physical activity.
Today, however, with the use of an electric mixer, one or two loaves of

bread can be prepared at one time, the extra loaf stored in the freezer for future use.

For the recipes in this book, the baked bread is cut into thick slices to make bread pudding, the unbaked dough rolled out and filled to make tarts and sweet rolls. To further enrich the flavor of the bread, you might like to add chopped candied orange peel and/or golden raisins to the dough. Mix the peel with the softened butter and continue with the recipe. Gerry Moss, who bakes the bread at Spago, Los Angeles, first experimented with this combination and it proved to boost the flavor of the bread. To make candied orange peel, see Candied Grapefruit Peel (page 188), substituting oranges for the grapefruit. After the last boiling, strain the orange peel, dry thoroughly, and chop. Do not roll in granulated sugar.

Read through the directions before starting and you should have perfect results every time. Make sure the yeast you use is fresh. (The expiration date is usually printed on every package.)

BASIC BRIOCHE

APRICOT ROLLS

PRUNE AND APPLE POCKETS

STICKY BUNS

APPLE BREAD PUDDING

CHOCOLATE BREAD PUDDING

RICOTTA FIG TART

Basic Brioche

EQUIPMENT

Electric mixer

Large bowl

Plastic wrap

2 loaf pans, 7 x 14 inches each

Rolling pin

Small bowl or cup

Whip

Pastry brush

INGREDIENTS

3⅓ cups all-purpose flour

½ cup cake flour

¼ cup granulated sugar

*2 teaspoons table salt
(not kosher salt)*

*2 tablespoons dry yeast
(2 packages) or 0.6 ounce
(1 package) cake yeast*

5 large eggs

*¼ cup cold water plus extra if
necessary*

*14 tablespoons (1¾ sticks)
unsalted butter, at room
temperature, cut into small cubes*

*1 egg plus 1 tablespoon cream for
egg wash*

*A*t Spago, Las Vegas, the bread department is adjacent to the pastry department, and the bakers are kind enough to bake brioche for us when we need it. However, when we wanted to include the recipe in the book, we had to bake it ourselves. It was fun working with the dough, but best of all, we found it exceedingly easy to make.

1. In the large bowl of an electric mixer, fitted with the dough hook, combine the all-purpose and cake flours and the sugar. Stop the machine and on 1 side of the bowl, on top of the mixture, carefully place the salt. On the opposite side, sprinkle the yeast. Do not allow the yeast and salt to touch. (The salt will destroy the yeast if it is combined at this stage.) Add the eggs and ¼ cup water and start the machine, slowly at first, then a little faster, until the dough comes away from the sides of the bowl and clings to the dough hook, 4 to 5 minutes. (If making bread in a dry climate, it may be necessary to add 1 or 2 tablespoons more water to the dough. Add the water 1 or 2 teaspoons at a time until the right texture is reached.)

2. With the machine running at medium speed, add the butter, 1 or 2 cubes at a time. As each addition is absorbed into the dough, add a little more until all the butter is used, scraping down sides of bowl and dough hook as necessary. It is important that the butter be absorbed completely. (Otherwise bits of butter will ooze through the dough and there will be dark spots on the bread.)

3. To make it easier to remove the dough, sprinkle a little flour over the dough and then turn out onto a lightly floured surface. Gently pat down the dough and fold all 4 sides

TO PREPARE AHEAD

THROUGH STEP 3, 1 DAY
AHEAD. WHEN BAKED, BREAD
CAN BE SLICED AND FROZEN.

toward, and meeting in, the center. Place in a large buttered bowl, seam side down, cover with plastic wrap, and refrigerate overnight.

4. When ready to use, divide the dough in half, 18 ounces each, refrigerating the unused half, covered, until needed.

5. To make bread, butter two 7 x 14-inch loaf pans and set aside. Preheat oven to 300 degrees, turn off oven, and let cool slightly.

6. On a lightly floured surface, roll out half of the dough to a 7 x 13- or 14-inch rectangle. Place the 14-inch side of the pan at the top of the dough and then roll each of the long sides of the dough in just enough to measure a little less than the length of the pan. Starting at the top, roll the dough about ¼ of the way and pinch down on the edges of the roll to seal, tucking in the ends as necessary. Repeat 2 more times, rolling, sealing, and tucking. The dough should be slightly smaller than the length of the pan. Pinch the seam again and set in the prepared pan, seam side down. Repeat with the remaining half of dough. To proof dough, set pans in turned-off oven, uncovered, until dough rises almost to the top of the pans, 1½ to 2 hours.

7. Remove pans from oven and keep in a warm spot. Preheat oven to 325 degrees. In a small bowl or cup, whisk together the egg and cream, brush over the top of the dough, and return pans to oven. Bake 20 minutes, turn pans front to back, and bake bread until top is golden brown, about 15 minutes longer. Cool on rack and use as needed.

Note: When making Sticky Buns, Apricot Rolls, Prune Apple Pockets, and the Ricotta Fig Tart, follow this recipe through step 3.

Apricot Rolls

MAKES 8 ROLLS

EQUIPMENT

Small and medium bowls

10-inch Pyrex pie plate

Medium and small saucepans

Whip

Strainer

Plastic wrap

Rolling pin

Parchment or wax paper

Food processor

INGREDIENTS

BOTTOM OF PAN

6 tablespoons (¾ stick) unsalted
butter, melted

⅓ cup brown sugar

3 tablespoons light corn syrup

FILLING

8 ounces dried apricots

1 cup milk

½ vanilla bean, split lengthwise

3 egg yolks

2½ tablespoons all-purpose flour,
sifted

18 ounces (½ recipe) brioche
dough (see page 140), removed
from refrigerator while preparing
pie plate and making filling

For these next recipes, you will be using unbaked brioche dough. These sweet rolls, usually associated with breakfast or lunch, will be equally welcome at teatime.

1. In a small bowl, stir together all the ingredients to be placed in the bottom of the pie pan and pour into the pan. Set aside.

2. Make the filling: In a medium saucepan, cover 1 pound apricots (half to be used for filling and half for sauce) with cold water and bring to a simmer. Poach until tender, about 10 minutes. Cool and drain, reserving ¾ cup liquid for sauce. Dry apricots thoroughly, divide in half, and set aside.

3. In a medium saucepan, scald the milk with the vanilla bean and its scrapings. In a medium bowl, using a wire whip, whisk together the egg yolks and sugar until mixture is pale yellow and forms a ribbon when whip is lifted. Whisk in the flour. Whisking continuously, pour about half the hot milk into the egg mixture. Pour back into the remaining milk in the saucepan and cook over medium heat, stirring all the while, until the mixture thickens and bubbles begin to appear on the surface. Strain into a clean small bowl and place a piece of plastic wrap directly on top of the cream to prevent a skin forming. Refrigerate until needed.

4. Make the roll: On a lightly floured surface, roll out the brioche dough to a 9 x 12-inch rectangle, placing the 12-inch side directly in front of you. Arrange half the poached apricots, rounded side up, on the dough, covering the entire surface. Spread the pastry cream over the apricots. Starting with the 12-inch side nearest you, carefully roll the dough, com-

SAUCE

8 ounces dried apricots

¾ cup poaching liquid

2 cups orange juice

¼ cup apricot brandy

Juice of 1 medium lemon

TO PREPARE AHEAD

THROUGH STEP 8. APRICOT ROLL SHOULD BE SERVED AT ROOM TEMPERATURE, SAUCE WARMED OVER LOW HEAT WHEN NEEDED.

pletely enclosing the filling. (A little may ooze out, but that's okay.) Transfer the roll to a sheet of parchment or wax paper a little larger than the roll, and wrap the paper around the roll, completely enclosing the dough. Freeze until firm enough to cut, about 1 hour. The colder the dough, the easier it will be to cut.

5. Remove from freezer, unwrap the roll of dough, and place on a cutting board. Straighten to make a 12-inch-long roll. Working as quickly as possible so that the dough remains firm, and with a very sharp knife, gently mark the top of the roll into 8 sections, each 1½ inches wide. Then cut through each mark, making 8 buns. Arrange in a circle, cut side down, in prepared pan. Let rise, uncovered, in a warm spot until almost doubled in volume, about 1 hour.

6. Position rack in center of oven and preheat oven to 350 degrees.

7. Bake until a rich golden brown, 35 to 40 minutes. Let rest 5 minutes, then carefully invert onto a large serving plate.

8. While apricot roll is baking, make the sauce: In a food processor fitted with a steel blade, combine the remaining poached apricots, ¾ cup reserved poaching liquid, the orange juice, apricot brandy, and lemon juice, and process until pureed. Transfer to a small saucepan and warm before serving.

9. To serve, cut each roll and place on a dessert plate. Spoon warm sauce over each serving.

Prune and Apple Pockets

MAKES TWENTY 4-INCH POCKETS

These pockets, filled with prunes, apples, and pine nuts, are folded like hamantashen for Purim. They are perfect for a brunch or buffet.

1. Make the filling: In a medium saucepan, combine prunes, apples, sugar, orange zest, and vanilla bean with its scrapings. Pour in water and bring to a boil. Lower heat to medium and cook until prunes are very soft, about 20 minutes, stirring often. As mixture thickens, heat may have to be turned down to very low to prevent burning.

2. Remove from heat and discard the vanilla bean. Stir in Armagnac, transfer to a medium mixing bowl, and let cool. Stir in the chopped pine nuts and set aside.

3. Roll out the brioche dough: Using half the dough at a time, keep the remaining half covered until needed. Roll the first half to a 14-inch square, trimming edges to even. Cut the dough into nine 4-inch squares, saving the scraps. Roll out the scraps to a 5-inch square and cut out the last 4-inch square.

4. Place 1 heaping tablespoon of filling in the center of each square and fold the corners toward the center, pinching the seams together (see illustration). Line 1 or 2 baking trays with parchment paper. As the pockets are completed, set on the prepared trays, about 2 inches apart. Repeat with the remaining half of the brioche dough and filling. Let rise in a warm spot until doubled in bulk, about 1 hour.

5. Position rack in center of oven and preheat oven to 350 degrees.

EQUIPMENT

Medium saucepan

Medium bowl

Rolling pin

Ruler

1 or 2 baking trays

Parchment paper

INGREDIENTS

FILLING

1 pound pitted prunes, cut in half

2 (about ¾ pound) Granny Smith apples, peeled, cored, and cut into chunks

½ cup granulated sugar, plus extra for tops of pockets

1 teaspoon orange zest

½ vanilla bean, split lengthwise

2 cups water

2 tablespoons Armagnac

½ cup coarsely chopped pine nuts

1 recipe brioche dough (see page 140), removed from refrigerator about 30 minutes before needed

1 egg, lightly whisked, for egg wash

Crystal sugar

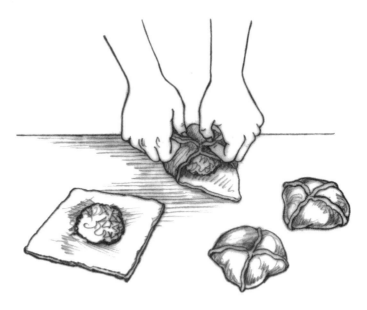

6. Brush each of the pockets with egg wash and sprinkle with crystal sugar. Bake until golden brown, about 25 minutes, reversing the trays halfway through.

7. To serve, serve warm as is or with softly whipped cream.

Sticky Buns

MAKES 8 BUNS

EQUIPMENT

Small and medium bowls

10-inch pie plate

Parchment or wax paper

Rolling pin

INGREDIENTS

BOTTOM OF PAN

⅓ cup brown sugar, packed

6 tablespoons (¾ stick) unsalted butter, melted

3 tablespoons light corn syrup

⅔ cup (about 3½ ounces) pecan halves

FILLING

½ cup (about 4 ounces) semisweet or milk chocolate chips

½ cup (about 2½ ounces) coarsely chopped pecans

⅓ cup brown sugar

¼ cup granulated sugar

4 tablespoons (½ stick) unsalted butter, melted

2 teaspoons ground cinnamon

18 ounces (½ recipe) brioche dough (see page 140), removed from refrigerator while preparing pie plate and making filling

*I*f you like a sweet breakfast roll, you will love these buns. The buns are best served warm, but if your family is like mine, they won't be able to wait.

1. In a small bowl, stir together the brown sugar, melted butter and corn syrup until well combined. Pour the sugar mixture into the pie plate. Arrange the pecans on the mixture, rounded sides down, close together and in circles, starting on the outside and working toward the center. Set aside.

2. Make the filling: In a medium bowl, stir together all the ingredients until well combined. Set aside.

3. On a lightly floured surface, roll out the brioche dough to a 9 x 12-inch rectangle, placing the 12-inch side directly in front of you. Spread the filling over the dough, covering the entire surface. Starting at the top 12-inch side, carefully roll the dough, enclosing the filling, tucking in the ends as necessary. Transfer to a sheet of parchment or wax paper and roll up in the paper, enclosing the dough. Refrigerate until firm enough to cut easily, about 1 hour.

4. Remove from refrigerator and place roll of dough on cutting board. Straighten to make an even 12-inch roll. With a very sharp knife, gently mark the top of the roll into 8 sections, each 1½ inches wide. Then cut through each mark, making 8 buns. Arrange the buns in a circle, cut side down, in prepared pie plate. Let rise, uncovered, in a warm spot until almost doubled in volume, about 1 hour.

5. Preheat oven to 350 degrees.

To Prepare Ahead

Through step 6

6. Bake until the brioche is a rich golden brown, about 35 minutes. Remove from oven, place on a cooling rack, and let rest 5 minutes. Then carefully invert onto a large serving plate. Syrup will run, so make sure there is enough room on the plate.

7. To serve, cut into portions and serve warm.

Apple Bread Pudding

SERVES 8

EQUIPMENT

10- or 12-inch skillet

Baking tray

Pastry brush

Medium nonreactive saucepan

Large bowl

2-quart, 9 x 12-inch oven-to-table porcelain baking dish

Baking pan larger than baking dish

Strainer

INGREDIENTS

2 pounds (about 5 medium) Granny Smith apples, peeled, cored, halved, and cut into thin slices

4 tablespoons (½ stick) unsalted butter

1 vanilla bean, split lengthwise

½ cup granulated sugar

1 loaf Basic Brioche (see page 140), baked

8 tablespoons (1 stick) unsalted butter, clarified (see page XX)

½ cup cinnamon sugar*

*B*read pudding is the ultimate comfort food, welcome after most meals. The sautéed apples give the pudding a little crunch. Half-and-half can be substituted for the heavy cream, if desired.

1. Caramelize the apples: In a 10- or 12-inch skillet, melt 2 tablespoons butter. Arrange half the apples in the skillet (if using one skillet, wash and dry between use) with half the vanilla bean plus its scrapings. Pour ¼ cup sugar on top of the apples and sauté over medium heat until apples and sugar are caramelized, turning to sauté all sides. Repeat with the remaining butter, vanilla bean, apples, and sugar. Set aside and let cool.

2. Position rack in center of oven and preheat oven to 350 degrees.

3. Carefully cut away the crust from all sides of the loaf of Brioche. Cut into 22 to 24 slices, each about ⅜ inch thick. Place slices of bread on a baking tray and lightly toast in the oven, turning to toast all sides, 4 to 5 minutes. Using a pastry brush, brush a little clarified butter over each slice of bread and then sprinkle with cinnamon sugar. Set aside.

4. Make the custard: In a medium saucepan, scald the cream with the vanilla bean and its scrapings, the nutmeg, and the cinnamon sticks. Meanwhile, in a large mixing bowl, whisk together the egg yolks, whole eggs, and sugar until the sugar is

---

*To make cinnamon sugar: In a small bowl, combine ½ cup granulated sugar with 1½ teaspoons ground cinnamon. Mix well. Cinnamon sugar will keep in a covered container indefinitely.

CUSTARD

2½ cups heavy cream

1 vanilla bean, split lengthwise

2 teaspoons freshly grated nutmeg

2 to 3 cinnamon sticks

5 egg yolks

2 whole eggs

1 tablespoon granulated sugar

TO PREPARE AHEAD

THROUGH STEP 4, PUDDING
CAN BE MADE EARLY IN THE
DAY AND WARMED AT SERVING
TIME.

dissolved. Slowly pour the scalded liquid over the eggs, whisking all the while. Strain into a clean bowl.

5. Make the pudding: Arrange 7 or 8 slices of bread on the bottom of the baking dish, cutting slices to fit tightly, and pour a little of the custard over the bread, pressing down on the slices to make sure that the bread has absorbed the custard and is well soaked. Top with a layer of half the apples. Repeat with layers of bread, custard, apples, bread, and the remaining custard, pressing down on each layer of bread after the custard is poured over. There will be 3 layers of bread, custard poured over each layer, and 2 layers of apples. Place baking dish in a larger pan and fill the pan with boiling water halfway up the sides of the porcelain dish. Bake until the pudding is golden brown, the sauce begins to bubble, and a small knife gently inserted in the center comes out clean, 50 to 60 minutes. Let rest about 15 minutes.

5. To serve, the pudding can be inverted onto a large plate or served directly from the baking dish. If inverting, run a sharp knife around the edges of the pudding and then invert onto a platter slightly larger than the pudding. Serve warm with softly whipped cream, Vanilla Ice Cream (see page 253), or Crème Anglaise (see page 6).

Chocolate Bread Pudding

SERVES 8

EQUIPMENT

Small and large heatproof bowls

Whip

Small and medium saucepans

2-inch cookie cutter

Large baking pan with sides

Eight ¾-cup custard cups

Slotted spoon

Strainer

INGREDIENTS

CUSTARD

6 ounces bittersweet chocolate

1½ ounces bitter chocolate

3 whole eggs

3 egg yolks

½ cup granulated sugar

2 cups half-and-half

SOAKING LIQUID

1½ cups half-and-half

1 cup plus 2 tablespoons
granulated sugar

⅓ cup unsweetened cocoa

Eight ½-inch-thick slices Basic
Brioche (see page 140)

*A*n absolutely marvelous melt-in-your-mouth pudding. Bread pudding seems to be served more during the colder months of the year, but it is a treat at any time.

1. Make the custard: In a small heatproof bowl set over simmering water, melt the two chocolates. When almost melted, turn off heat and let melt completely, stirring occasionally.

2. In a large heatproof bowl, whisk together the whole eggs and egg yolks. Gradually whisk in the sugar and beat until fluffy.

3. Meanwhile, in a small saucepan, bring the half-and-half to a rolling boil. Slowly whisk into the egg mixture. Scrape in the melted chocolate and whisk until incorporated. Chill over ice cubes and cold water and then refrigerate, covered, until needed. (Prepare the custard the day before so that it thickens.)

4. Make the circles of bread: In a medium saucepan, combine the soaking liquid ingredients and heat until the cocoa dissolves completely. Using a 2-inch cookie cutter, cut 2 circles out of each slice of bread. You now have 16 circles of bread. Arrange the circles in a pan with sides, large enough to hold the circles in 1 layer. Pour the soaking liquid over and soak, turning slices, until the bread absorbs as much of the liquid as possible but remains intact.

5. Position rack in center of oven and preheat oven to 350 degrees. Butter, or coat with vegetable spray, eight ¾-cup custard cups.

TO PREPARE AHEAD

THROUGH STEP 3, CUSTARD
SHOULD BE MADE 1 DAY
AHEAD. THROUGH STEP 6,
MAKE PUDDING EARLY IN
THE DAY.

6. Make the pudding: Spoon a layer of custard, about 2 ounces, into the bottom of each of the 8 cups. Using a slotted spoon, remove a circle of bread and set in the custard. Cover with a second layer of custard, then a second circle of bread, and top with a final layer of custard. Repeat this procedure, filling the remaining cups with custard and bread circles. Arrange the cups in the large baking pan and fill the pan with boiling water, halfway up the sides of the cups. Bake 30 minutes. Remove cups from the water, cool, and then refrigerate, covered, until needed.

7. To serve, dust the puddings with sifted powdered sugar and pass a bowl of unsweetened whipped cream.

Ricotta Fig Tart

MAKES ONE 10-INCH TART
SERVES 8

*U*nbaked brioche dough is rolled out for the crust and blind-baked. It is a rustic-looking dessert. The crust is golden brown, with pieces of fig poking through the filling. We prefer to use black Mission figs for this tart.

1. Preheat oven to 350 degrees.

2. On a lightly floured surface, roll out Brioche dough to a circle about 12 inches in diameter. Fit into the pan and trim the edges. Line with parchment paper and fill with pie weights (see page XXII). Bake for 20 minutes, take from the oven, and carefully remove the paper with the weights. Return to the oven and bake another 10 minutes. Set aside.

3. Meanwhile, make the filling: Remove the stems from the figs and cut in half, from top to bottom. In a small bowl, marinate the figs in rum or Armagnac until needed.

4. In the large bowl of an electric mixer, on high speed, combine the ricotta and cream cheeses until smooth. Gradually add the sugar and again beat until smooth. Add the whole eggs and egg yolk, 1 at a time. Stop the machine, add the lemon juice, orange zest, vanilla, cardamom, and salt and mix, on low speed, just to combine.

5. With a slotted spoon, transfer the figs to the baked shell. (If a little of the liquid comes with them, that's okay.) Scrape the filling over the figs and smooth.

6. Combine the almond meal and 1 tablespoon sugar and sprinkle evenly over the filling. Bake until the filling is firm to

EQUIPMENT

Rolling pin

10-inch tart pan or Pyrex pie plate

Parchment paper, aluminum foil, or large coffee filter papers

Pie weights or dried beans

Electric mixer

Slotted spoon

INGREDIENTS

18 ounces Basic Brioche dough (see page 140)

FILLING

¾ pound (about 2 cups) dark dried figs

¾ cup dark rum or Armagnac

¾ pound ricotta cheese

3 ounces cream cheese, at room temperature, cut into small pieces

¾ cup granulated sugar

2 whole eggs

1 egg yolk

3 tablespoons lemon juice

1 tablespoon orange zest

1 teaspoon vanilla extract

½ teaspoon ground cardamom

Pinch of salt

2 tablespoons almond meal (see footnote on page 108)

1 tablespoon granulated sugar

the touch and is lightly golden, about 1 hour. Cool on a rack and then refrigerate. Remove from refrigerator about 15 minutes before serving.

TO PREPARE AHEAD

THROUGH STEP 6

VIII

Brownies

Almost everyone has a favorite brownie recipe, and each recipe holds a special memory. People make brownies as a simple dessert for dinner or as a treat for the entire household. They can be made with or without nuts, with different kinds of chocolate, different-flavored chocolate chips; they can be fudgy or cakelike. Brownies keep well and travel well. They are truly an all-American dessert.

Our brownie is of the fudgy variety, with lots of flavor. It can be made into squares for munching, or into a Brownie Pie, or into our very special Blond Brownie Sundae. When I was working at Spago, Los Angeles, I tried to put brownies on the dessert menu, but every time Wolfgang held up a brownie, he would say, in his inimitable accent, "You know, I don't think I like these square chocolate things." And so the brownies never made it. But when Spago, Las Vegas, opened, I experimented with an ice cream sundae, using the Blond Brownie as its base. It was an instant success, and in the first month Spago was open, we sold more Brownie Sundaes than any other dessert.

BASIC BROWNIES

BLOND BROWNIE SUNDAES

BLOND BROWNIES

BROWNIE PIE

MARBLED BROWNIES

MILK CHOCOLATE BROWNIES

Basic Brownies

MAKES 9 BROWNIES, ABOUT 2½ INCHES EACH

The brownies can be made in a 9-inch round pan, as well as in a square pan, cutting in slices rather than squares. These are dense brownies, fudgy and rich.

1. Position rack in center of oven and preheat oven to 350 degrees. Butter, or coat with vegetable spray, an 8-inch square baking pan. Dust with flour, tapping out excess flour. Set aside.

2. In the top of a double boiler or medium heatproof bowl set over simmering water, combine chocolate, butter, and espresso (if desired), stirring occasionally until almost melted. Turn off the heat, stir, and let melt completely.

3. Sift together the flour, baking powder, and salt. Set aside.

4. In a large heatproof mixing bowl set over simmering water, whisk the eggs, sugar, and vanilla until the sugar dissolves. Transfer to the large bowl of an electric mixer and, on high speed, using paddle or beaters, beat until pale yellow. Lower speed to medium, scrape in the chocolate mixture, and beat until well mixed. On low speed, gradually add flour mixture and beat just until combined. Add ¾ cup of walnuts and again, on low speed, beat just until combined. Scrape into prepared pan and sprinkle remaining walnuts over top of cake.

5. Bake until edges of cake pull away from sides of pan and tester, gently poked into center of cake, comes out clean, 40 to 45 minutes. Cool on rack.

6. To serve, cut the brownies into 9 squares, each about 2½ inches. Serve as is or with softly whipped cream or ice cream of your choice.

EQUIPMENT

8-inch square baking pan

Medium and large heatproof bowls

Sifter

Whip

Electric mixer

INGREDIENTS

¾ pound bittersweet chocolate, coarsely chopped

8 ounces (2 sticks) unsalted butter, cut into small pieces

1 teaspoon instant espresso, optional

1½ cups all-purpose flour

1 teaspoon baking powder

½ teaspoon salt

4 eggs

2 cups granulated sugar

1 teaspoon vanilla extract

2 cups coarsely chopped walnuts

TO PREPARE AHEAD

THROUGH STEP 5

Note: Cookies can also be made out of the dough. Drop teaspoonfuls of dough on a parchment-paper-lined baking tray and bake in a 350-degree oven 10 to 12 minutes. Cool on a rack.

Blond Brownie Sundaes

SERVES 9

EQUIPMENT

Electric mixer or whip

Ice cream scoop

INGREDIENTS

2 cups heavy cream

Blond Brownies (see page 160)

Vanilla Ice Cream (see page 253)

Hot Fudge Sauce (see page 231)

2 cups chopped nuts (walnuts, pecans, unblanched almonds, or a combination)

9 whole strawberries or 1 basket raspberries

TO PREPARE AHEAD

THROUGH STEP 2. CREAM CAN BE WHIPPED 1 HOUR AHEAD, BROWNIES BAKED 1 DAY AHEAD.

This brownie dessert is the perfect ending to almost any meal, whether simple or elegant.

1. In the large bowl of an electric mixer, using the whip, beat the heavy cream to soft peaks. Refrigerate, covered, until needed. When ready to build the sundaes, whip cream lightly, if necessary.

2. Make the Blond Brownies, cool and cut into nine 2½-inch squares.

3. To build the sundaes, arrange 1 brownie on each of 9 dessert plates. Place a scoop of Vanilla Ice Cream on each portion, spoon Hot Fudge Sauce over, top with a generous amount of whipped cream, a sprinkling of nuts, and finally a whole strawberry or a few raspberries. Serve immediately.

Blond Brownies

MAKES NINE 2½-INCH BROWNIES

When I was twelve years old, my cousin Charlene taught me how to make these brownies. It was the first dessert I ever attempted, and it is still one of my favorites.

1. Position rack in center of oven and preheat oven to 350 degrees. Butter, or coat with vegetable spray, an 8-inch square baking pan. Dust with flour, tapping out any excess. Set aside.

2. Sift together the flour, baking powder, and salt. Set aside.

3. In a clean large bowl of an electric mixer, using the paddle or beaters, beat together the butter and sugar. Start on low speed until the sugar is incorporated, then turn speed to high and beat until fluffy, scraping down sides of bowl and under beaters as necessary. Turn speed to medium and add eggs, 1 at a time, sour cream, and vanilla and beat until well combined. Turn speed to low and add flour mixture, beating just until mixed. Add walnuts and chocolate chips, and again beat just until mixed.

4. Scrape batter into prepared pan and level with spatula. Bake until top is firm to the touch and tester, gently poked into center of cake, comes out clean, about 45 minutes. Cool on rack.

5. When completely cool, using a sharp knife, run knife around inside edges of baking pan. Invert cake onto foil-lined rack and then back onto a firm, flat surface. Carefully cut away the hard outside edges of the cake. Cut the cake into 9 pieces, each piece about 2½ inches square.

6. To serve, dust top with sifted powdered sugar or top with a dollop of whipped cream, or as part of a Blond Brownie Sundae (see page 159).

Brownie Pie

MAKES ONE 9-INCH PIE   SERVES 8

EQUIPMENT

Rolling pin

9-inch Pyrex pie plate

2 medium heatproof bowl

Whip

Electric mixer

INGREDIENTS

1 pound Pâte Sucrée (see page 76)

6 ounces bittersweet chocolate, roughly chopped

4 ounces (1 stick) unsalted butter, cut into small pieces

½ teaspoon instant espresso, optional

¾ cup all-purpose flour

½ teaspoon baking powder

¼ teaspoon salt

2 eggs

1 cup granulated sugar

½ teaspoon vanilla extract

1 cup coarsely chopped walnuts or pecans

⅓ cup chocolate chips

TO PREPARE AHEAD

THROUGH STEP 1, PASTRY SHELL CAN BE MADE 1 DAY AHEAD. OR PREPARE THROUGH STEP 6.

This fudgy, chewy pie consists of half the Basic Brownie recipe piled into a Pâte Sucrée crust.

1. Roll out the pastry: On a lightly floured surface, flouring the rolling pin as necessary, roll out the Pâte Sucrée to an 11-inch round, about ¼-inch thick. Coat a 9-inch Pyrex pie plate with vegetable spray. Roll the pastry around the rolling pin, fit into the pan, and trim the edges. Refrigerate until needed.

2. Position rack in center of oven and preheat oven to 350 degrees.

3. In a medium heatproof bowl set over simmering water, combine chocolate, butter, and espresso (if desired), stirring occasionally, until almost melted, 5 to 7 minutes. Remove from heat, stir, and let melt completely.

4. Sift together the flour, baking powder, and salt. Set aside.

5. In a clean heatproof mixing bowl set over simmering water, whisk the eggs, sugar, and vanilla until the sugar dissolves, about 5 minutes. Transfer to the large bowl of an electric mixer and, on high speed, using paddle or beaters, beat until pale yellow. Lower speed to medium, scrape in the chocolate mixture, and beat until well mixed. On low speed, gradually add flour mixture and beat just until combined. Add ½ cup walnuts, and again, on low speed, beat just until combined. Scrape into Pâte Sucrée shell and sprinkle the remaining ½ cup walnuts and the chocolate chips over the top.

6. Bake 30 minutes, remove pie from oven, cover top with foil, and return to oven for 10 minutes longer. Cool on a rack.

7. To serve, cut pie into slices and serve with ice cream.

Marbled Brownies

MAKES 10 BROWNIES,
EACH ABOUT 3½ X 1½-INCHES

EQUIPMENT

8-inch square baking pan

Sifter

Medium heatproof bowl

Wooden spoon

Electric mixer

Spatula

INGREDIENTS

DARK CHOCOLATE
BROWNIE BATTER

*¾ cup plus 1 tablespoon
all-purpose flour*

½ teaspoon baking powder

¼ teaspoon salt

*5 ounces bittersweet chocolate, cut
into small pieces*

*3 ounces (6 tablespoons) unsalted
butter, at room temperature, cut
into small pieces*

2 eggs

*½ cup plus 1 tablespoon
granulated sugar*

½ teaspoon vanilla extract

*¾ cup semisweet or milk chocolate
chips*

*I*n this recipe, we decided to swirl the Blond Brownie batter through the Dark Chocolate Brownie batter, resulting in a marbled effect. The cake can be served as described below, or just cut into small or large squares. No decoration is necessary. These go great with a glass of milk.

1. Position rack in center of oven and preheat oven to 350 degrees. Butter, or coat with vegetable spray, an 8-inch square baking pan. Dust with flour, tapping out any excess. Set aside.

2. Make the dark chocolate brownie batter: Sift together the flour, baking powder, and salt. Set aside.

3. In a medium heatproof bowl set over simmering water, melt together the chocolate and butter, stirring occasionally with a wooden spoon until almost melted. Turn off the heat and let melt completely.

4. In the large bowl of an electric mixer, using the paddle or beaters, beat together the eggs and sugar until light in color. Start on medium speed, raising speed to high when sugar is incorporated, scraping down sides of bowl as necessary. Turn speed down to low, add the vanilla extract, scrape in the melted chocolate, and mix well. Gradually add the flour mixture and, last of all, the chocolate chips, beating until just combined. Pour into the prepared pan and level with a spatula. Set aside.

5. Make the blond brownie batter: Sift together the flour, baking powder, and salt. Set aside.

BLOND BROWNIE BATTER

¾ cup plus 1 tablespoon
all-purpose flour

¾ teaspoon baking powder

Pinch of salt

3 ounces (6 tablespoons) unsalted
butter, at room temperature, cut
into small pieces

½ cup light brown sugar, packed,

1 egg

¼ cup sour cream

¾ teaspoon vanilla extract

⅓ cup (about 2 ounces) coarsely
chopped walnuts

⅓ cup chocolate chips

Vanilla ice cream (see page 253)

Hot Fudge Sauce (see page 231)

TO PREPARE AHEAD

THROUGH STEP 6 OR 7,
CUTTING THE CAKE ABOUT 1
HOUR BEFORE SERVING

6. In a clean large bowl of the electric mixer, using the paddle or beaters, beat together the butter and sugar. Start on low speed until the sugar is incorporated, then turn speed to high and beat until fluffy, scraping down sides and under beaters as necessary. Turn speed to medium and add egg, sour cream, and vanilla and beat until well combined. Turn speed to low and add flour mixture, beating just until mixed. Add walnuts and chocolate chips and again beat just until mixed. Space large spoonfuls of blond brownie batter on top of the dark chocolate brownie batter and swirl through the dark chocolate, giving it a marbled effect. Bake until top is firm to the touch and tester, gently poked in center of cake, comes out clean, about 50 minutes. Cool on rack.

7. When completely cool, using a serrated knife, run the knife around the inside edges of the baking pan. Invert cake onto foil-lined rack and then back onto a flat plate or cutting board. Carefully cut away the hard edges around the sides of the cake. Cut the cake into 10 pieces, each piece about 3½ inches long and 1½ inches wide. The easiest way to do this is to cut the cake in half, each half about 7 x 3½ inches. Then cut each half into 5 pieces, each about 3½ x 1½ inches.

8. To serve, place 1 brownie in the center of each plate. Top with a scoop of Vanilla Ice Cream and spoon Hot Fudge Sauce over all.

Milk Chocolate Brownies

EQUIPMENT

8-inch square baking dish

Medium and large heatproof bowls

Sifter

Electric mixer

Whip

INGREDIENTS

9 ounces milk chocolate

6 ounces (1½ sticks) unsalted butter, cut into small pieces

1 teaspoon instant espresso, optional

2¼ cups all-purpose flour

1 teaspoon baking powder

½ teaspoon salt

3 eggs

1½ cups granulated sugar

1 teaspoon vanilla

1½ cups semisweet chocolate chips

TO PREPARE AHEAD

THROUGH STEP 5

Whether made with milk chocolate or bittersweet chocolate, brownies are addictive. These are rich, but not quite as dense as the Basic Brownies (see page 158).

1. Position rack in center of oven and preheat oven to 350 degrees. Butter or coat an 8-inch square baking pan with vegetable spray, and then sprinkle flour all over, tapping out excess flour. Set aside.

2. In a medium heatproof bowl set over simmering water, melt chocolate, butter, and espresso (if desired) until *almost* melted, stirring occasionally. Remove from heat, stir, and let melt completely.

3. Meanwhile, sift together the flour, baking powder, and salt. Set aside.

4. In a large heatproof bowl set over simmering water, whisk the eggs, sugar, and vanilla until the sugar dissolves. (Test by carefully placing a finger in a spoonful of the mixture, making sure the sugar is dissolved.)

5. Transfer to the large bowl of an electric mixer, fitted with paddle or beaters, and beat on high speed for about 1 minute. Lower speed to medium, scrape in the melted chocolate mixture, and mix well. On low speed, gradually add the flour mixture and beat just until combined. Add the chocolate chips, again beating just until combined. Scrape into the prepared pan and bake until top of cake is firm to the touch and tester, gently poked into the center of the cake, comes out moderately clean, about 50 minutes. Cool on a rack.

6. To serve: Invert onto foil-lined rack and then back onto a flat, firm surface. Trim the hard outside edges of the cake and cut into 2½-inch squares. Or, if you prefer smaller brownies, cut to desired size. Serve as is or dusted with sifted confectioners' sugar, or for a really luscious dessert, spoon Hot Fudge Sauce (see page 231) over and top with a dollop of whipped cream.

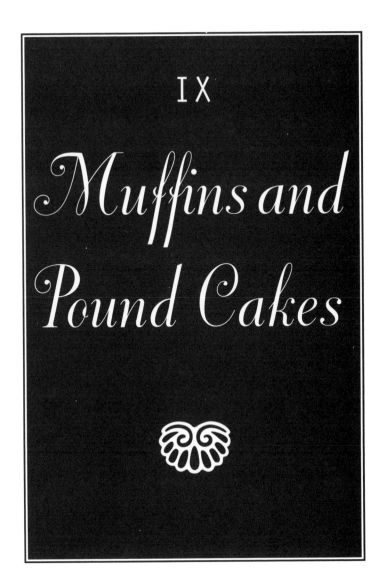

IX

Muffins and Pound Cakes

Brunch is served on Saturdays and Sundays at Spago Las Vegas. To complement the brunch, baskets of tiny muffins and miniature pound cakes are set on each table. At the meal's end (and sometimes sooner), the baskets are empty. These are easy and quick to prepare, since the batter ingredients are combined in a saucepan and no rising time is required before baking.

Almost any fruit or toasted nut of choice can be folded into the muffins. The batter can be baked in small loaf pans, if desired (see Banana Muffins, page 173), until a tester, inserted into the center of the loaf, comes out clean, about 40 minutes.

At Spago these "quick breads" are freshly baked the day they are served. However, if it is more convenient, they can be baked, wrapped well in airtight plastic bags, and kept in a cupboard overnight, refrigerated up to 3 or 4 days, or frozen. Defrost, wrapped, and then warm in a 350-degree oven as needed.

CHUNKY APPLE MUFFINS

Streusel

BLUEBERRY MUFFINS

BANANA MUFFINS

SPICED MUFFINS

STRAWBERRY MUFFINS

BUTTERMILK LEMON POUND CAKE

ORANGE POPPY SEED LOAF

Chunky Apple Muffins

MAKES 12 LARGE MUFFINS

These are moist, tasty muffins that can be prepared in record time. Pears can be substituted for the apples.

1. Position rack in center of oven and preheat oven to 350 degrees. Butter, or coat with vegetable spray, 12 muffin cups. Set aside. (Muffin cups can also be lined with paper cups, if desired, in which case no spray or butter is necessary to coat pan.)

2. In a small saucepan, combine the apples with ¼ cup brown sugar, the water, orange juice, orange zest, and ½ teaspoon cinnamon. Cook over medium heat, stirring occasionally, until apples are just tender. Don't let them get too soft. Drain and set aside.

3. Meanwhile, sift together the flour, baking soda, remaining ½ teaspoon cinnamon, and salt. Set aside.

4. In a medium saucepan, melt the butter. Over medium heat, using a wooden spoon, blend in the granulated and remaining brown sugars. Remove from the heat, add the sour cream, then the eggs and vanilla, stirring until smooth. Stir in the flour mixture. Fold in the cooked apples and pecans.

5. Spoon batter into the prepared muffin pan, filling to the top of each cup. Sprinkle Streusel over the top of each muffin. Bake until muffins are golden brown and cake tester comes out clean when poked into 1 or 2 muffins, 25 to 30 minutes. Let rest in pan about 5 minutes, then remove muffins, 1 at a time, to a rack to cool.

EQUIPMENT

12-cup muffin pan, each cup 2¾ x 1¼ inches

Small and medium saucepans

Sifter

Wooden spoon

INGREDIENTS

1 pound (about 3 medium) Granny Smith apples, peeled, cored, and cut into 1-inch chunks

¾ cup light brown sugar, packed

½ cup water

½ cup orange juice

1½ teaspoons grated orange zest

1 teaspoon ground cinnamon

2 cups all-purpose flour

1 teaspoon baking soda

½ teaspoon salt

4 ounces (1 stick) unsalted butter, cut into small pieces

½ cup granulated sugar

½ cup sour cream

2 eggs, lightly beaten

1 teaspoon vanilla extract

1 cup toasted pecans, coarsely chopped

¼ cup Streusel (see page 171)

TO PREPARE AHEAD

THROUGH STEP 5

Streusel

MAKES 1¾ CUPS

EQUIPMENT

Baking tray

Metal spatula

Food processor

Medium bowl

INGREDIENTS

¼ cup (2 ounces) unblanched whole almonds

⅓ cup all-purpose flour

2 tablespoons dark brown sugar

2 tablespoons granulated sugar

1½ teaspoons ground cinnamon

¾ teaspoon freshly grated nutmeg

Pinch of ground cardamom

4 tablespoons (½ stick) unsalted butter, chilled and cut into small pieces

⅓ cup quick oats

TO PREPARE AHEAD

THROUGH STEP 4, THIS WILL KEEP, REFRIGERATED, 2 TO 3 WEEKS. STREUSEL CAN ALSO BE FROZEN AND WILL KEEP 2 TO 3 MONTHS.

*S*treusel is a crumbly, nutty, and somewhat spicy topping that we sprinkle on coffee cakes, cobblers, and many other desserts. This is a handy item to keep in your freezer; take it out and use as needed.

1. Position rack in center of oven and preheat oven to 350 degrees.

2. Arrange almonds on baking tray and toast, 15 to 18 minutes, turning occasionally with a metal spatula. Cool. Chop coarsely and set aside.

3. In a food processor, fitted with the steel blade, combine the flour, brown and granulated sugars, cinnamon, nutmeg, and cardamom with a few on/off turns. Add the butter and process just until the mixture comes together.

4. Transfer to a medium bowl and stir in the oats and almonds. Refrigerate, covered, until needed.

INGREDIENTS

2 cups all-purpose flour

1 teaspoon baking soda

½ teaspoon salt

½ teaspoon ground cinnamon

⅛ teaspoon ground nutmeg

*4 ounces (1 stick) unsalted butter,
cut into small pieces*

½ cup granulated sugar

½ cup dark brown sugar, packed

½ cup orange juice

2 eggs, lightly beaten

1 teaspoon vanilla extract

*1 cup (about 5½ ounces)
blueberries, rinsed, patted dry,
any stems removed*

*1½ tablespoons grated, or finely
chopped, orange peel*

TO PREPARE AHEAD

THROUGH STEP 4

Blueberry Muffins

MAKES 12 LARGE MUFFINS

When I was young, my mother would bring home blueberry muffins from Filene's in Boston. I loved them. When we began to serve Saturday and Sunday brunch at Spago, Las Vegas, I re-created the muffins, and I think you will enjoy them as much as our weekend diners do. If you have Streusel (see page 171) in your freezer, sprinkle a little over the top before baking.

1. Position rack in center of oven and preheat oven to 350 degrees. Butter, or coat with vegetable spray, 12 muffin cups, each cup 2¾ x 1¼ inches. Set aside. (Muffins can also be baked in paper-cup-lined muffin cups, if desired.)

2. Sift together the flour, baking soda, salt, cinnamon, and nutmeg. Set aside.

3. In a medium saucepan, melt the butter. Over medium heat, using a wooden spoon, blend in the sugars. Remove from heat, stir in the orange juice, then the eggs and vanilla. Stir in the flour mixture and, last of all, fold in the blueberries and orange peel.

4. Spoon batter into the prepared muffin pan, filling almost to the top of each cup. Bake until muffins are golden brown and cake tester, gently poked into 1 or 2 muffins, comes out clean, about 25 minutes. Let rest in pan about 5 minutes, then remove muffins, 1 at a time, to a rack to cool.

Banana Muffins

MAKES 12 LARGE MUFFINS

❀

EQUIPMENT

*12-cup muffin pan, each cup
2¾ x 1¼ inches*

Sifter

Medium saucepan

Wooden spoon

INGREDIENTS

1 cup all-purpose flour

1 cup whole wheat flour

1 teaspoon baking soda

½ teaspoon salt

*4 ounces (1 stick) unsalted butter,
cut into small pieces*

½ cup granulated sugar

½ cup light brown sugar, packed

*1 cup (2 medium) mashed ripe
bananas*

2 eggs, lightly beaten

1 teaspoon vanilla extract

½ cup coarsely chopped walnuts

*1½ tablespoons grated, or finely
chopped, orange peel*

TO PREPARE AHEAD

THROUGH STEP 4

If you prefer, you can use 2 cups all-purpose flour instead of all-purpose and whole wheat flours. The batter can also be spooned into small muffin cups, baked about 20 minutes, or into mini bread tins (7½ x 3½ inches), baked 40 to 45 minutes.

1. Position rack in center of oven and preheat oven to 350 degrees. Butter, or coat with vegetable spray, 12 muffin cups. Set aside. (Muffins can also be baked in paper-cup-lined muffin pan, if desired, in which case cups do not have to be coated.)

2. Sift together the all-purpose and whole wheat flours, baking soda, and salt. Set aside.

3. In a medium saucepan, melt the butter. Over medium heat, using a wooden spoon, blend in the sugars. Remove from heat and stir in the bananas, then the eggs and vanilla, stirring until smooth. Stir in the flour mixture and fold in the nuts and orange peel.

4. Spoon batter into the prepared muffin pan, filling almost to the top of each cup. Bake until muffins are golden brown and cake tester comes out clean when gently poked into 1 or 2 muffins, about 25 minutes. Let rest in pan about 5 minutes, then remove muffins, 1 at a time, to a rack to cool.

Spiced Muffins

MAKES 12 LARGE MUFFINS

EQUIPMENT

*12-cup muffin pan, each cup
2¾ x 1¼ inches*

Sifter

Medium saucepan

Wooden spoon

INGREDIENTS

2 cups all-purpose flour

1½ teaspoons ground ginger

1½ teaspoons ground cinnamon

1 teaspoon baking soda

1 teaspoon ground nutmeg

½ teaspoon salt

*4 ounces (1 stick) unsalted butter,
cut into small pieces*

½ cup granulated sugar

½ cup dark brown sugar, packed

¼ cup orange juice

Peel of 1 medium orange, grated

2 eggs, lightly beaten

1 cup raisins

1 cup coarsely chopped walnuts

TO PREPARE AHEAD

THROUGH STEP 4

*W*ith the addition of a few fragrant spices, these muffins take on a wonderful flavor.

1. Position rack in center of oven and preheat oven to 350 degrees. Butter, or coat with vegetable spray, 12 muffin cups. Set aside. (Muffins can also be baked in paper-cup-lined muffin cups, if desired.)

2. Sift together the flour, ginger, cinnamon, baking soda, nutmeg, and salt. Set aside.

3. In a medium saucepan, melt the butter. Over medium heat, using a wooden spoon, blend in the sugars. Remove from heat and stir in the orange juice, grated peel, then the eggs. Stir in the flour mixture and fold in the raisins and nuts.

4. Spoon batter into the prepared muffin pan, filling almost to the top of each cup. Bake until muffins are golden brown and cake tester comes out clean when gently poked into the center of 1 or 2 muffins, 20 to 25 minutes. Let rest in pan about 5 minutes, then remove muffins, 1 at a time, to a rack to cool.

Strawberry Muffins

Makes 12 large muffins

❀

Equipment

*12-cup muffin pan, each cup
2¾ x 1¼ inches*

Sifter

Small baking tray

Medium bowl

Medium saucepan

Wooden spoon

Ingredients

2 cups all-purpose flour

1 teaspoon baking soda

½ teaspoon salt

*¾ cup shredded coconut,
preferably unsweetened*

*1 cup (about ¾ pint) strawberries,
hulled*

*4 ounces (1 stick) unsalted butter,
cut into small pieces*

½ cup granulated sugar

½ cup dark brown sugar, packed

2 eggs, lightly beaten

1 teaspoon vanilla extract

To Prepare Ahead

Through step 6

*M*uffins can be baked in regular or mini muffin pans. Bake the smaller muffins about 15 minutes, or until a tester inserted into the center comes out clean.

1. Position rack in center of oven and preheat oven to 350 degrees. Butter, or coat with vegetable spray, 12 muffin cups. Set aside. (Muffins can also be baked in paper-cup-lined muffin cups, if desired.)

2. Sift together the flour, baking soda, and salt. Set aside.

3. Spread coconut on the baking tray and toast just until golden, 8 to 10 minutes. Set aside, reserving about 2 tablespoons for the tops of the muffins.

4. Mash the berries in the bowl with a fork. Berries do not have to be pureed, just mashed. Set aside.

5. In a medium saucepan, melt the butter. Over medium heat, using a wooden spoon, blend in the sugars. Remove from heat and stir in the strawberries, then the eggs and vanilla, stirring until smooth. Stir in the flour mixture and fold in all but 2 tablespoons toasted coconut.

6. Spoon batter into the prepared muffin pan, filling almost to the top of each cup. Divide the remaining coconut and sprinkle over each muffin. Bake until muffins are golden brown and cake tester comes out clean when poked into 1 or 2 of the muffins, about 25 minutes. Let rest in pan about 5 minutes, then remove muffins, 1 at a time, to a rack to cool.

Buttermilk Lemon Pound Cake

MAKES 2 LOAVES

EQUIPMENT

2 loaf pans, 8½ x 3½ x 2½ inches

Sifter

Electric mixer

INGREDIENTS

3 cups all-purpose flour

1 teaspoon salt

½ teaspoon baking powder

½ teaspoon baking soda

½ teaspoon ground cinnamon

⅛ teaspoon ground or a few scrapings of fresh nutmeg

8 ounces (2 sticks) unsalted butter, at room temperature, cut into small pieces

2 cups granulated sugar

1 tablespoon lemon zest

4 eggs

2 tablespoons fresh lemon juice

1 cup buttermilk

1 cup fresh blueberries, rinsed, dried, and picked over or 1 cup caramelized apple slices (see page 98, step 2; you will need about two large Granny Smiths), cut into small chunks

TO PREPARE AHEAD

THROUGH STEP 6

*T*his lemony cake makes good eating any time of the day, whether for breakfast, lunch, tea, or late-night snack. At Spago we serve it for brunch on Saturdays and Sundays.

1. Position rack in center of oven and preheat oven to 350 degrees. Butter, or coat well with vegetable spray, 2 loaf pans, each 8½ x 3½ x 2½ inches. Dust with flour, tapping out any excess. Set aside.

2. Sift together the flour, salt, baking powder, baking soda, cinnamon, and nutmeg. Set aside.

3. In the large bowl of an electric mixer, on medium speed, using paddle or beaters, soften the butter. Gradually add the sugar and the lemon zest, and continue to beat until fluffy.

4. Add the eggs, 1 at a time, and the lemon juice, and beat until well combined.

5. Alternate adding the flour mixture and buttermilk, starting and ending with the flour mixture (3 additions of flour and 2 of buttermilk). With the last addition of flour, add the fruit and beat just until incorporated.

6. Divide the batter and scrape into the prepared pans. The batter should reach about ⅔ up sides of pans. Bake until tops are golden brown and skewer, gently poked into the center of cake, comes out clean, about 1 hour. Cool on rack. To remove from pan, run a knife around inside of pan and invert onto a flat surface, then invert again onto a serving plate, right side up.

7. To serve, serve as is, or dust with confectioners' sugar and cut into slices.

Orange Poppy Seed Loaf

MAKES 2 LOAVES

The batter can be spooned into a muffin pan for a quick breakfast treat. Bake 25 to 30 minutes. Serve with marmalade or jelly.

1. Position rack in center of oven and preheat oven to 350 degrees. Butter, or coat well with vegetable spray, both loaf pans. Dust with flour, tapping out any excess. Set aside.

2. Sift together flour, salt, baking powder, and baking soda. Set aside.

3. In the large bowl of an electric mixer, using the paddle or beaters, on medium speed, soften the butter. Gradually pour in the sugar, add the orange zest, and continue to beat until fluffy.

4. Add the eggs, 1 at a time, and the orange juice and beat until well combined.

5. Alternate adding the flour mixture and buttermilk, starting and ending with the flour mixture (3 additions of flour and 2 of buttermilk). With the last addition of flour, add the poppy seeds and beat just until incorporated.

6. Divide the batter and scrape into the prepared pans. The batter should reach about ⅔ up the sides of the pans. Bake until tops are golden brown and a skewer, gently poked into the center of cake, comes out clean, about 1 hour. Cool on rack. To remove from pan, run a knife around inside of the pan and invert onto a flat surface, then invert again onto a serving plate, right side up.

7. To serve, serve as is, or dust with confectioners' sugar and cut into slices.

X

Truffles and Candied Fruit

Truffles are probably the easiest of all sweets to make. They are very rich, made with chocolate, cream, butter, and liqueur. They can be small or large, but since they are rich, a small size is preferred. Truffles can be set in tiny paper or foil cups, arranged on a small tray, and passed, as an added bonus, with coffee.

They freeze well and can be prepared up to 3 months ahead, removed from the freezer, and served at a few moments' notice.

Since the most important ingredient is chocolate, only the best chocolate should be used (see list of purveyors, page 263). After the truffles are formed, they can be rolled in sifted cocoa and placed in the refrigerator or freezer.

Candied fruit peel, arranged around a slice of cake or over scoops of ice cream or sorbet, makes a simple and decorative garnish. Orange or lemon peel can be candied in the same way as the grapefruit peel. The peel can be cut into thick or julienne slices. Use the unused fruit to make sorbet, if desired.

CHOCOLATE HAZELNUT TRUFFLES

CHOCOLATE TRUFFLES WITH BRANDIED APRICOTS

CHAMBORD CHOCOLATE TRUFFLES

MILK CHOCOLATE TRUFFLES

CANDIED GRAPEFRUIT PEEL

CANDIED FRESH GINGER

Chocolate Hazelnut Truffles

MAKES ABOUT 6 DOZEN TRUFFLES

*A*ll the truffles in this chapter can be frozen. Freeze in a tightly covered tin and remove from freezer about 20 minutes before you intend to serve them. Frangelico, which is used in this recipe, is a hazelnut-flavored liqueur.

1. Position rack in center of oven and preheat oven to 350 degrees.

2. Toast hazelnuts: Spread hazelnuts on a baking tray and toast in oven, about 15 minutes, turning nuts after 7 or 8 minutes to toast evenly. Cool. Place a few nuts at a time in a clean towel and rub with the towel, removing as much of the skins as possible. Finely chop the nuts and set aside.

3. Make the truffle base: Melt chocolate in a medium heatproof bowl set over simmering water. When the chocolate is almost melted, turn off the heat and let stand until completely melted, stirring as necessary.

4. In a small saucepan, heat the cream and Frangelico.

5. Set melted chocolate on side of stove and whisk in the alcohol mixture just until combined.

6. Remove bowl from side of stove and dot top with bits of butter. Do not stir, just let butter melt into the warm mixture. When melted, stir to combine well. Let cool *completely*, then cover with plastic wrap and refrigerate overnight.

7. Form the truffles: Remove truffle base from the refrigerator. Fill a small bowl with hot water and line a large baking tray with parchment paper. Dip the melon baller into the hot

EQUIPMENT

Large baking tray

Medium heatproof bowl

Wooden spoon

Small saucepan

Whip

Small bowl

Parchment paper

Plastic wrap

Large baking tray

1-inch-diameter melon baller

INGREDIENTS

1 cup (about 4½ ounces) hazelnuts

1 pound milk chocolate, cut into small pieces

¾ cup heavy cream

½ cup Frangelico

6 tablespoons (¾ stick) unsalted butter, cut into small pieces

Sifted unsweetened cocoa, optional

TO PREPARE AHEAD

THROUGH STEP 6, MAKING THE BASE. THROUGH STEP 7, REFRIGERATING FOR UP TO 1 WEEK OR FREEZING FOR UP TO 3 MONTHS.

water, tapping out excess water. Scoop out a truffle and quickly roll between the palms of your hands. As the truffles are formed, place on the prepared baking tray. Wash your hands in cold water as necessary, drying thoroughly, to prevent the chocolate from sticking to your hands. Continue to dip and scoop, changing water as it cools, until all the truffles are formed. (If the truffle base begins to soften too much, refrigerate or freeze until firm.) Refrigerate truffles. Before serving, the truffles can be rolled in sifted unsweetened cocoa, if desired, or dipped in melted white, milk, or dark chocolate. After dipping, place truffles on wax paper and refrigerate for 10 minutes.

EQUIPMENT

Small saucepan

Large heatproof bowl

Whip

Wooden spoon

Large baking tray

Parchment paper

Small bowl

Small melon baller

INGREDIENTS

*1 cup (4 ounces) dried apricots,
cut into small dice*

¾ cup heavy cream

½ cup apricot brandy

*1 pound bittersweet chocolate, cut
into small pieces*

*6 tablespoons (¾ stick) unsalted
butter, cut into small pieces*

*Sifted unsweetened cocoa or melted
white chocolate*

TO PREPARE AHEAD

THROUGH STEP 4, MAKING
THE BASE. THROUGH STEP 5,
TRUFFLES CAN BE
REFRIGERATED FOR UP TO 1
WEEK AND FROZEN FOR UP TO
3 MONTHS.

Chocolate Truffles
with Brandied Apricots

MAKES ABOUT 6 DOZEN TRUFFLES

*W*olfgang used to make this truffle years ago. He loves the combination of apricots and chocolate.

1. Make the truffle base: In a small saucepan, bring the apricots, cream, and apricot brandy to a simmer. Remove from the heat and let steep 1 to 2 hours. (To enable the apricots to soften and to absorb the flavor of the brandy, you must allow them to steep the specified time.)

2. Melt chocolate in a large heatproof bowl set over gently simmering water. When chocolate is almost melted, turn off heat and let melt completely, stirring occasionally. Set on side of stove and whisk in the apricot mixture until combined.

3. Remove bowl from side of stove and dot top with bits of butter. Do not stir at this point, just let butter melt into the warm mixture. When melted, stir to combine well.

4. Let cool completely. Cover with plastic wrap and refrigerate overnight.

5. Form the truffles: Line a large baking tray with parchment paper and place near where you will be forming the truffles. Fill a small bowl with hot water. Remove truffle base from refrigerator. Dip the melon baller into the hot water, tapping out excess water. Scoop out a truffle, making certain 1 or 2 pieces of apricot are included, and quickly roll between the palms of your hands. Place on the prepared baking tray. Wash your hands in cold water as necessary to prevent the chocolate from sticking to your hands and dry thoroughly. Dip and scoop, changing hot water as it cools, until all the truffles are formed. If the truffle base begins to soften too much, refrigerate or freeze until firm, then continue to dip and scoop. Refrigerate truffles until firm.

6. If you like, truffles can be rolled in sifted cocoa or drizzled with melted chocolate before serving.

Chambord Chocolate Truffles

MAKES 75 TO 80 SMALL TRUFFLES

*M*ilk chocolate can be substituted for the bittersweet chocolate and Bailey's Irish Cream, a chocolate-flavored liqueur, for the Chambord. Truffles can be placed in small colored paper or foil cups, if desired.

1. Make the truffle base: Melt chocolate in a medium heatproof bowl set over simmering water. When almost melted, turn off heat and let melt completely, stirring as necessary.

2. In a small saucepan, heat cream and Chambord.

3. Set melted chocolate on side of stove and whisk in the alcohol mixture just until combined.

4. Remove bowl from side of stove and dot top with bits of butter. Do not stir at this point, just let butter melt into the warm mixture. When melted, stir to combine well.

5. Let cool completely. (If not completely cool, chocolate will have streaks running through it.) Cover with plastic wrap and refrigerate overnight.

6. Form the truffles: The next day, line a large baking tray with parchment paper and place it near where you will be forming the truffles. Remove truffle base from refrigerator. Fill a small bowl with hot water. Dip the melon baller into the hot water, tapping out excess water. Scoop out a truffle and, as the truffles are formed, roll in sifted cocoa powder and arrange on prepared tray. Continue to dip and scoop, changing water as it cools, until all the truffles are formed. Truffles do not have to be a uniform size and may or may not be rolled into a perfect ball. (If you want a round truffle, roll between the palms of your hands, rinsing and drying hands as necessary.) Refrigerate until firm.

EQUIPMENT

Medium heatproof bowl

Small saucepan

Wooden spoon

Whip

Large baking tray

Parchment paper

Small bowl

1-inch-diameter melon baller

Small colored paper or foil cups, optional

INGREDIENTS

1 pound bittersweet chocolate, cut into small pieces

¾ cup heavy cream

½ cup Chambord or Grand Marnier

6 tablespoons (¾ stick) cold unsalted butter, cut into small bits

Sifted unsweetened cocoa

TO PREPARE AHEAD

THROUGH STEP 5, MAKING THE BASE. THROUGH STEP 6, REFRIGERATING FOR UP TO 1 WEEK OR FREEZING IN A COVERED CONTAINER FOR UP TO 3 MONTHS.

Milk Chocolate Truffles

MAKES ABOUT 5 DOZEN TRUFFLES

EQUIPMENT

Large heatproof bowl

Small saucepan

Whip

Wooden spoon

Shallow pan

Small bowl

Large baking tray

Parchment paper

1-inch-diameter melon baller

INGREDIENTS

*1 pound milk chocolate, cut into
small pieces*

½ cup Bailey's Irish Cream

¾ cup heavy cream

*6 tablespoons (¾ stick) unsalted
butter, cut into small bits*

TO PREPARE AHEAD

THROUGH STEP 2, TRUFFLES
CAN BE FROZEN FOR UP TO 3
MONTHS.

We flavor these truffles with Bailey's Irish Cream, a chocolate-flavored liqueur, but if you have another favorite, the choice is yours.

1. Make the truffle base: Melt chocolate in a heatproof bowl set over simmering water. When the chocolate is almost melted, turn off the heat and let stand until completely melted.

2. In a small saucepan, bring the Bailey's and cream just to a simmer.

3. Set melted chocolate on side of stove and whisk in the alcohol mixture just until combined.

4. Place the small bits of butter around the chocolate mixture and let melt. When completely melted, stir to incorporate. Pour mixture into a shallow pan, giving you a 1-inch-thick layer of chocolate. Refrigerate or freeze until very firm.

5. Form the truffles: Have a small bowl of very hot water ready and replace the water as it cools down. Line a large baking tray with parchment paper. Remove truffle base from the refrigerator. Before scooping out a ball of chocolate, dip the melon baller into the hot water, shaking to remove any excess water. Scoop out a truffle, tapping the melon baller on a firm surface to release the truffle. Quickly roll between the palms of your hands and place on the prepared baking tray. You will have to wash your hands in cold water often to prevent the chocolate from sticking to your hands. Repeat this procedure until all the balls have been scooped and rolled. If the truffle base begins to soften too much, refrigerate or freeze until firm, and then continue to scoop out the truffles. Place in a covered container and refrigerate or freeze until needed.

Candied Grapefruit Peel

EQUIPMENT

Sharp paring knife

Small nonreactive saucepan

Fine strainer

INGREDIENTS

1 large (about 1 pound) grapefruit

*1¾ cups granulated sugar plus
about ½ cup extra for coating*

TO PREPARE AHEAD

THROUGH STEP 6, 1 DAY
AHEAD, KEEPING THE PEEL
IN THE SYRUP, COVERED.
THROUGH STEP 7, CANDIED
PEEL SHOULD BE STORED IN
AN AIRTIGHT CONTAINER.

*L*emon or orange peel can be candied in the same way. These bittersweet fruits are softened and sweetened, then coated with sugar and allowed to dry on a rack. When dry, the peels will keep for weeks in an airtight container.

1. Cut a slice from the top and bottom ends of the grapefruit. Place the grapefruit, cut side down, on a flat, firm surface. Peel the grapefruit with a sharp paring knife, starting at the top, cutting down in one large strip (see illustration). Turn the grapefruit as you cut off all the peel. Use the grapefruit as desired, in fruit salad, for juice or sorbet.

2. Cut the peel into strips, about 2 inches long and ¾ inch wide. Carefully cut away as much of the white pith as you can on each piece of the grapefruit. (You will end up with about 3 ounces of peel after you trim.)

3. Place the peel in a small nonreactive saucepan and pour in 2 cups cold water. Bring to a boil, boil for 5 minutes, and then strain through a fine strainer.

4. For the second boil, return peel to pan, add 2 cups cold water and ¼ cup sugar. Bring to a boil and boil 5 minutes. Again strain.

5. For the third boil, return peel to pan, add 2 cups cold water and ½ cup sugar. Bring to a boil and boil 5 minutes. Strain.

6. For the fourth and final boil, return peel to pan, add 1½ cups cold water and 1 cup sugar. Bring to a boil, lower heat to medium, and boil until the peel is very tender, about 10 minutes. Let cool in syrup and then strain.

7. Place about ½ cup sugar, adding more if necessary, on a flat plate. Toss the grapefruit peels in the sugar, coating all sides. As the pieces are coated, remove to a piece of aluminum foil to dry. Use as needed.

Candied Fresh Ginger

MAKES ABOUT ½ CUP

EQUIPMENT

Peeler

Small nonreactive saucepan

Fine-mesh strainer

INGREDIENTS

4 ounces gingerroot

1¾ cups granulated sugar plus about ½ cup extra for coating

TO PREPARE AHEAD

THROUGH STEP 5, 1 DAY AHEAD, KEEPING THE PEEL IN THE SYRUP, COVERED. THROUGH STEP 6, CANDIED PEEL SHOULD BE STORED IN AN AIRTIGHT CONTAINER.

*C*andied ginger or fruit peel can be sprinkled over ice cream or fruit tarts or served with truffles on an assorted sweet tray.

1. Peel gingerroot and cut into julienne or ⅛-inch-thick slices.

2. Place ginger in a small nonreactive saucepan with 2 cups cold water. Bring to a boil and boil 5 minutes. Strain and return ginger to saucepan.

3. For the second boil, add 2 cups cold water and ¼ cup sugar, and bring to a boil. Lower heat to medium and boil 35 minutes. Strain and return ginger to saucepan.

4 For the third boil, add 2 cups cold water and ½ cup sugar. Bring to a boil and boil 5 minutes. Strain and return ginger to saucepan.

5. For the fourth and final boil, add 4 cups cold water and 1 cup sugar. Bring to a boil, lower heat to medium, and boil until about 1 cup liquid remains and ginger is very tender, about 45 minutes. Let cool in the syrup and then strain.

6. Place about ½ cup sugar on a flat plate. Toss the ginger in the sugar, coating well. As the pieces are coated, remove to a piece of aluminum foil to dry. Use as needed.

XI

Cooked Fruits

With so many people on special diets, we decided to include a few fat-free recipes that can be produced easily and quickly. We started experimenting with baked apples and found them overwhelmingly popular. The others followed.

Many fruits can be poached . . . peaches, pears, apples, oranges, grapes. If the wine you use is sweet, sugar may not be needed. Let your taste be your guide. Poaching and baking fruit are best done in a heavy nonreactive pan, allowing the fruit to maintain its shape. If the fruit is ripe, cooking time will be shorter. When ready, the fruit should be tender but still firm.

Cooked fruit is at its best served at room temperature. If refrigerated, remove 1 or 2 hours before serving.

BAKED APPLES WITH CRÈME ANGLAISE

STRAWBERRIES IN PORT WINE

PEAR AND DRIED SOUR CHERRY COMPOTE

TANGERINE SOUP

SERVES 8

EQUIPMENT

Apple corer

10- or 12-inch nonreactive, heavy-duty pot with 4-inch sides

Small bowl

Aluminum foil

INGREDIENTS

8 medium (about 3 pounds) Granny Smith apples

8 small cinnamon sticks

1½ cups golden brown sugar, packed

1 cup Calvados or applejack brandy

1 cup water

1½ tablespoons finely chopped lemon zest

½ teaspoon freshly ground nutmeg

½ vanilla bean, split lengthwise

Crème Anglaise (see page 6)

½ cup Streusel (see page 171), toasted*

8 small sprigs fresh mint

TO PREPARE AHEAD

THROUGH STEP 4, APPLES CAN BE BAKED UP TO A FEW HOURS BEFORE SERVING.

*W*e didn't realize how much people loved baked apples until we tested this recipe. Everyone in the kitchen came running over to make sure the "sample" was worthy of being sent out to the restaurant. The verdict was unanimous—great! The first day we put the apples on the menu, we had to make a second batch to accommodate all the requests. The Crème Anglaise certainly adds to the flavor, but you can eliminate it if you are counting calories.

1. Place rack in lower third of oven and preheat oven to 325 degrees.

2. Using an apple corer, remove core of each apple, from top through bottom

3. In a 10- or 12-inch nonreactive, heavy-duty pot with 4-inch sides, arrange apples in 1 layer. Place 1 cinnamon stick in hollowed-out opening of each apple. In a small bowl, combine the sugar, Calvados, water, lemon zest, nutmeg, and vanilla bean with its scrapings and pour around the apples. Partially cover pot with aluminum foil, and bring to a boil on top of stove.

4. Cover tightly with foil, transfer to oven, and bake until apples are tender, 30 to 35 minutes. Baking time depends on size of each apple. (Peel may crack slightly as apples bake, but that's okay.) Remove the vanilla bean. Reserve the liquid.

---

*To toast Streusel, spread on a baking sheet and bake in 325-degree oven for 5 to 10 minutes to crisp.

5. Apples should be served warm or at room temperature. To serve, spoon ¼ cup Crème Anglaise into each of 8 large shallow soup bowls. Carefully place 1 apple in the center of each bowl, cinnamon stick still in the opening. Spoon reserved liquid into each apple. Sprinkle some of the toasted Streusel over the apple and around the Crème Anglaise, and garnish each serving with a sprig of mint.

Strawberries in Port Wine

Serves 4

*T*he combined flavors of port wine, cinnamon, and strawberries make this a wonderful topping for ice cream. It is also delicious served in bowls by itself.

1. Arrange strawberries in a 12-inch heavy-duty skillet or sauté pan. Add sugar, orange zest, cinnamon stick, and vanilla bean with its scrapings, and finally pour in the wine. Over high heat, cook for 10 minutes. Strawberries should be very soft and sauce should be slightly thickened. Remove vanilla bean and cinnamon stick, stir in the lemon juice, and correct seasoning to taste.

2. To serve, spoon into shallow soup bowls and float a small scoop of vanilla ice cream on top of the berries, if desired.

Equipment

12-inch heavy-duty skillet or sauté pan

Ingredients

2 pints strawberries, hulled and cut into ¼-inch slices

1 cup granulated sugar

2 tablespoons orange zest

1 cinnamon stick

½ vanilla bean, split lengthwise

2½ cups dry red wine

1 tablespoon lemon juice

To Prepare Ahead

Through step 1, strawberries can be prepared up to 2 hours ahead.

Pear and Dried Sour Cherry Compote

SERVES 8 TO 10

EQUIPMENT

Medium bowl

12-inch skillet

INGREDIENTS

3¾ pounds (8 large) ripe Bartlett or Bosc pears, quartered, peeled, and cored

3 tablespoons fresh lemon juice

1 cup (about 4 ounces) dried sour cherries

½ vanilla bean, split lengthwise

2 cups Gewürztraminer or Riesling

8 small sprigs fresh mint

TO PREPARE AHEAD

THROUGH STEP 2, PEARS CAN BE PREPARED EARLY IN THE DAY.

The sweetness for this dessert comes from the wine. No sugar is added to the fruit. You can also make this with whole, peeled Seckel pears, leaving the stems intact. Two pears can be used for each serving. Cut a small slice from the bottoms of the pears so that they will not topple, and cook in a sauté pan with 2- to 3-inch sides.

1. In a medium bowl, toss pears in lemon juice. Arrange in a 12-inch skillet in 1 layer, add the cherries and vanilla bean with its scrapings, and pour the wine over. Let marinate at room temperature, covered, for about 1 hour.

2. Transfer to stove and, over low heat, cook, still covered, until pears are barely tender, about 15 minutes. Cooking time depends on ripeness of fruit.

3. Pears should be served at room temperature. To serve, arrange 3 or 4 pear quarters in each serving bowl. Spoon the cherries, together with sauce, over the pears and garnish each portion with a sprig of mint.

Sticky Buns

Pear Cherry Napoleon with Phyllo Nests

Top: Ricotta Fig Tart
Right: Fresh Cherry Lattice Tart; Lemon Tart; Cherry Clafouti
Bottom: Fresh Cherry Tart (without lattice top)

Blond Brownie Sundae

Chunky Apple Muffins with Streusel; Blueberry Muffins; slices of Orange Poppy Seed Loaf

Assorted cookies

Spago Banana Split

Assorted ice creams and sorbets with biscotti

Tangerine Soup

EQUIPMENT

Heavy-duty 12-inch sauté pan

INGREDIENTS

1 pound tangerines, seeded, peeled, and cut into segments

¼ cup granulated sugar

½ vanilla bean, split lengthwise

4 cups orange or tangerine juice

2 tablespoons chopped fresh mint leaves

Chocolate Sorbet (see page 242)

TO PREPARE AHEAD

THROUGH STEP 1, SOUP CAN BE SERVED JUST WARMED OR COLD.

This fruit soup, made with tangerines, is a refreshing way to end a meal. When the menu lists this as Sautéed Tangerines with Chocolate Sorbet, people are eager to try it, but as Tangerine Soup, there are usually no takers. No matter the name, it makes a delicious light dessert. Eating oranges, seeded, peeled, and cut into segments, can be substituted for the tangerines.

1. Arrange tangerine segments in a heavy-duty 12-inch sauté pan. Add the sugar and the vanilla bean and its scrapings, and cook over medium-high heat until sugar begins to bubble, about 5 minutes. Lower heat and cook until segments begin to soften, about 10 minutes longer. Pour the juice over and warm slightly.

2. To serve, place a scoop of Chocolate Sorbet in the center of each of 8 shallow soup bowls. Spoon soup into bowls, dividing tangerine segments equally around the sorbet. Serve immediately.

XII

Cookies, Biscotti, and Macaroons

For many people, making cookies is their introduction to baking. For the first time, they measure ingredients, crack eggs, sift flour, drop the dough onto the pan, and somehow the result is edible.

In all of Wolfgang's restaurants, hundreds of cookies are baked every day. Not only must they taste good, but they must look as good as they taste. Most of the cookie dough is either rolled into logs of predetermined length and width, the dough sliced before baking, or rolled into small balls, all the same diameter, ensuring a uniform size for each type of cookie. Logs or balls can be made in large quantities, wrapped well, refrigerated, and baked to order. We do not freeze cookie dough at Spago, but the logs and balls can be frozen, wrapped well, for up to 2 months.

The recipes in this chapter include examples of both kinds of cookies with helpful tips on how to make them. Remember: <u>Always</u> store baked cookies in airtight containers!

Biscotti come to us via Italy. They are twice-baked, resulting in a crisp cookie that, in Italy, is served with and dipped into wine. Stored in an airtight container, biscotti will keep for up to 1 month.

BASIC BUTTER COOKIES

CHOCOLATE COCONUT COOKIES

MACADAMIA BUTTER COOKIES

CINNAMON SUGAR COOKIES

GINGER SPICE COOKIES

OATMEAL CURRANT COOKIES

PEANUT BUTTER COOKIES

BLACK SNOWBALLS

CHOCOLATE CHIP COOKIES

CHOCOLATE CHOCOLATE CHIP COOKIES

CHOCOLATE PEANUT BUTTER CHOCOLATE CHIP
COOKIES

CHOCOLATE BISCOTTI

BISCOTTI WITH CHOCOLATE CHUNKS,
RAISINS, AND NUTS

PISTACHIO BISCOTTI

APRICOT COCONUT MACAROONS

Basic Butter Cookies

MAKES ABOUT 6½ DOZEN COOKIES

EQUIPMENT

Sifter

Electric mixer

Plastic wrap

1 or 2 baking trays

Parchment paper

Wide metal spatula

INGREDIENTS

4 cups all-purpose flour

¼ teaspoon salt

1 pound unsalted butter, at room temperature, cut into small pieces

1 cup granulated sugar

4 egg yolks

2 teaspoons vanilla extract

About ¼ cup crystal sugar

TO PREPARE AHEAD

THROUGH STEP 4 OR 6. THE LOGS CAN BE WRAPPED WELL AND FROZEN, THE COOKIES BAKED WITHIN 10 DAYS.

This is a most versatile cookie. It can be served plain, with a sprinkling of crystal sugar, or it can be made into a sandwich cookie with a thin layer of frosting between two layers, chopped crystallized ginger added to the batter. The variations are infinite.

1. Sift together the flour and salt. Set aside.

2. In the large bowl of an electric mixer, using paddle or beaters, beat together the butter and sugar until very creamy. Start on low speed and, when combined, raise speed to high and mix until fluffy. On medium, add the egg yolks, then the vanilla. Add the flour mixture and beat just until combined. Dough will clog the paddle or beaters, but it will be creamy.

3. Remove dough from bowl and wrap in plastic wrap. Refrigerate until slightly firm, about 1 hour.

4. Remove from refrigerator and divide in half, each half about 1½ pounds. Roll each half into a log about 12 inches long and 2 inches in diameter. Wrap each log in plastic wrap and refrigerate for about 2 to 3 hours, or better still, overnight.

5. Place rack in top third of oven and preheat oven to 350 degrees. Line 1 or 2 baking trays with parchment paper.

6. Working with 1 log at a time, cut into about 40 cookies, each about ¼ inch thick. Arrange cookies on prepared tray, about 2 inches apart, and sprinkle the tops with crystal sugar. Bake until the edges of the cookies are lightly brown, 10 to 11 minutes. Remove cookies from trays with a wide metal spatula and cool on rack. Repeat with remaining log and crystal sugar. If using the same baking tray, allow to cool before arranging cookies on the pan.

Chocolate Coconut Cookies

MAKES ABOUT 5 DOZEN COOKIES

EQUIPMENT

Sifter

Electric mixer

Plastic wrap

1 or 2 baking trays

Parchment paper

Wide metal spatula

INGREDIENTS

1⅓ cups all-purpose flour

¾ cup unsweetened cocoa

¾ teaspoon ground cinnamon

⅛ teaspoon salt

⅛ teaspoon ground black pepper

⅛ teaspoon ground cayenne pepper

6 ounces (1½ sticks) unsalted butter, at room temperature, cut into small pieces

1 cup granulated sugar

1 egg

1½ teaspoons vanilla extract

1 cup unsweetened shredded coconut

TO PREPARE AHEAD

THROUGH STEP 3 OR 5

*T*his is the Mexican version of our chocolate cookies, flavored with pinches of black pepper and cayenne pepper.

1. Sift together the flour, cocoa, cinnamon, salt, and black and cayenne peppers. Set aside.

2. In the large bowl of an electric mixer, using paddle or beaters, and on medium speed, soften the butter. Add the sugar, raising the speed to high when the sugar is incorporated, and continue to mix until fluffy, scraping down sides of bowl as necessary. Lower the speed to medium, add the egg and vanilla, and beat just to combine. Lower speed, gradually pour in the flour mixture, and mix just until combined.

3. Scrape dough out of the machine and onto a flat work surface. (If too soft to roll, refrigerate, wrapped, for 1 hour.) With very lightly floured hands, roll into a log, about 15 inches long and 1 inch in diameter. Sprinkle coconut on the work surface and then roll the log in the coconut, coating the entire log with shredded coconut. Wrap in plastic wrap and refrigerate until well chilled and very firm, at least 2 to 3 hours or, better still, overnight.

4. Position rack in center of oven and preheat oven to 350 degrees. Line 1 or 2 baking trays with parchment paper.

5. Remove the paper from the log and reroll log in the coconut as necessary. With a very sharp knife, cut the log into about 60 slices, each about ¼ inch wide, and arrange on the baking trays, about 1 inch apart. (These cookies do not spread very much.) Bake until the coconut is lightly toasted, about 10 minutes, reversing trays front to back after 5 minutes. Remove from trays with a wide metal spatula and cool on rack.

Macadamia Butter Cookies

MAKES ABOUT 5½ DOZEN COOKIES

❀

*T*hese are buttery and crisp, the macadamia nuts giving them a very distinctive flavor.

1. In the large bowl of an electric mixer, using paddle or beaters, on low speed, beat the butter until it begins to soften. Add the sugar, raising speed to high when the sugar is incorporated, and continue to beat until light and fluffy.

2. Meanwhile, sift the flour and set aside.

3. Lower speed to medium, add the egg yolks to the butter and sugar, and beat just until combined. On low speed, add the honey, then the flour, and beat until incorporated. Add the nuts and beat just to mix. Scrape dough out of bowl, wrap in plastic wrap, and refrigerate until firm, 2 to 3 hours or overnight.

4. Position rack in center of oven and preheat oven to 350 degrees. Line 1 or 2 baking trays with parchment paper and set aside.

5. Divide dough in half, each half about 1½ pounds. Roll each half into a log, about 12 inches long and 2 inches in diameter. (If not firm after rolling, rewrap and refrigerate for about 30 minutes.) Keep a log refrigerated while slicing the first one. Cut the log in slices about ⅓ inch wide. Arrange slices on prepared baking trays, spaced 2 inches apart. Repeat with the remaining log. Bake until golden, about 10 minutes, reversing cookie sheets front to back after 5 minutes. Remove cookies from trays with a wide metal spatula and cool on rack.

Cinnamon Sugar Cookies

MAKES ABOUT 5½ DOZEN COOKIES

❧

Since we usually serve an assortment of cookies, the dough is rolled into ½-ounce balls. However, if you prefer larger cookies, use 1 ounce of dough for each cookie, but keep them well separated when baking, since they will spread.

1. Sift together the flour, cinnamon, cream of tartar, baking soda, and salt. Set aside.

2. In the large bowl of an electric mixer, using paddle or beaters, on medium speed, soften the butter. Add the sugar, raising the speed to high when the sugar is incorporated, and continue to mix until fluffy, scraping down sides of bowl and under beaters as necessary. Add the eggs, 1 at a time, and the vanilla and beat well, again scraping down sides of bowl as necessary. Turn speed to low, gradually pour in the flour mixture, and beat just until combined. Scrape out of bowl, wrap in plastic wrap, and refrigerate until firm, 2 to 3 hours or, better still, overnight.

3. When ready to bake, position rack in center of oven and preheat oven to 350 degrees. Line 1 or 2 baking trays with parchment paper.

4. Remove dough from refrigerator and divide into mounds, about ½ ounce each and 1 inch in diameter. Roll between the palms of your hands, forming small balls of dough. Place the cinnamon sugar on a small, flat plate and as each ball is formed, roll in the cinnamon sugar and arrange the balls on the prepared baking trays, about 2 inches apart. Bake until golden brown around the edges and slightly firm to the touch, 14 to 15 minutes, reversing trays front to back after 7 minutes to ensure even baking. Remove cookies from trays with a wide metal spatula and cool on rack. If reusing a baking tray, cool slightly before arranging balls of dough on it.

Ginger Spice Cookies

MAKES ABOUT 6 DOZEN SMALL COOKIES

❧

*F*resh and ground ginger are combined with other spices, giving the cookies a slightly pungent taste.

1. Sift together the flour, ground ginger, baking soda, cinnamon, nutmeg, and cloves. Set aside.

2. In the large bowl of an electric mixer, using paddle or beaters, on medium speed, soften the butter. Add the granulated and brown sugars, raising the speed to high when the sugar is incorporated, and continue to mix until fluffy, scraping down sides of bowl and under beaters as necessary. Lower speed to medium, and add the grated ginger and molasses and mix until well combined. Add the egg and continue to mix. Turn speed to low, gradually pour in the flour mixture, and beat just until combined. Scrape out of the bowl, wrap in plastic wrap, and refrigerate until firm, 2 to 3 hours or, better still, overnight.

3. When ready to bake, position rack in center of oven and preheat oven to 350 degrees. Line 1 or 2 baking trays with parchment paper.

4. Remove dough from refrigerator and divide into mounds, about ½ ounce each. Roll between the palms of your hands, forming balls about 1 inch in diameter, and arrange on prepared baking trays, about 2 inches apart. Bake until edges and bottom of cookies are lightly brown and cookies are just firm to the touch, 14 to 15 minutes, reversing trays front to back after 6 to 7 minutes to ensure even baking. Remove cookies from trays with a wide metal spatula and cool on rack. If reusing a tray, cool slightly before arranging balls of dough on it.

EQUIPMENT

Sifter

Electric mixer

Grater

Plastic wrap

1 or 2 baking trays

Parchment paper

Wide metal spatula

INGREDIENTS

2¾ cups all-purpose unbleached flour

3 tablespoons ground ginger

1½ teaspoons baking soda

1 teaspoon ground cinnamon

½ teaspoon freshly grated nutmeg

½ teaspoon ground cloves

8 ounces (2 sticks) unsalted butter, at room temperature, cut into 1-ounce pieces

½ cup granulated sugar

½ cup brown sugar, packed

2 tablespoons fresh gingerroot, peeled and grated

½ cup molasses

1 egg

TO PREPARE AHEAD

THROUGH STEP 2 OR 4

Oatmeal Currant Cookies

MAKES ABOUT 4 DOZEN COOKIES

*C*urrants, which are a little more delicate than raisins, are added to these cookies. If you prefer raisins, they can be substituted.

1. Sift together the flour, cinnamon, baking soda, baking powder, allspice, and salt. Set aside.

2. In the large bowl of an electric mixer, using paddle or beaters, on medium speed, soften the butter. Add the granulated and brown sugars, raising the speed to high after the sugar is incorporated, and continue to mix until fluffy, stopping machine and scraping down sides of bowl and under beaters as necessary. Lower speed to medium and add eggs, 1 at a time. Add the flour mixture and beat just until combined. Add the remaining ingredients and again beat just until combined.

3. Scrape out of bowl and wrap in plastic wrap. Refrigerate 2 to 3 hours or, better still, overnight.

4. Position rack in center of oven and preheat oven to 350 degrees. Line 1 or 2 baking trays with parchment paper.

5. Remove dough from refrigerator and divide into mounds, about 1 ounce each. Roll between the palms of your hands, forming about 48 balls. As balls are rolled, arrange on prepared trays, about 2 inches apart. Bake until slightly firm to the touch, 13 to 15 minutes, reversing trays front to back after 7 to 8 minutes to ensure even baking. Remove cookies from trays with a wide metal spatula and cool on rack. If reusing a baking tray, cool slightly before arranging balls of dough on it.

Peanut Butter Cookies

Equipment

Sifter

Electric mixer

Plastic wrap

1 or 2 baking trays

Parchment paper

Wide metal spatula

Ingredients

2 cups plus 1 tablespoon
all-purpose flour

2 teaspoons baking soda

8 ounces (2 sticks) unsalted butter,
at room temperature, cut into
small pieces

1 cup granulated sugar

1 cup brown sugar

1 cup peanut butter (10 ounces),
chunky or smooth

2 whole eggs

1½ cups dried currants

To Prepare Ahead

Through step 2 or 4

*N*ext to chocolate, most people love peanut butter cookies. Toasted, chopped unsalted peanuts can be added to the batter, if desired. To toast peanuts, arrange 1 cup peeled peanuts on a baking tray and set in a preheated 350-degree oven for 10 to 12 minutes. Cool and then coarsely chop.

1. Sift together the flour and baking soda and set aside.

2. In the large bowl of an electric mixer, using paddle or beaters, on medium speed, soften the butter. Add the granulated and brown sugars, raising the speed to high when the sugar is incorporated, and continue to mix until fluffy, stopping machine and scraping down sides of bowl and under beaters as necessary. Add the peanut butter and beat until thoroughly combined. Lower speed to medium and add eggs, 1 at a time. Turn speed to low, and add the sifted ingredients, beating just until combined. Remove bowl and fold in the currants. Scrape out of bowl and wrap in plastic wrap. Refrigerate 2 to 3 hours or, better still, overnight.

3. Position rack in center of oven and preheat oven to 350 degrees. Line 1 or 2 baking trays with parchment paper.

4. Remove dough from refrigerator and divide into mounds, about 1 ounce each. Roll between the palms of your hands, forming about 48 small balls. (Dough can be rolled, placed on trays, and refrigerated until needed. The balls then can be baked to order, if desired.) As balls are rolled, arrange on parchment-lined baking trays, about 2 inches apart. Bake until slightly firm to the touch, 12 to 14 minutes, reversing trays front to back after 6 to 7 minutes. Remove cookies from trays with a wide metal spatula and cool on rack. If reusing a baking tray, cool slightly before arranging balls of dough on it.

Black Snowballs

EQUIPMENT

Small and large mixing bowls

*Double boiler or medium
heatproof bowl*

Whip

Parchment paper

1 or 2 baking trays

Sifter

Wide metal spatula

INGREDIENTS

*1 cup almond meal (see footnote,
page 108)*

*½ cup plus 2 tablespoons
all-purpose flour*

¾ teaspoon baking powder

*12 ounces bittersweet chocolate,
cut into small pieces*

*4 tablespoons (½ stick) unsalted
butter, at room temperature, cut
into pieces*

3 eggs

1 cup granulated sugar

*¼ cup plus 2 tablespoons flavored
liqueur (Amaretto, Chambord, or
crème de menthe) or strong coffee*

*About ⅓ cup sifted confectioners'
sugar*

TO PREPARE AHEAD

THROUGH STEP 4 OR 6

*I*n the pastry kitchen, we have a special name for these
cookies, but it is unprintable. In spite of our pet name,
the cookies are deliciously soft and chewy.

1. In a small bowl, combine the almond meal, flour, and baking powder. Set aside.

2. In a double boiler or medium heatproof bowl placed over
simmering water, heat the chocolate and butter until almost
melted. Turn off heat and let stand over warm water until
completely melted, stirring occasionally.

3. While the chocolate and butter are melting, in a large mixing bowl, whisk together the eggs and ½ cup of the sugar. Stir
in the flavoring of your choice. Whisk the melted chocolate
into the egg mixture, then fold in the reserved flour mixture.
Refrigerate at least 2 to 3 hours, up to overnight.

4. Roll into small balls, about ½ ounce each and 1 inch in
diameter. Arrange on one or two parchment-paper-lined baking trays. Refrigerate at least 30 minutes.

5. When ready to bake, position rack in center of oven and
preheat oven to 350 degrees.

6. Pour the remaining ½ cup granulated sugar onto one large
plate and about ⅓ cup sifted powdered sugar on another. Roll
each cookie first in the granulated sugar, then in the confectioners' sugar. Return to baking trays, placing about 2 inches
apart. Bake until slightly firm to the touch and the tops of the
cookies start to crack, 10 to 11 minutes. Remove cookies
from trays with a wide metal spatula and cool on rack. If
reusing baking trays, let them cool slightly between use.

Chocolate Chip Cookies

MAKES ABOUT 3 DOZEN COOKIES

These chocolate chip cookies have been on the menu since January 1982, when Spago first opened its doors. Wolfgang likes crisp cookies, so this recipe makes crisp ones. However, if you prefer a softer variety, bake only 10 to 11 minutes. (Or you can form larger balls and bake the same number of minutes.)

1. Sift together the flour, baking soda, and salt. Set aside.

2. In the large bowl of an electric mixer, using paddle or beaters, and on medium speed, soften the butter. Add the brown and granulated sugars, raising the speed to high when the sugar is incorporated, and continue to mix until fluffy, scraping down sides of bowl and under beaters as necessary. Add the eggs, 1 at a time, and the vanilla. Turn speed to low, gradually pour in the flour mixture, then add the nuts and chocolate chips and mix just until combined. Remove dough, wrap in plastic wrap, and refrigerate until firm, 2 to 3 hours or, better still, overnight.

3. Position rack in center of oven and preheat oven to 350 degrees. Line 1 or 2 baking trays with parchment paper.

4. Remove dough from refrigerator and divide into mounds, about 1 ounce each. Roll between the palms of your hands, forming about 36 balls. Arrange on prepared trays, about 2 inches apart. Bake until golden brown and slightly firm to the touch, 12 to 14 minutes, reversing trays front to back after 6 to 7 minutes to ensure even baking. Remove cookies from trays with a wide metal spatula and cool on rack. If reusing a tray, cool slightly before arranging balls of dough on it.

Chocolate Chocolate Chip Cookies

MAKES ABOUT 4½ DOZEN COOKIES

EQUIPMENT

Sifter

Electric mixer

Plastic wrap

1 or 2 baking trays

Parchment paper

Wide metal spatula

INGREDIENTS

1¾ cups all-purpose flour

½ cup unsweetened cocoa

¾ teaspoon baking soda

¼ teaspoon salt

8 ounces (2 sticks) unsalted butter, at room temperature, cut into small pieces

1 cup brown sugar

¾ cup granulated sugar

2 eggs

1½ teaspoons vanilla extract

1½ ounces bittersweet chocolate, melted (see page XXI)

2 cups (½ pound) coarsely chopped pecans or walnuts or toasted and cooled unsalted peanuts, coarsely chopped

1¾ cups (¾ pound) semisweet chocolate chips

TO PREPARE AHEAD

THROUGH STEP 2 OR 4

If you like chocolate cookies, you will love these, made with bittersweet chocolate, semisweet chocolate chips, and chopped pecans.

1. Sift together the flour, cocoa, baking soda, and salt. Set aside.

2. In the large bowl of an electric mixer, using paddle or beaters, and on medium speed, soften the butter. Add the brown and granulated sugars, raising the speed to high when the sugar is incorporated, and continue to mix until fluffy, stopping machine and scraping down sides of bowl and under beaters as necessary. Lower speed to medium, add the eggs, 1 at a time, and the vanilla. Stop machine, scrape in the melted chocolate, and beat until thoroughly combined. Turn speed to low, gradually pour in the flour mixture, and beat just until combined. Add the nuts and chocolate chips, and again beat just until combined. Scrape out of bowl and wrap in plastic wrap. Refrigerate until firm, 2 to 3 hours or, better still, overnight.

3. Position rack in center of oven and preheat oven to 350 degrees. Line 1 or 2 baking trays with parchment paper.

4. Remove dough from refrigerator and divide into mounds, 1 ounce each. Roll between the palms of your hands, forming about 54 small balls. (Dough can be rolled, placed on trays, and refrigerated until needed.) Arrange the rolled balls on the prepared baking trays, about 2 inches apart. Bake until slightly firm to the touch, about 15 minutes, reversing trays front to back after 7 to 8 minutes. Remove cookies from trays with a wide metal spatula and cool on rack. If reusing a baking tray, cool slightly before arranging balls of dough on it.

EQUIPMENT

Sifter

Medium bowl

Electric mixer

1 or 2 baking trays

Parchment paper

Wide metal spatula

INGREDIENTS

1½ cups all-purpose unbleached
flour

⅓ cup plus 1 tablespoon
unsweetened cocoa

1 teaspoon baking soda

½ teaspoon salt

8 ounces (2 sticks) unsalted butter,
at room temperature, cut into
small pieces

½ cup granulated sugar

½ cup dark brown sugar, packed

½ cup peanut butter, creamy or
chunky

2 eggs

1 teaspoon vanilla extract

2 ounces bittersweet chocolate,
melted (see page XXI)

1 cup toasted peanuts (or walnuts,
pecans, or macadamia nuts),
coarsely chopped

1 cup semisweet chocolate chips

Chocolate Peanut Butter Chocolate Chip Cookies

MAKES ABOUT 3½ DOZEN COOKIES

*T*hese cookies combine the two ingredients most people favor: chocolate and peanut butter. The recipe can easily be doubled, if desired. Unbaked balls can be frozen in airtight plastic bags and baked to order.

1. In a medium bowl, sift together the flour, cocoa, baking soda, and salt. Set aside.

2. In the large bowl of an electric mixer, using paddle or beaters, on medium speed, beat the butter. Add the granulated and brown sugars, and when the sugar is incorporated, raise the speed to high and continue to mix until fluffy, scraping down sides of bowl and under beaters as necessary. Add the peanut butter and beat well.

3. Lower speed to medium, add the eggs, 1 at a time, the vanilla, and the melted chocolate, and beat until well mixed, scraping down sides of bowl as necessary. Turn speed to low, gradually pour in the flour mixture, and beat just until combined. Add nuts and chocolate chips, and again beat just until combined. Scrape out of bowl, wrap in plastic wrap, and refrigerate until firm, 2 to 3 hours or, better still, overnight.

4. Position rack in center of oven and preheat oven to 350 degrees.

5. Line 1 or 2 baking trays with parchment paper. Pinch off about 1 ounce cookie dough and roll into a ball, about 1 inch in diameter. Place on the prepared baking trays and repeat

(continued)

CHOCOLATE PEANUT BUTTER CHOCOLATE CHIP COOKIES *(continued)*

TO PREPARE AHEAD

THROUGH STEP 5

with the remaining dough, arranging the balls about 2 inches apart. Bake until cookies feel *almost* firm to the touch, 14 to 15 minutes, reversing trays back to front after 7 to 8 minutes. Remove to rack to cool with a wide metal spatula.

Chocolate Biscotti

MAKES 3 LOGS, EACH ABOUT 1 POUND, 3 OUNCES, EACH CUT INTO 28 TO 30 SLICES

EQUIPMENT

Sifter

Electric mixer

Plastic wrap

1 or 2 baking trays

Parchment paper

1 or 2 racks to fit into baking trays

Long, serrated knife

INGREDIENTS

4 cups all-purpose flour

1 cup unsweetened cocoa

1 tablespoon baking powder

8 ounces (2 sticks) unsalted butter, at room temperature, cut into pieces

1¼ cups granulated sugar

4 eggs plus 1 egg white, lightly beaten, for egg wash

2 teaspoons brandy

The chocolate adds another dimension to the biscotti, giving them a cookielike dense texture.

1. Sift together the flour, cocoa, and baking powder. Set aside.

2. In the large bowl of an electric mixer, with paddle or beaters, beat the butter and sugar. Start on low speed until slightly blended, then raise speed to high and continue to beat until fluffy.

3. Turn speed to medium, and add eggs, 1 at a time, beating just to combine after each addition. Add brandy and vanilla. On low speed, slowly pour in the sifted ingredients and beat just until combined. Add the nuts and chocolate chips, again beating just until incorporated into the batter.

4. Divide dough into 3 equal portions, each about 1 pound, 3 ounces. With lightly floured hands and on a lightly floured surface, form each portion into a log, about 15 inches long and 1

1½ teaspoons vanilla extract

About 2 cups (½ pound)
walnut halves

1 cup chocolate chips

About 3 tablespoons crystal sugar

TO PREPARE AHEAD

THROUGH STEP 6, LOGS CAN
BE FROZEN. DEFROST,
WRAPPED, IN
REFRIGERATOR, AND
CONTINUE WITH RECIPE.
THROUGH STEP 8, BISCOTTI
WILL KEEP WELL FOR 2 TO 3
WEEKS.

inch in diameter. Wrap each log in plastic wrap, place on a baking tray, and refrigerate until firm, 2 to 3 hours.

5. Position rack in center of oven and preheat oven to 325 degrees.

6. When firm, unwrap one of the logs and place on a baking tray lined with parchment paper. If placing 2 logs on the tray, arrange them about 4 inches apart, since the logs will spread during the baking process. (The chocolate log does not spread as much as the pistachio log.) Brush each log with egg wash and sprinkle about 1 tablespoon crystal sugar down the length of the log. Bake until slightly firm to the touch, about 35 minutes. (There will be cracks in the log. That's okay.) Place tray on a rack and let logs cool. Do not remove log from tray while hot, since it might break. When completely cool, wrap in plastic wrap, and carefully set logs on a flat surface in refrigerator overnight.

7. The next day, preheat oven to 275 degrees. Fit a rack into a baking tray.

8. Unwrap a log and place on a cutting board. Using a sawing motion, and on a sharp angle, cut off one of the ends. Carefully cut slices at a sharp angle, a scant ½ inch thick, about 4 inches long, making 28 to 30 slices. (Ends can be used, too, if desired.) As each log is sliced, arrange the slices on the rack in the baking tray. Bake until the slices harden, about 35 minutes. At first the slices will be soft, but they will harden as they bake. Repeat with the remaining logs. Cool on the rack. Store in an airtight container.

Biscotti with Chocolate Chunks, Raisins, and Nuts

MAKES 3 LOGS, EACH ABOUT 1 POUND, 4 OUNCES,
EACH CUT INTO 30 TO 32 SLICES

EQUIPMENT

Sifter

Electric mixer

Plastic wrap

1 or 2 baking trays

1 or 2 racks to fit into baking trays

Parchment paper

Long, serrated knife

INGREDIENTS

4 cups all-purpose flour

1½ teaspoons baking powder

8 ounces (2 sticks) unsalted butter, at room temperature, cut into small pieces

1¾ cups granulated sugar

4 eggs plus 1 egg white, lightly beaten, for egg wash

1½ teaspoons vanilla extract

8 ounces bittersweet chocolate, cut into very small chunks

¾ cup raisins, dark or golden

¾ cup (about 3 ounces) pecan halves, toasted* and cooled

2 tablespoons cinnamon sugar

3 teaspoons unsweetened cocoa, sifted

*T*his dough is a little softer and stickier than other biscotti dough. The raisins can be dark or golden, the nuts walnut halves, toasted almonds, or hazelnuts, but the chocolate should be a good bittersweet chocolate rather than chocolate chips, as the small chunks melt into the dough, adding to the flavor and texture.

1. Sift together the flour and baking powder. Set aside.

2. In the large bowl of an electric mixer, with paddle or beaters, beat the butter and sugar. Start on low speed until slightly blended, then raise speed to high and continue to beat until fluffy.

3. Turn speed to medium, add eggs, 1 at a time, beating just to combine after each addition, and the vanilla. On low speed, slowly pour in the sifted ingredients and finally add the chocolate, raisins, and pecans, beating just until incorporated into the batter.

4. Divide the dough into 3 equal portions, each about 1 pound, 4 ounces. On a lightly floured surface, with lightly floured hands, roll out each portion into a log, about 15 inches long and 1 inch in diameter. Wrap each log in plastic wrap, place on a baking tray, and refrigerate until firm, 2 to 3 hours.

* To toast, arrange nuts on a small baking tray and bake in a preheated 350-degree oven for 15 minutes, turning nuts after 7 to 8 minutes to toast evenly.

To Prepare Ahead

THROUGH STEP 4, LOGS CAN
BE FROZEN. DEFROST,
WRAPPED, IN REFRIGERATOR
AND CONTINUE WITH RECIPE.
THROUGH STEP 9, BISCOTTI
WILL KEEP 2 TO 3 WEEKS.

5. Position rack in center of oven and preheat oven to 325 degrees.

6. In a small cup, stir together the cinnamon sugar and sifted cocoa. Set aside.

7. When firm, unwrap one of the logs and place on a baking tray lined with parchment paper. If placing more than 1 log on the tray, arrange them about 4 inches apart, since the logs will spread during the baking process. Brush each log with egg wash and spoon a generous amount of the cinnamon mixture down the length of the log. Bake until golden, 35 to 40 minutes. (There will be cracks on the surface of the log. That's okay.) Place tray on a rack and let logs cool. Do not remove logs from tray while hot, as they might break. When completely cool, wrap in plastic wrap and carefully set in the refrigerator overnight. Repeat with the remaining logs, egg wash, and cinnamon mixture.

8. The next day, preheat oven to 275 degrees and fit a rack into a baking tray.

9. Unwrap a log and place on a cutting board. Using a sawing motion, and on a sharp angle, cut off one of the ends. Continue to cut slices at a sharp angle, about ½ inch thick and about 4 inches long, making 30 to 32 slices. (Ends can be used, too.) As the log is sliced, arrange the slices on the rack in the baking tray. Bake until the biscotti are lightly golden around the edges, about 35 minutes. At first the biscotti will be soft, but as they bake they will harden. Remove from oven and let cool on the rack. Repeat with the remaining logs. When completely cool, store in an airtight container.

Pistachio Biscotti

MAKES 3 LOGS, EACH ABOUT 1 POUND, 3 OUNCES,
EACH CUT INTO 28 TO 30 SLICES

EQUIPMENT

Sifter

Electric mixer

Plastic wrap

1 or 2 baking trays

Parchment paper

1 or 2 racks to fit into baking trays

Long, serrated knife

INGREDIENTS

5 cups all-purpose flour

1 tablespoon baking powder

1 tablespoon crushed anise seed

*8 ounces (2 sticks) unsalted butter,
cut into pieces, at room
temperature*

1¼ cups granulated sugar

*4 eggs plus 1 egg white, lightly
beaten, for egg wash*

2 teaspoons Amaretto

1½ teaspoons vanilla extract*

1½ cups (½ pound) pistachio nuts

About 3 tablespoons crystal sugar

Whole hazelnuts or unblanched almonds can be substituted for the pistachio nuts. Lightly toast the nuts and remove as much of the skins as possible. Biscotti can be cut into thinner or thicker slices, if desired. Baking time will remain the same. Biscotti, after the first baking, should be refrigerated overnight.

1. Sift together the flour and baking powder. Add crushed anise seed to sifted ingredients. Set aside.

2. In the large bowl of an electric mixer, with paddle or beaters, beat the butter and sugar. Start on low speed until slightly blended, then raise speed to high and continue to beat until fluffy, scraping down sides of bowl and under beaters as necessary.

3. Lower speed to medium and add eggs, 1 at a time, beating just to combine after each addition. Add Amaretto and vanilla. Turn speed to low, slowly pour in the sifted ingredients, add the nuts, and beat just until incorporated into the batter.

4. Divide dough into 3 equal portions, about 1 pound, 3 ounces each. With lightly floured hands and on a lightly floured surface, roll each portion into a log, about 15 inches long and 1 inch in diameter. Wrap each log in plastic wrap, place on a baking tray, and refrigerate until firm, 2 to 3 hours.

5. Position rack in center of oven and preheat oven to 325 degrees.

*If alcohol is not used, increase amount of vanilla to 3½ teaspoons.

TO PREPARE AHEAD

THROUGH STEP 4, LOGS CAN
BE FROZEN. DEFROST,
WRAPPED, IN REFRIGERATOR
AND CONTINUE WITH RECIPE.
THROUGH STEP 8, BISCOTTI
WILL KEEP 2 TO 3 WEEKS.

6. When firm, unwrap one of the logs and place on a baking tray lined with parchment paper. If placing more than 1 log on the tray, arrange them about 4 inches apart, since the logs will spread during the baking process. Brush each log with egg wash and sprinkle about 1 tablespoon crystal sugar down the length of the roll. Bake until lightly golden, about 35 minutes. There will be cracks on the surface of the log. That's okay. Place tray on a rack and let logs cool. Do not remove log from tray while hot; it might break. When completely cool, wrap in plastic wrap, and carefully set in the refrigerator overnight. Repeat with the remaining logs, egg wash, and crystal sugar.

7. The next day, preheat oven to 275 degrees and fit a rack into a baking tray.

8. Unwrap a log and place on a cutting board. Using a sawing motion and, on a sharp angle, cut off one of the ends. Continue to cut slices at a sharp angle, a scant ½ inch thick, about 4 inches long, making 28 to 30 slices.* (Ends can be used, if desired . . . the taste is just as good.) As the roll is sliced, arrange the slices on the rack in the baking tray. Bake until the slices are lightly golden around the edges, about 35 minutes. At first the biscotti will be soft, but as they bake, they will harden. Remove from oven and let cool on the rack. Repeat with the remaining logs, egg wash, and crystal sugar. Store in an airtight container.

*The roll can be sliced straight across, if desired, resulting in smaller slices.

Apricot Coconut Macaroons

MAKES ABOUT 2 DOZEN MACAROONS

*T*hese macaroons were created originally for the Passover seder held at Spago every year. However, they proved to be so popular that now they are baked and served all year round. These are flavorful and moist. The unsweetened coconut used in the recipe can usually be obtained in health food stores.

1. Position rack in center of oven and preheat oven to 350 degrees. Line 1 or 2 baking trays with parchment paper.

2. In a small saucepan, combine the apricots, water, and 1 tablespoon sugar. Over medium heat, poach the apricots until tender and about 1 tablespoon of water remains. Cool slightly and transfer to a food processor fitted with the steel blade.

3. Add the remaining ¾ cup sugar, the egg whites, and ½ cup coconut, and process until the apricots are pureed. Start with on/off turns and then let the machine run. Transfer to the large bowl of an electric mixer fitted with paddle or beaters. Add the remaining 4 cups of coconut and, on medium speed, beat until the coconut is well combined. Stop the machine and check the texture—the mixture should hold together when pinched. Continue to mix as necessary.

4. Form the macaroons: With lightly moistened fingers, using 2 ounces of the mixture for each macaroon, shape 24 to 26 small pointed haystacks. Pinch the top of each haystack (see illustration) and arrange on prepared baking trays, about 2 inches apart. Bake until the tops are well browned, 15 to 20 minutes. Cool on a rack and use as needed.

EQUIPMENT

1 or 2 baking trays

Parchment paper

Small saucepan

Food processor

Electric mixer

INGREDIENTS

3 ounces (½ cup, packed) dried apricots, each cut into 3 or 4 pieces

½ cup water

¾ cup plus 1 tablespoon granulated sugar

3 egg whites

4½ cups (11 ounces) unsweetened shredded coconut

TO PREPARE AHEAD

THROUGH STEP 4. STORE IN AIRTIGHT CONTAINER.

XIII

Shortcakes

Shortcakes are the flaky biscuits that top cobblers or serve as the base for strawberry shortcake. Ours are rich and cakelike in texture. Not only are they a significant part of cobblers and fruit shortcakes, they can be split, warmed, and eaten with your favorite preserve.

Cobblers are deep-dish fruit pies, usually with shortcakes arranged on the fruit. However, at Spago, we sometimes top the cobblers with nests of phyllo dough.

Because the fruit, when baked, oozes so much liquid, the tops of the cobblers are sprinkled with Streusel (see page 171), which absorbs some of the liquid and adds crunch to the cobbler.

BASIC SHORTCAKES

STRAWBERRY SHORTCAKES

PEACH AND BERRY COBBLER

SUMMER FRUIT COBBLER WITH SHORTCAKES

CHOCOLATE SHORTCAKES

SPAGO BANANA SPLIT

Hot Fudge Sauce

SUMMER FRUIT COBBLER WITH PHYLLO NESTS

Phyllo Pastry Circles

Basic Shortcakes

MAKES 10 SHORTCAKES

Since shortcakes can be eaten alone, with sweet butter or with softly whipped cream and a fresh fruit preserve, you might want to add raisins or bits of candied ginger to the batter.

1. Position rack in center of oven and preheat oven to 375 degrees. Line 1 or 2 baking trays with parchment paper.

2. In a food processor fitted with the steel blade, combine the flour, ¼ cup sugar, orange zest, baking powder, and salt with 2 or 3 on/off turns. Arrange the butter around the blade and process just until combined. With the motor running, pour the cream through the feed tube, stopping just before the dough forms a ball.

3. Turn out the dough onto a lightly floured surface and gently knead, forming a smooth ball. Do not overwork. With the rolling pin, roll out the dough to a ¾-inch-thick round. Using a 3-inch cookie or biscuit cutter, cut out 7 circles, dipping the cutter into flour as necessary. Arrange on the baking trays as they are cut out, about 2 inches apart. Knead the scraps together, roll again to a ¾-inch-thick round, and cut out 3 more circles. Arrange on the baking trays.

4. Using a clean, dry pastry brush, brush the tops of the circles with cream and sprinkle lightly with sugar. Bake 5 minutes, reduce the heat to 350 degrees, and bake until the cakes are golden and firm to the touch, 25 to 30 minutes longer. Cool on a rack.

5. When ready to serve, split each shortcake in half and warm slightly.

Strawberry Shortcakes

SERVES 10

*W*hen I was a child, I always ordered strawberry shortcake when I was taken to a restaurant. The cakes were packaged, the fruit out of the freezer compartment, but I loved the way it all looked. Now that I know better, this is truly one of my favorite desserts, made with flaky biscuits and fresh fruit, and served with softly whipped cream.

1. Line 1 or 2 baking trays with parchment paper.

2. Make the compote: In a medium nonreactive saucepan, combine berries, sugar, and cinnamon sticks. Cook over medium-high heat until compote thickens slightly and just coats the back of a spoon, about 15 minutes. Cool.

3. On a lightly floured surface, roll out Basic Shortcake dough to a circle ¾ inch thick. Using a 2-inch cookie cutter, dipped in flour, cut out as many rounds as possible. Gently knead the scraps together, reroll the dough, and continue to cut out rounds. Repeat as necessary until there are 20 rounds. Arrange on prepared baking trays, about 2 inches apart. Brush tops with cream and sprinkle with crystal sugar. Bake until shortcakes are golden brown and firm to the touch, about 35 minutes. Cool on rack.

4. Pour cream into large bowl of electric mixer (or you can use a wire whip and large bowl) and with beater or whip, whip to firm peaks.

5. To serve, cut each shortcake in half with a serrated knife and warm slightly. For each serving, arrange 2 shortcake bot-

EQUIPMENT

1 or 2 baking trays

Parchment paper

Medium nonreactive saucepan

Rolling pin

2-inch cookie or biscuit cutter

Pastry brush

Electric mixer or whip

Large bowl

Serrated knife

INGREDIENTS

STRAWBERRY COMPOTE

Three 1-pint baskets strawberries, hulled and cut into thick slices

¾ cup granulated sugar

1½ cinnamon sticks

1 recipe Basic Shortcakes (see page 224)

Crystal sugar for sprinkling

About 2 cups chilled heavy cream

(continued)

STRAWBERRY SHORTCAKES *(continued)*

TO PREPARE AHEAD

THROUGH STEP 1, COMPOTE
CAN BE MADE THE DAY
BEFORE. THROUGH STEP 5,
SHORTCAKES CAN BE MADE
EARLY IN THE DAY AND
WARMED AS NEEDED. CREAM
CAN BE WHIPPED 1 TO 2
HOURS AHEAD OF TIME AND
REFRIGERATED, COVERED.
WHISK ONCE OR TWICE JUST
BEFORE SERVING.

toms on a plate and top with a little of the compote and a large dollop of whipped cream. Cover with the remaining halves of the shortcake and spoon the remaining compote around. Serve immediately.

Peach and Berry Cobbler

SERVES 12

EQUIPMENT

1 or 2 baking trays

Parchment paper

Rolling pin

2½-inch cookie cutter

Pastry brush

Large bowl

An oven-to-table baking dish, approximately 8½ x 13½ x 2½ inches

*W*hen summer fruit is abundant, cobblers are a most welcome dessert. They are wonderfully homey, and the fruit can be as varied as the market and imagination allow.

1. Make the shortcakes: Preheat oven to 375 degrees. Line 1 or 2 baking trays with parchment paper.

2. Roll out the dough to ½-inch thickness. Using a 2½-inch cutter, and rerolling the dough as necessary, cut out 12 circles. Arrange the circles on the prepared tray, brush the tops with cream, and sprinkle lightly with sugar. Bake 5 minutes, reduce the oven temperature to 350 degrees, and continue baking just until lightly golden, 15 to 20 minutes.

INGREDIENTS

*1 recipe Basic Shortcakes
(see page 224)*

Heavy cream

Sugar

FILLING

*3 pounds (8 or 9 large) ripe
peaches*

*4 cups (2 baskets) blackberries,
blueberries, or raspberries (or a
combination)*

3 tablespoons dark brown sugar

3 tablespoons all-purpose flour

3 tablespoons lemon juice

*2 tablespoons kirsch or Grand
Marnier*

½ teaspoon ground cinnamon

Pinch of freshly grated nutmeg

⅓ cup Streusel (see page 171)

TO PREPARE AHEAD

THROUGH STEP 5, REHEATING
WHEN READY TO SERVE

3. Make the filling: Blanch the peaches*, peel, cut in half, and remove the pits. Cut each half into 4 slices and place in a large mixing bowl. Combine with the remaining ingredients, except Streusel, and gently toss to combine thoroughly. Let sit 20 to 30 minutes.

4. Raise oven temperature to 375 degrees.

5. Lightly butter an oven-to-table baking dish, approximately 8½ x 13½ x 2½ inches. Spoon the fruit into the dish, spreading it as evenly as possible. Sprinkle the Streusel over and arrange the shortcakes on top. (There will be 3 rows, 4 shortcakes in each row). Bake until the shortcakes are nicely browned, about 40 minutes.

6. To serve: Warm the cobbler, if made earlier in the day. Serve with softly whipped cream or your favorite ice cream or as is, with sifted confectioners' sugar sprinkled over just before serving.

---

*To blanch peaches, bring a large pot of water to a boil. Turn off heat, and place 2 or 3 peaches in water for 30 seconds so that peel comes off easily. (The riper the peach, the more easily the peel can be removed.) Immediately refresh the blanched peaches in cold water. Bring water back to a boil and continue blanching peaches 2 or 3 at a time.

Summer Fruit Cobbler with Shortcakes

SERVES 10

This is a variation of Strawberry Shortcake made by sautéeing the summer fruit and spooning it over shortcakes.

1. Make 10 shortcakes and set aside.

2. In a large sauté pan, over medium heat, brown the butter with the vanilla bean and its scrapings. (When the butter begins to have a nutty aroma and turns golden brown, it is ready.) Sprinkle the sugar over but *do not* stir. Add the nectarines, berries, cinnamon stick, and lemon juice, and pour in the wine. Cook until the fruit is tender, 10 to 15 minutes, stirring frequently but gently, keeping the fruit intact. Excessive stirring will break up the fruit. Remove from heat and let cool.

3. To serve, cut shortcakes in half with a serrated knife, place on a baking tray, and warm slightly in a low oven. Arrange the bottom half on a dessert plate or bowl, top with a scoop of Vanilla Ice Cream, and spoon about ½ cup fruit mixture over the ice cream. Cover with the remaining half of shortcake and sift a little confectioners' sugar over, if desired. Repeat with the remaining shortcakes, ice cream, fruit, and sifted sugar.

Chocolate Shortcakes

EQUIPMENT

Food processor

Rolling pin

2-inch cookie cutter

Parchment paper

Baking tray

INGREDIENTS

2 cups all-purpose flour

1 cup unsweetened cocoa

⅓ cup granulated sugar

*1 tablespoon plus 1 teaspoon
baking powder*

1 teaspoon salt

*6 ounces (1½ sticks) unsalted
butter, chilled, cut into small
pieces*

½ cup semisweet chocolate chips

1 cup heavy cream

TO PREPARE AHEAD

THROUGH STEP 4

*T*his is the base we use for the Spago Banana Split (see page 230).

1. In a food processor fitted with the steel blade, combine the flour, cocoa, sugar, baking powder, and salt with a few on/off turns. Add the butter, arranging around the bowl, and process until mixture resembles fine meal. Add the chocolate chips and process with on/off turns. With the motor running, pour the cream through the feed tube until the dough comes together in a mass. Remove from processor and wrap in plastic wrap. Refrigerate until firm, 2 to 3 hours.

2. When firm, on a very lightly floured surface, roll out dough to an 8-inch round or square that is about 1 inch thick. Using a 2-inch cookie cutter, cut out 7 circles. Dip the cookie cutter into flour before cutting out each cake to prevent dough from sticking. As cakes are cut out, arrange on a parchment-paper-lined baking tray. Reroll the dough into a 5-inch round and cut out 3 more circles. Do not reroll more than once or cakes will not bake evenly and will crack more readily. Refrigerate cakes for about 30 minutes.

3. Position rack in center of oven and preheat oven to 350 degrees.

4. Bake until tester, gently poked into the center of 1 of the cakes, comes out clean, about 30 minutes, reversing baking tray after 15 minutes. Cool on rack. Use for Spago Banana Split or as desired.

Spago Banana Split

SERVES 8

EQUIPMENT

One or two 12-inch skillets

Baking tray

Serrated knife

INGREDIENTS

*½ cup plus 2 tablespoons
granulated sugar*

*8 large bananas, peeled, ends
discarded, cut into ½-inch round
slices*

*2 tablespoons banana liqueur,
Grand Marnier, or liqueur of your
choice*

*8 Chocolate Shortcakes
(see page 229), baked*

Vanilla Ice Cream (see page 253)

Hot Fudge Sauce (see page 231)

Sifted confectioners' sugar

TO PREPARE AHEAD

THROUGH STEP 1

*T*his is one of our more popular desserts. At Spago the banana split is made with vanilla ice cream, but you can choose your favorite flavor. Top with a dollop of whipped cream.

1. Caramelize the bananas: (If you have only 1 large skillet, wash and dry between uses.) In a 12-inch skillet, spread ¼ cup sugar. Arrange bananas in circles, starting at the outside edge of the skillet, working toward the very center. Sprinkle 1 tablespoon sugar over the circles of bananas. Cook over medium-high heat just until sugar caramelizes, 2 to 3 minutes. (Don't allow the bananas to get too soft.) Remove from heat, spoon 1 tablespoon liqueur over, and immediately spread out on baking tray to cool. Repeat with the remaining sugar, bananas, and liqueur.

2. Make the banana split: With a serrated knife, cut the short-cakes in half and place the bottom half in the center of each of 8 dessert plates. Build the banana split. Start with a scoop of Vanilla Ice Cream, Hot Fudge Sauce, a generous dollop of whipped cream if desired, and scatter some of the caramelized bananas around. Place the remaining half of cake on top and sprinkle with sifted confectioners' sugar. Serve immediately.

Hot Fudge Sauce

MAKES ABOUT 4½ CUPS

❧

If kept refrigerated, covered, this sauce will last for up to 2 weeks.

1. In a small heatproof bowl, set over barely simmering water, melt the chocolate until almost melted. Then turn off the heat and let stand over the warm water until completely melted, stirring occasionally.

INGREDIENTS

15 ounces bittersweet chocolate, cut into small pieces

½ cup granulated sugar

1 cup light corn syrup

1 cup plus 2 tablespoons cold water

1½ cups unsweetened cocoa powder

1½ tablespoons instant coffee

6 tablespoons cognac or brandy, optional

2. Meanwhile, in a large saucepan, combine the sugar, corn syrup, water, cocoa, and instant coffee and bring to a boil. Simmer for 1 to 2 minutes, stirring constantly to prevent burning on the bottom. When the surface is covered with bubbles, remove from the heat and whisk in the melted chocolate. Reduce, over low heat, until the mixture thickens. Stir in the cognac, if desired, and pour through a fine strainer. Use as needed. When cool, refrigerate, covered.

TO PREPARE AHEAD

THROUGH STEP 2. WHEN NEEDED, REHEAT OVER SIMMERING WATER OR OVER A VERY LOW FLAME.

Summer Fruit Cobbler with Phyllo Nests

SERVES 8

EQUIPMENT

8 ramekins, each 4½ x 1 inch

Medium saucepan

Small and large bowls

Baking pan large enough to hold the 8 ramekins

Baking tray

Parchment paper

INGREDIENTS

PHYLLO PASTRY CIRCLES

Package of phyllo pastry

⅓ cup granulated sugar

½ teaspoon ground cinnamon

Vegetable spray

FRUIT COBBLER

2 pounds (about 6 medium) nectarines, halved, pitted, and cut into ¼-inch slices

1 pound cherries, pitted and kept whole

¾ pound (about 8 medium) apricots, halved, pitted, and cut into thin slices

1½ cups granulated sugar

¼ cup fresh lemon juice

¼ cup all-purpose flour

1 vanilla bean, split lengthwise

At Spago we make our cobblers in individual ramekins, but this can also be assembled in a 2-quart oven-to-table baking dish. Nests of baked phyllo pastry are placed on top. When serving, spoon out individual portions onto dessert plates and serve with Crème Anglaise (see page 6) spooned over.

1. Position rack in center of oven and preheat oven to 350 degrees. Coat eight 4½ x 1-inch ramekins with vegetable spray. Set aside.

2. Make the phyllo nests: Do not unroll the pastry. Place the roll on a firm surface and cut into strips, about ¼ inch wide each. Toss the strips together as if you were tossing fettuccine. You should have about 8 cups.

3. You will need 1 cup loosely packed strips of phyllo to make each 4-inch circle. In a small bowl, combine the cinnamon and sugar and set aside.

4. On a parchment-paper-lined baking tray, arrange 1 cup loosely packed phyllo strips into a 4-inch circle. Repeat until you have 8 circles. Sprinkle each circle with cinnamon sugar and then lightly spray with vegetable spray. Bake until crispy and golden brown, 15 to 20 minutes. Cool on a rack.

5. Make the cobbler: In a medium saucepan, combine the nectarines, cherries, apricots, sugar, lemon juice, flour, vanilla bean with its scrapings, cinnamon stick, and freshly grated nutmeg. Cook, stirring occasionally, just until the fruit

1 cinnamon stick

About 6 scrapings of fresh nutmeg

Two 1-pint baskets blackberries

About ⅓ cup Streusel

(see page 171)

TO PREPARE AHEAD

THROUGH STEP 4, THE
PHYLLO NESTS CAN BE MADE
EARLY IN THE DAY. IN STEP
6, RAMEKINS CAN BE FILLED
EARLY AS WELL. CONTINUE
WITH RECIPE ABOUT AN HOUR
BEFORE SERVING SO THAT
THE COBBLER WILL STILL BE
WARM WHEN NEEDED.

is *al dente* and the juice thickens, about 5 minutes. (The fruit shouldn't be soft, since it will be baked.)

6. Transfer the fruit to a large bowl and remove the vanilla bean and cinnamon stick. Stir in the blackberries. Divide the fruit among the prepared ramekins and sprinkle a little Streusel on top. Set in a baking pan and pour boiling water halfway up the sides of the ramekins. Bake until the juices thicken, about 30 minutes. Remove the ramekins from the baking pan, cool slightly, and place a circle of baked phyllo pastry on top of each ramekin.

7. To serve, serve warm, setting a ramekin on each of 8 dessert plates.

XIV

Frozen Desserts

It wasn't too long ago that making ice cream or sorbet at home was an ordeal. If you were lucky enough to own an ice cream maker, it was one that required ice and salt and a strong arm with which to crank the contraption. Today, with the advent of the electric ice cream machine, those of us who love to eat as well as prepare these tempting frozen desserts can do so with a great deal of ease.

The fruit sorbets are all made with a sugar syrup, the fruit cooked in the syrup. We use only seasonal fruit—apples, grapes, pineapples, bananas, lemons, and oranges during the winter months; plums, apricots, melon, and assorted berries during the summer. Sorbets made with fruit juice require no cooking. Alcohol, added to some of the sorbets, gives an extra boost to the flavor, but alcohol can be optional.

The ice creams we have selected for this book are the ones most in demand at Spago. All have the same base, but the variations are limitless. Chocolate and/or marshmallow bits can be added to Chocolate Ice Cream; broken pieces of amaretto cookies to Peach Ice Cream; dried fruit soaked in brandy or Armagnac and then pureed can be combined with Vanilla or Chocolate Ice Cream.

Sorbets and ice creams are at their best when churned the day they are being served. The base, however, can be made 1 or 2 days ahead and refrigerated, covered, until needed.

APPLE GRAPE SORBET

BANANA SORBET

Simple Sugar Syrup

CHOCOLATE SORBET

GRAPEFRUIT VODKA SORBET

MIXED BERRY SORBET

PINEAPPLE DAIQUIRI SORBET

STRAWBERRY DAIQUIRI SORBET

TEQUILA SUNRISE SORBET

CHOCOLATE ICE CREAM

CINNAMON ICE CREAM

EGGNOG ICE CREAM

HONEY ICE CREAM

PEACH ICE CREAM

VANILLA ICE CREAM

MILK CHOCOLATE MALT ICE CREAM

STRAWBERRY ICE CREAM

WHITE CHOCOLATE MINT ICE CREAM WITH WHITE
CHOCOLATE MINT TRUFFLES

White Chocolate Mint Truffles

VANILLA PARFAIT WITH STRAWBERRY SAUCE

RED, WHITE, AND BLUE PARFAIT

Apple Grape Sorbet

MAKES ABOUT 1 QUART

❧

*T*his combination of two very available fruits results in a flavorful and refreshing sorbet. Red, white, or black grapes and apples of your choice can be used. Because the seeds of apples can give a bitter taste to the finished product, remove them before cooking the fruit.

EQUIPMENT

Large nonreactive saucepan

Food processor or blender

Strainer

Large bowl

Ice cream maker

INGREDIENTS

2 pounds grapes, stemmed

1½ pounds (5 medium) apples, seeded and cut into quarters

2 cups granulated sugar

1 tablespoon orange zest (from about 2 oranges), chopped fine

1 large or 2 small cinnamon sticks

1 cup water

TO PREPARE AHEAD

THROUGH STEP 2, THE DAY BEFORE NEEDED, REFRIGERATING BASE, COVERED, AND CONTINUING WITH RECIPE THE NEXT DAY. OR THROUGH STEP 3, SORBET CAN BE MADE EARLY IN THE DAY AND PLACED IN FREEZER. TRANSFER FROM FREEZER TO REFRIGERATOR ABOUT 30 MINUTES BEFORE YOU ARE READY TO SCOOP.

1. In a large nonreactive saucepan, combine all the ingredients. Cook over medium heat until the fruit is very soft, about 30 minutes. Cool slightly and remove cinnamon stick(s).

2. Puree in food processor or blender, in 2 or 3 batches so that the puree does not run out of the machine. Strain into a large bowl and chill over ice cubes and water.

3. Transfer to ice cream maker and freeze according to the manufacturer's directions. Scrape into chilled container, cover, and freeze until needed.

4. To serve, place 1 or 2 scoops of sorbet in a small bowl. If desired, serve with slices of caramelized apples (see step 1, page 148), spooned over and around sorbet.

Banana Sorbet

EQUIPMENT

Medium nonreactive saucepan

Food processor or blender

Ice cream maker

INGREDIENTS

*2 cups Simple Sugar Syrup
(see page 241)*

3 tablespoons fresh lemon juice

*1¾ pounds ripe bananas, peeled
and sliced*

1 cup water

¼ cup rum, optional

TO PREPARE AHEAD

THROUGH STEP 3, SORBET
CAN BE MADE EARLY IN THE
DAY AND PLACED IN THE
FREEZER UNTIL NEEDED.
TRANSFER TO REFRIGERATOR
ABOUT 30 MINUTES BEFORE
YOU ARE READY TO SCOOP.

Select bananas that are very ripe but not brown. Freeze immediately after pureeing the bananas because, like peeled bananas, the base will turn brown if left exposed to air too long.

1. In a medium nonreactive saucepan, heat sugar syrup with lemon juice. Add the sliced bananas and cook for 5 minutes. Stir in the water.

2. In a food processor or blender, puree in batches so that the puree does not overflow the machine. Do not strain. Stir in the rum, if desired.

3. Pour into the ice cream maker and freeze according to the manufacturer's directions. Scrape into a chilled container and freeze, covered, until needed.

4. To serve, place 1 or 2 scoops in a small bowl and top with caramelized bananas (see step 1, page 230) if desired. Serve immediately.

Simple Sugar Syrup

MAKES ABOUT 3 CUPS

❧

EQUIPMENT

Medium saucepan

INGREDIENTS

3 cups water

2⅓ cups granulated sugar

TO PREPARE AHEAD

THROUGH STEP 1, SUGAR
SYRUP, REFRIGERATED,
WILL KEEP ALMOST
INDEFINITELY.

*M*any of our sorbets are made with sugar syrup, and a large container of syrup is always on hand in our walk-in refrigerator. Sugar syrup can be used to sweeten iced tea, iced coffee, and cold lemonade.

1. In a medium saucepan, stir together the water and sugar. Over medium heat, bring to a boil and boil until the mixture is clear and the sugar dissolves completely, 3 to 5 minutes. Pour into a clean jar and let cool. Refrigerate, covered, and use as needed.

Chocolate Sorbet

MAKES ABOUT 1¹/₂ QUARTS

At Spago we use Valrhona bittersweet chocolate and cocoa. Use the very best chocolate and cocoa you can find. It makes a difference in the flavor of the sorbet.

1. In a large saucepan, combine the water and sugar and bring to a boil. Let boil until the sugar dissolves, 3 to 5 minutes. Remove from heat, stir in the chocolate and cocoa, and continue to stir until the chocolate is completely melted. Strain into a large bowl and chill over ice cubes and cold water.

2. Pour into an ice cream maker and freeze according to the manufacturer's directions. Scrape into a chilled container and place in the freezer, covered, until needed.

3. To serve, place 1 or 2 scoops in a small bowl. Surround with seeded tangerine slices or Candied Grapefruit Peel (see page 188) and serve immediately.

EQUIPMENT

Large saucepan

Strainer

Large bowl

Ice cream maker

INGREDIENTS

1 quart water

1¾ cups granulated sugar

1 pound bittersweet chocolate, cut into very small pieces

1 cup unsweetened cocoa

TO PREPARE AHEAD

THROUGH STEP 1, REFRIGERATING, COVERED, OVERNIGHT AND CONTINUING WITH RECIPE THE NEXT DAY. OR THROUGH STEP 2, PLACING IN REFRIGERATOR 30 MINUTES BEFORE SCOOPING.

Grapefruit Vodka Sorbet

MAKES ABOUT 2 QUARTS

EQUIPMENT

Large bowl

Ice cream maker

INGREDIENTS

4 cups fresh grapefruit juice

*3 cups Simple Sugar Syrup
(see page 241)*

1¼ cups vodka

2 tablespoons fresh lemon juice

TO PREPARE AHEAD

THROUGH STEP 2, SORBET
CAN BE MADE EARLY IN THE
DAY AND PLACED IN
FREEZER. TRANSFER TO
REFRIGERATOR ABOUT 30
MINUTES BEFORE YOU ARE
READY TO SCOOP.

This is the sorbet version of a Greyhound, a popular bar drink made from grapefruit juice and vodka. Use only freshly squeezed grapefruit juice for best results.

1. In a large bowl, combine all the ingredients. Taste and add more vodka, if necessary, by tablespoons, 1 at a time, but no more than ¼ cup.

2. Transfer to the ice cream maker and freeze according to the manufacturer's directions. Scrape into chilled container, cover, and freeze until needed.

3. To serve, place 1 or 2 scoops of sorbet in a small bowl. Top with a few Candied Grapefruit Peels (see page 188) if desired. Serve immediately.

Mixed Berry Sorbet

MAKES ABOUT 1 QUART

EQUIPMENT

Medium nonreactive saucepan

Food processor or blender

Strainer

Medium bowl

Ice cream maker

INGREDIENTS

*2 baskets (about 3 pounds)
strawberries, rinsed and hulled*

1¼ cups water

1¼ cups granulated sugar

*2 baskets (about 2½ pounds)
raspberries, rinsed or patted clean*

1 tablespoon lemon juice

TO PREPARE AHEAD

THROUGH STEP 2, BASE CAN
BE REFRIGERATED,
COVERED, THE DAY BEFORE
NEEDED AND RECIPE
CONTINUED THE NEXT DAY.
OR THROUGH STEP 3, SORBET
CAN BE MADE EARLY IN THE
DAY AND PLACED IN
FREEZER. TRANSFER TO
REFRIGERATOR ABOUT 30
MINUTES BEFORE YOU ARE
READY TO SCOOP.

*A*ny fruit can be combined in a mixed fruit sorbet, which makes this a perfect way to use leftover fruit. If tropical fruit is added, the sorbet will taste like a fruit punch.

1. In a medium nonreactive saucepan, combine the strawberries, water, and sugar and cook over medium heat. After 5 minutes, add the raspberries and continue to cook until berries are very soft, about 5 minutes longer. Remove from heat and let cool.

2. In a food processor or blender, puree the mixture. Strain into a medium bowl and flavor with lemon juice.

3. Transfer to ice cream maker and freeze according to the manufacturer's directions. Scrape into chilled container, cover, and freeze until needed.

4. To serve, place 1 or 2 scoops of sorbet in a small bowl and top with sliced or whole assorted berries. Serve immediately.

Pineapple Daiquiri Sorbet

MAKES ABOUT 2 QUARTS

❧

Large nonreactive saucepan

Food processor or blender

Fine-mesh strainer

Large bowl

Ice cream maker

2 pineapples, 3½ to 4 pounds each, peeled and cored, cores reserved

2 cups water

1½ cups granulated sugar

⅓ cup dark rum

3 tablespoons lime juice

Fresh mint sprigs

1 basket fresh raspberries, rinsed or patted clean

THROUGH STEP 2, REFRIGERATING, COVERED, UNTIL NEEDED. OR THROUGH STEP 3, TRANSFERRING TO REFRIGERATOR 30 MINUTES BEFORE SCOOPING.

*F*or this refreshing dessert, use only ripe, fresh pineapples.

1. Cut pineapples and the cores into 1-inch pieces. In a large nonreactive saucepan, combine pineapple, water, and sugar. Over medium heat, bring to a boil and cook, stirring occasionally, until fruit is soft, 15 to 20 minutes. Remove from heat and allow to cool.

2. When cool, puree, in 2 or 3 batches, in food processor or blender. Strain, through a fine strainer, into a large bowl. Stir in rum and lime juice.

3. Freeze in ice cream maker according to the manufacturer's directions. Scrape into chilled container, cover, and place in freezer until needed.

4. To serve, place 1 or 2 scoops in a small bowl. Garnish with a small sprig of fresh mint and a few raspberries. Serve immediately.

Strawberry Daiquiri Sorbet

MAKES 1½ QUARTS

EQUIPMENT

Heavy medium saucepan

Food processor or blender

Strainer

Medium bowl

Ice cream maker

INGREDIENTS

1½ cups water

1 cup granulated sugar

Four 1-pint baskets strawberries, rinsed and hulled

¼ cup dark rum plus additional, optional

2 tablespoons fresh lime juice

2 tablespoons orange liqueur (Triple Sec or Grand Marnier)

TO PREPARE AHEAD

THROUGH STEP 2, THE DAY BEFORE NEEDED, REFRIGERATING, COVERED, AND CONTINUING WITH RECIPE THE NEXT DAY. OR THROUGH STEP 3, SORBET CAN BE MADE EARLY IN THE DAY AND PLACED IN FREEZER. TRANSFER TO REFRIGERATOR ABOUT 30 MINUTES BEFORE YOU ARE READY TO SCOOP.

The rum should be added to taste. Start with ¼ cup, taste, and adjust accordingly.

1. Make sugar syrup: In a heavy medium saucepan, combine water and sugar. Over high heat, bring to a boil and let boil until sugar dissolves completely, stirring as necessary, 2 to 3 minutes. Remove from heat and cool slightly.

2. Puree strawberries in food processor or blender. Strain into medium bowl and stir in the rum, lime juice, liqueur, and sugar syrup.

3. Transfer to ice cream maker and freeze according to the manufacturer's directions. Scrape into chilled container, cover, and freeze until needed.

4. To serve, place 1 or 2 scoops of sorbet in a small bowl and surround with sliced fresh strawberries or mixed berries. Additional liqueur can be spooned over, if desired. Serve immediately.

Tequila Sunrise Sorbet

MAKES ABOUT 2 QUARTS

EQUIPMENT

Large bowl

Ice cream maker

INGREDIENTS

4 cups fresh orange juice

*1½ cups Simple Sugar Syrup
(see page 241)*

¾ cup tequila

3 tablespoons grenadine syrup

2 tablespoons lemon juice

Fresh mint leaves

1 orange, cut into slices

TO PREPARE AHEAD

THROUGH STEP 3. TRANSFER
TO REFRIGERATOR ABOUT 30
MINUTES BEFORE YOU ARE
READY TO SCOOP.

When Patrón tequila was first introduced to the United States, J. P. Dejoria asked Wolfgang to create an entire menu using the tequila. This is one of the desserts we served that night.

1. In a large bowl, combine all the ingredients except the mint leaves and the orange. Pour into the ice cream maker and freeze according to the manufacturer's directions.

2. Scrape into 1 or 2 chilled containers and place in the freezer until needed.

3. To serve, place 1 or 2 scoops in a small bowl and garnish with a few orange slices and mint leaves. Serve immediately.

Chocolate Ice Cream

MAKES ABOUT 1½ QUARTS

EQUIPMENT

Large nonreactive saucepan

Large heatproof bowl

Whip

Wooden spoon

Strainer

Large bowl

Ice cream maker

INGREDIENTS

2 cups heavy cream

2 cups milk

1 vanilla bean, split lengthwise

8 egg yolks

⅓ cup granulated sugar

8 ounces bittersweet chocolate, cut into small pieces and melted

¼ cup bourbon, optional

TO PREPARE AHEAD

IN STEP 2, DO NOT STRAIN BEFORE YOU REFRIGERATE OVERNIGHT. STRAIN JUST BEFORE FREEZING. FREEZE A FEW HOURS BEFORE SERVING. OR PREPARE THROUGH STEP 3. REMOVE ICE CREAM FROM FREEZER AND PLACE IN REFRIGERATOR 15 TO 30 MINUTES BEFORE YOU ARE GOING TO SERVE IT.

*I*ce cream, once frozen, has a short storage life, lasting no more than 2 days for maximum flavor. However, the base will last up to 4 days. We've selected the most popular Spago flavors for this book.

1. In a large nonreactive saucepan, bring to a boil the cream, milk, and vanilla bean with its scrapings.

2. In a large heatproof bowl, whisk together the egg yolks and sugar until thoroughly combined. Slowly whisk the hot cream mixture into the egg yolks and then return to the saucepan. Over low heat, stirring constantly with a wooden spoon, cook until the mixture heavily coats the back of the spoon. Stir in the melted chocolate and return to the bowl. Chill over ice cubes and cold water, replacing the ice cubes as they dissolve. Strain into a clean large bowl and stir in the bourbon, if desired.

3. Freeze in an ice cream maker according to the manufacturer's directions. Scrape into a large chilled container and freeze, covered, until needed.

Cinnamon Ice Cream

EQUIPMENT

Large nonreactive saucepan

Large stainless steel bowl

Whip

Wooden spoon

Fine-mesh strainer

Ice cream maker

INGREDIENTS

2 cups heavy cream

2 cups milk

2 cinnamon sticks

8 egg yolks

½ cup granulated sugar

TO PREPARE AHEAD

THROUGH STEP 2, REFRIGERATING, COVERED, OVERNIGHT AND FREEZING A FEW HOURS BEFORE SERVING. OR PREPARE THROUGH STEP 3, TRANSFERRING THE ICE CREAM TO THE REFRIGERATOR ABOUT 15 MINUTES BEFORE NEEDED.

MAKES ABOUT 1½ QUARTS

❦

We use Cinnamon Ice Cream at Spago to accompany our apple tarts and blueberry cobbler. We also place a scoop on our ice cream and cookie plates.

1. In a large heavy saucepan, combine the cream, milk, and cinnamon sticks. Bring to a boil, turn off heat, and let steep for 20 minutes.

2. In a large stainless steel bowl, using a whip or rotary beater, whip the egg yolks. Gradually whisk in the sugar until thoroughly combined. Slowly whisk the hot cream mixture into the egg yolks and then pour back into the saucepan. Over low heat, stirring constantly with a wooden spoon, cook until the mixture heavily coats the back of the spoon. Return to the bowl and chill over ice cubes and cold water.

3. Strain into a clean bowl and freeze in an ice cream maker according to the manufacturer's directions. When ready, spoon into a large chilled container, cover, and place in the freezer until needed.

4. To serve, place a scoop of ice cream next to a slice of Apple Pear Tarte Tatin (see page 128) and serve immediately. Or serve 2 or 3 small scoops in a bowl.

Eggnog Ice Cream

MAKES ABOUT 1½ QUARTS

🌰

Large nonreactive saucepan

2 large bowls, 1 stainless steel

Whip

Wooden spoon

Strainer

Ice cream maker

2 cups half-and-half

2 cups heavy cream

1 vanilla bean, split lengthwise

8 egg yolks

⅔ cup granulated sugar

1 teaspoon ground nutmeg, preferably freshly ground

¼ cup bourbon

¼ cup dark rum

TO PREPARE AHEAD

IN STEP 2, DO NOT STRAIN BEFORE YOU REFRIGERATE OVERNIGHT. STRAIN JUST BEFORE YOU POUR INTO THE ICE CREAM MAKER. OR PREPARE THROUGH STEP 3. REMOVE THE ICE CREAM FROM THE FREEZER AND PLACE IN THE REFRIGERATOR 15 TO 30 MINUTES BEFORE YOU ARE GOING TO SCOOP.

Kevin Ripley is the chef at Granita and this is an adaptation of his mother's recipe. A favorite at Christmas, eggnog ice cream accompanies Pumpkin Pie with Cranberry Marmalade (see page 112), Pecan Pie (see page 116), and Apple and Dried Cherry Turnovers (see page 100).

1. In a large nonreactive saucepan, bring to a boil the half-and-half, cream, and vanilla bean with its scrapings.

2. In a large stainless steel bowl, whisk the egg yolks. Gradually whisk in the sugar and nutmeg until thoroughly combined. Slowly whisk in the hot cream mixture and then return to the saucepan. Over low heat, stirring constantly with a wooden spoon, cook until the mixture heavily coats the back of the spoon. Return to the bowl and chill over ice cubes and cold water, replacing the ice cubes as they dissolve. Strain into a clean bowl and stir in the bourbon and rum.

3. Freeze in an ice cream maker according to the manufacturer's directions. Scrape into a large chilled container and place in the freezer, covered, until needed.

Honey Ice Cream

MAKES ABOUT 1½ QUARTS

EQUIPMENT

Large nonreactive saucepan

Stainless-steel bowl

Whip

Wooden spoon

Fine strainer

Ice cream maker

INGREDIENTS

2 cups heavy cream

2 cups milk

8 egg yolks

½ to ¾ cup honey (clover or orange), or to taste

TO PREPARE AHEAD

THROUGH STEP 2, REFRIGERATING, COVERED, OVERNIGHT OR UNTIL NEEDED, CHURNING 2 TO 3 HOURS BEFORE SERVING. OR PREPARE THROUGH STEP 3. REMOVE THE ICE CREAM FROM THE FREEZER AND PLACE IN THE REFRIGERATOR ABOUT 15 MINUTES BEFORE YOU ARE GOING TO SERVE IT.

*A*lone or paired with fruit and/or cookies, this is a "sweet" way to conclude your dinner.

1. In a large nonreactive saucepan, bring the cream and milk to a boil. In a large stainless-steel bowl, whisk the egg yolks. Gradually pour the heated liquid into the bowl, whisking all the while. Return to the saucepan and cook over medium heat, stirring with a wooden spoon, until the mixture coats the back of the spoon.

2. Remove from the heat and stir in the honey to taste. Pour into a clean bowl and chill over ice cubes and cold water.

3. Strain into the bowl of an ice cream maker and freeze according to the manufacturer's directions. Transfer to a clean chilled container and place in the freezer, covered, until needed.

Peach Ice Cream

MAKES ABOUT 2 QUARTS

EQUIPMENT

2 large nonreactive saucepans

Large stainless steel mixing bowl

Whip

Food processor

Ice cream maker

Wooden spoon

Fine strainer

INGREDIENTS

COMPOTE

3 pounds ripe (about 8 large) peaches, pitted and cut into slices

1¾ cups granulated sugar

1 whole cinnamon stick

¼ cup lemon juice

BASE

2 cups milk

2 cups heavy cream

1 vanilla bean, split lengthwise

8 egg yolks

½ cup granulated sugar

TO PREPARE AHEAD

THROUGH STEP 4.

S elect ripe peaches for the ice cream. As soon as the peaches are cooked, stir into the base and freeze. Fruit ice creams should always be frozen immediately.

1. Make the compote: In a large saucepan, combine the peaches, sugar, cinnamon stick, and lemon juice. Cook, over medium heat, stirring occasionally, until the peaches are very soft and mixture begins to thicken, about 30 minutes. Watch carefully during the last 10 minutes to prevent scorching.

2. Make the base: While the peaches are cooking, in a clean large saucepan, bring the milk, cream, and vanilla bean with its scrapings to a boil. In a large mixing bowl, whisk the egg yolks. Gradually whisk in the sugar until thoroughly combined. Slowly whisk in half the hot cream mixture and then pour back into the saucepan. Over low heat, stirring constantly with a wooden spoon, cook until mixture thickens and evenly coats the back of the spoon. (Do not overcook or the mixture will break and you will have to start over.)

3. Stir the peach compote into the base and combine thoroughly. Let steep about 10 minutes. Strain into the large mixing bowl, pressing down on the mixture to extract as much flavor as possible. Set the bowl in ice cubes and cold water to chill, stirring occasionally.

4. Freeze in an ice cream maker according to the manufacturer's directions. Transfer to a container, cover, and freeze. If made the night before, transfer ice cream from freezer to refrigerator about 30 minutes before serving.

5. To serve, arrange 1 or 2 scoops of ice cream in a chilled serving dish. Surround with slices of peeled fresh peaches and a few fresh raspberries and serve immediately.

Vanilla Ice Cream

MAKES ABOUT 1½ QUARTS

*V*anilla ice cream is not only a popular choice, but it is extremely versatile. With the addition of bits of chocolate, raisins, or chopped toffee, a new flavor is created. Using vanilla beans, rather than extract, gives the ice cream its unique taste.

1. In a large nonreactive saucepan, bring to a boil the milk, cream, and vanilla beans with their scrapings.

2. In a large stainless steel bowl, whisk the egg yolks. Gradually whisk in the sugar until thoroughly combined. Slowly whisk the hot cream mixture into the egg yolks and then return to the saucepan. Over low heat, stirring constantly with a wooden spoon, cook until the mixture heavily coats the back of the spoon. Pour into the bowl and cool over ice cubes and cold water.

3. Strain into an ice cream maker and freeze according to the manufacturer's directions. Scrape into a large chilled container and place in the freezer, covered, until needed.

Note: To make rum raisin ice cream, in a small saucepan, warm ½ cup raisins in ½ cup dark rum. Turn off heat and let steep until cool. Add to vanilla ice cream after it has been strained and is ready for the ice cream maker.

EQUIPMENT

Large nonreactive saucepan

Large stainless steel bowl

Whip

Wooden spoon

Strainer

Ice cream maker

INGREDIENTS

2 cups milk

2 cups heavy cream

2 vanilla beans, split lengthwise

8 egg yolks

½ cup granulated sugar

TO PREPARE AHEAD

THROUGH STEP 2, BOWL CAN BE REFRIGERATED, COVERED, OVERNIGHT. CONTINUE WITH RECIPE A FEW HOURS BEFORE SERVING. THROUGH STEP 3, PLACING ICE CREAM IN REFRIGERATOR 15 TO 30 MINUTES BEFORE SCOOPING.

Milk Chocolate Malt Ice Cream

MAKES ABOUT 1½ QUARTS

EQUIPMENT

Large nonreactive saucepan

Large and small heatproof bowls

Whip

Long-handled wooden spoon

Fine strainer

Ice cream maker

INGREDIENTS

2 cups milk

2 cups heavy cream

8 egg yolks

10 ounces milk chocolate, broken or cut into small chunks

½ cup Horlicks malt powder*

Hot Fudge Sauce (see page 231)

TO PREPARE AHEAD

THROUGH STEP 3, REFRIGERATING, COVERED, OVERNIGHT. CONTINUE WITH RECIPE THE NEXT DAY. OR PREPARE THROUGH STEP 4, PLACING CONTAINER IN REFRIGERATOR ABOUT 30 MINUTES BEFORE NEEDED.

Many years ago, when I first started to work at Spago, this was one of the first ice creams that Nancy Silverton taught me to make. It is so different and so delicious that I usually prepare this whenever I want a chocolate ice cream to complement dessert.

1. In a large nonreactive saucepan, bring the milk and cream to a boil.

2. In a large heatproof bowl, whisk the egg yolks. Gradually pour the heated liquid into the bowl, whisking all the while. Return to the saucepan and cook, over medium heat, stirring occasionally with a wooden spoon, until the mixture coats the back of the spoon.

3. Meanwhile, melt the chocolate in a small heatproof bowl set over simmering water. Scrape into the heated milk mixture and whisk until well combined. Remove 1 cup of liquid (you can use the same small bowl) and dissolve the malt powder in it. Return to the saucepan and mix well. Strain into a clean large bowl and chill over ice cubes and cold water.

4. Freeze in an ice cream maker according to the manufacturer's directions. Scrape into a chilled container and place in freezer until needed.

5. To serve, place 1 or 2 scoops in a small bowl. Spoon Hot Fudge Sauce over and top with a little shaved chocolate. Serve immediately. (You can pass whipped cream if you dare.)

*Horlicks malt powder can be found in specialty food stores or in many Asian markets.

Strawberry Ice Cream

MAKES ABOUT 2½ QUARTS

EQUIPMENT

2-quart nonreactive saucepan

Large saucepan

Large heatproof bowl

Whip

Wooden spoon

Strainer

Ice cream maker

INGREDIENTS

COMPOTE

4 pints strawberries, hulled

1¾ cups granulated sugar

¼ cup lemon juice (4 medium lemons)

1 vanilla bean, split lengthwise

ICE CREAM BASE

2 cups heavy cream

2 cups milk

1 vanilla bean, split lengthwise

8 egg yolks

½ cup granulated sugar

TO PREPARE AHEAD

THROUGH STEP 4,

Make this when strawberries are very ripe. To develop the fullest flavor, prepare the base the day before and refrigerate, covered. Then continue with the recipe the next day.

1. Make the compote: In a 2-quart nonreactive saucepan, combine all the compote ingredients. Cook over medium-high heat, stirring occasionally, about 45 minutes, skimming off foam that forms on top. Lower heat and cook until compote thickens, 15 minutes longer. Set aside.

2. Make the ice cream base: In a large saucepan, bring to a boil the cream, milk, and vanilla bean with its scrapings.

3. Meanwhile, in a large heatproof bowl, whisk together the egg yolks and ½ cup sugar. Whisk the cream mixture into the yolks and return to the saucepan. Cook, over medium heat, stirring all the while with a wooden spoon, until the mixture coats the back of the spoon. Strain quickly into a clean bowl and stir in the reserved compote. Chill over ice cubes and water.

4. Freeze in an ice cream maker according to manufacturer's directions. Scrape into 1 or 2 chilled containers, cover with plastic wrap, and place in the freezer. If ice cream is frozen overnight, remove from the freezer to the refrigerator about 1 hour before serving.

5. To serve, place 1 or 2 scoops of ice cream in a chilled bowl. Pass bowls of softly whipped cream and sliced fresh strawberries.

White Chocolate Mint Ice Cream with White Chocolate Mint Truffles

MAKES ABOUT 1½ QUARTS

*T*he white chocolate mint truffles are softer than other truffles in this book so they will not harden when frozen in the ice cream. They are added after the ice cream has been churned, just before going into the freezer.

1. In a large saucepan, bring to a boil the cream, milk, and vanilla bean with its scrapings.

2. Meanwhile, in a large heatproof bowl, whisk together the egg yolks and sugar. Whisk in half the cream mixture and pour back into the saucepan. Cook, over medium heat, stirring all the while with a wooden spoon, until the mixture coats the back of the spoon. Remove from heat and stir in the mint leaves. Let steep until *very* flavorful, about 30 minutes. (The amount of time depends on the strength of the mint leaves.)

3. Melt the chocolate in a clean large heatproof bowl set over simmering water. Pour the steeped mint mixture into the chocolate and stir to combine. Immediately strain into a clean large bowl, pressing down on the leaves to extract all the flavor possible. Chill over ice cubes and water.

4. Freeze in an ice cream maker according to the manufacturer's directions. Remove the ice cream from the machine to a large bowl. Gently fold the white chocolate mint truffles into the ice cream, a few at a time. Transfer to 1 or 2 chilled containers, cover, and place in the freezer. If ice cream is frozen overnight, remove from the freezer to the refrigerator 30 to 40 minutes before serving.

EQUIPMENT

Large nonreactive saucepan

1 or 2 large heatproof bowls

Whip

Wooden spoon

Strainer

Ice cream maker

INGREDIENTS

2 cups heavy cream

2 cups milk

1 vanilla bean, split lengthwise

8 egg yolks

¼ cup granulated sugar

2 cups chopped (1 large or 2 small bunches) fresh mint leaves

8 ounces white chocolate, cut into small pieces

White Chocolate Mint Truffles (see opposite; use as many or as few as you wish)

TO PREPARE AHEAD

THROUGH STEP 3, BASE CAN BE MADE 1 DAY AHEAD AND REFRIGERATED, COVERED. OR PREPARE THROUGH STEP 4.

5. To serve, place 1 or 2 scoops of ice cream in a chilled bowl. Pour a little crème de menthe over, if desired, and decorate with a mint leaf or a small sprig of mint leaves.

White Chocolate Mint Truffles

MAKES 45 TO 50 SMALL TRUFFLES

EQUIPMENT

Large heatproof bowl

Small saucepan

Wooden spoon

Strainer

Whip

Shallow pan

Small bowl

Baking tray

Parchment paper

Small melon baller, 1 inch in diameter

INGREDIENTS

½ pound white chocolate, cut into small pieces

½ cup, packed, fresh mint leaves (green or white)

¼ cup heavy cream

2 tablespoons crème de menthe

6 tablespoons (¾ stick) unsalted butter, cut into small pieces

1. Make the truffles: In a large heatproof bowl set over gently simmering water, melt the chocolate. When chocolate is almost melted, turn off the heat and let stand until completely melted, stirring occasionally.

2. Meanwhile, in a small saucepan, steep mint leaves in cream and crème de menthe until liquid is very flavorful (amount of time depends upon the strength of the mint leaves). Then bring just to a simmer, strain, pressing down on the mint leaves to give as much flavor as possible, and whisk into the melted chocolate. Place the pieces of butter around the warm mixture and let the butter melt. When melted, stir to mix well. Pour mixture into a shallow pan, giving you a 1-inch-thick layer of chocolate. Cool completely and then refrigerate or freeze until very firm.

3. Form the truffles: Have a small bowl of very hot water ready and replace the water as it cools down. Line a baking tray with parchment paper. Remove truffle base from the refrigerator or freezer. Before scooping out a ball of chocolate, dip the melon baller into the hot water, shaking to remove any excess water. Scoop out a truffle, tapping the melon baller on a firm surface to release the truffle. Quickly

(continued)

WHITE CHOCOLATE MINT TRUFFLES *(continued)*

roll between the palms of your hands and place on the pre-pared baking tray. You will have to wash your hands in cold water often to prevent the chocolate from sticking to your hands. Repeat this procedure until all the balls have been scooped and rolled. If the truffle base begins to soften too much, refrigerate or freeze until firm and then continue to scoop out the truffles. Refrigerate or freeze until needed.

Vanilla Parfait with Strawberry Sauce

SERVES 10

EQUIPMENT

10 x 15 x ¾-inch jelly-roll pan

Wax or parchment paper

Electric mixer

2 medium nonreactive saucepans

Double boiler or heatproof bowl

Wooden spoon

Fine-mesh strainer

Offset spatula

Medium bowl

4-inch cookie or biscuit cutter

I served this on Valentine's Day, cutting out the parfait with a heart-shaped cookie cutter. It made a *lovely* dessert.

1. Butter a 10 x 15 x ¾-inch jelly-roll pan. Line with wax or parchment paper.

2. Make the parfait: In an electric mixer, using the paddle or beaters, beat the egg yolks and sugar on high speed until thick and pale yellow, about 10 minutes.

3. Meanwhile, in a medium saucepan, combine 1¼ cups heavy cream, half-and-half, and the vanilla bean with its scrap-ings and bring to a boil. Turn off heat and let steep, covered, about 10 minutes.

PARFAIT

12 egg yolks

½ cup granulated sugar

2¼ cups heavy cream

1¼ cups half-and-half

1 vanilla bean, split lengthwise

2 ounces white chocolate, cut into small pieces

STRAWBERRY SAUCE

2 pints fresh strawberries or 1 pound frozen sliced strawberries, thawed

½ cup granulated sugar

2 tablespoons dark rum

1 medium cinnamon stick

TO PREPARE AHEAD

THROUGH STEP 7, PARFAIT AND SAUCE CAN BE MADE 1 DAY AHEAD, THE ROUNDS CUT OUT WHEN READY TO SERVE.

4. In a double boiler or small heatproof bowl set over simmering water, melt the chocolate. Remove from heat and set aside in a warm spot.

5. Reduce mixer speed to low and slowly pour the hot cream mixture into the yolk mixture. Turn off machine and scrape contents of bowl into saucepan. Over medium heat, bring to a boil, stirring constantly with a wooden spoon, the spoon always touching the bottom of the pan to prevent burning. Immediately strain through a fine strainer into a clean mixing bowl. Add the melted chocolate and mix on low to medium speed until the outside of the bowl is completely cool to the touch, about 20 minutes.

6. Whip the remaining 1 cup of heavy cream until firm and refrigerate, covered, until needed. When the parfait is cool, fold in the whipped cream. Pour into the prepared jelly-roll pan and, using an offset spatula, spread evenly in the pan. Carefully place on a flat surface in freezer and freeze, covered, 6 to 8 hours or overnight.

7. Make the strawberry sauce: In a clean medium saucepan, combine all the ingredients and cook, over medium heat, until thickened, stirring occasionally with a wooden spoon. Remove cinnamon stick and transfer to medium bowl to cool. Refrigerate, covered, until needed.

8. To serve, remove parfait from freezer and, with a 4-inch cookie cutter, cut out 10 circles. Place 1 parfait round on each of 10 chilled dessert plates. Spoon 2 tablespoons strawberry sauce over each parfait, spooning additional sauce along one side.

Red, White, and Blue Parfait

SERVES 8 TO 10

EQUIPMENT

Cardboard and aluminum foil

10 x 3 x 4-inch loaf pan

Wax or parchment paper

Food processor

Fine-mesh strainer

*1 small, 1 large, and
2 medium bowls*

*Small and large nonreactive
saucepans*

Electric mixer

Whip

Large bowl

Metal spatula

INGREDIENTS

*2 pint baskets fresh raspberries plus
a few extra as garnish*

*1 pint basket fresh blueberries plus
a few extra as garnish*

*½ cup plus 2 tablespoons
granulated sugar*

2¾ cups heavy cream

12 egg yolks

1¼ cups half-and-half

1 vanilla bean, split lengthwise

*2 ounces white chocolate, cut into
small pieces and melted*

One year, Wolfgang did a *Good Morning America* show around a Fourth of July theme. He wanted a dessert with a red, white, and blue motif for the occasion. Consequently, this parfait!

1. Measure a piece of cardboard to fit the top of the loaf pan, about 10 x 4 inches, and wrap with aluminum foil. Set aside. Coat a 10 x 3 x 4 inch loaf pan with vegetable spray. Cut wax or parchment paper to fit the sides and bottom of the loaf pan and press into the pan. Set aside.

2. Make the raspberry puree: In a food processor fitted with the steel blade, puree the raspberries until liquid. Strain into a medium bowl. Set aside ¼ cup for the red layer, reserving the remaining puree, covered, in a small bowl until needed.

3. In a small saucepan, combine the blueberries with 2 tablespoons water and 2 tablespoons sugar. Over low heat, bring to a boil. (Cooking the blueberries gives them a nicer color.) In the clean bowl of a food processor fitted with the steel blade, puree the blueberries, strain into the second medium bowl, and set aside.

4. Whip 1½ cups heavy cream to soft peaks and refrigerate, covered, until needed. You should have about 3 cups whipped cream.

5. In the large bowl of an electric mixer, using whip or beaters, beat the egg yolks and the remaining ½ cup sugar until thick, about 10 minutes. Start on slow speed and as mixture thickens, turn speed to high.

TO PREPARE AHEAD

THROUGH STEP 8

6. Meanwhile, in a large nonreactive saucepan, combine the remaining 1¼ cups heavy cream, half-and-half, and the vanilla bean with its scrapings and bring to a boil. Turn off heat and let steep, covered, for about 10 minutes.

7. Turn mixer speed to low and slowly pour the hot cream mixture into the thickened yolks. Turn off the machine and scrape the contents of the bowl back into the saucepan. Bring to a boil, stirring constantly. Strain through a fine strainer into a large clean bowl. Immediately stir in the melted white chocolate. (You should have about 3¾ cups of mixture.) Divide the mixture evenly. To make the red layer, stir 1¼ cups into the bowl with raspberry puree. To make the blue layers, stir 1¼ cups into the bowl with blueberry puree. Pour 1¼ cups into the empty bowl. Stir each mixture until very smooth. Refrigerate, covered, until chilled. Remove the whipped cream and the 3 bowls from the refrigerator. Whisk the cream a few times, then fold 1 cup whipped cream into each bowl. Each layer of the mold needs to set up before you add another layer, so refrigerate until needed, but whisk the contents of each bowl before pouring into the mold.

8. Assemble the parfait: Pour the blueberry puree into the pan and set in the freezer until firm, about 2 hours. Remove from freezer, pour in the plain mixture, and return to freezer for 2 more hours until firm. Again remove from freezer, and pour in the raspberry puree. Cover and freeze overnight.

9. Unmold the parfait: Invert the parfait onto the reserved foil-covered piece of cardboard. Wet a towel with very hot water and wring well to remove all the water. Place the hot towel around the pan for a few seconds and tap the pan gently until the parfait separates from the pan and comes out onto the cardboard. (You may have to repeat wetting the towel.) Work

(continued)

RED, WHITE, AND BLUE PARFAIT *(continued)*

as quickly as you can so that the parfait doesn't melt. Return to the freezer until ready to serve. Chill 8 to 10 dessert plates.

10. To serve, place parfait and chilled plates on a flat work space. Ladle a little raspberry puree onto a plate and mirror the plate by tilting the plate in all directions until a thin coating of sauce covers the surface. Repeat with the remaining sauce and plates. Place a metal spatula under hot running water and smooth sides by running the spatula around the sides of the parfait. Cut into ½-inch slices with a warm knife (between slices run hot water over blade). Arrange 1 slice of parfait in the center of each mirrored plate. Garnish with whole raspberries and blueberries and serve immediately.

Resources

AMERICAN SPOON FOOD
P.O. Box 566
Petoskey, MI 49770
800-222-5886

Flours, preserves, dried berries, nuts, and honeys

AVERY SERVICES
905 E. Second Street
Los Angeles, CA 90001
213-624-7832

Gourmet cookware, small and large appliances

BRIDGE KITCHENWARE
214 E. 52nd Street
New York, NY 10022
212-688-4220

Gourmet cookware

CAVIAR & FINE FOODS
321 N. Robertson
West Hollywood, CA 90048
310-271-6300

Imported chocolate and gourmet groceries

CHEF'S CATALOG
3005 N. Clark Street
Chicago, IL 60657
312-327-5210

Gourmet cookware and small appliances

DEAN & DeLUCA
560 Broadway
New York, NY 10017
212-431-1691

Specialty foods and gourmet cookware

GOURMAND
5873 Blackwelder
Culver City, CA 90230
310-839-9222

Imported chocolate and gourmet groceries

R. HIRT
3000 Chrysler
Detroit, MI 48207
313-831-2020

Dried fruits

S. E. RYKOFF CO.
P.O. Box 21467, Market Street Station
Los Angeles, CA 90021
800-421-9873

Specialty foods and gourmet cookware

SOMIS NUTHOUSE
4475 Los Angeles Avenue
Somis, CA 93066
805-386-1211

Nuts

VANILLA SAFFRON IMPORTS
949 Valencia Street
San Francisco, CA 94110
415-648-8990

Vanilla beans

VAN REX
13365 Estelle Street
Corona, CA 91719
909-273-9980

Imported chocolate and gourmet groceries

WILLIAMS-SONOMA
P.O. Box 7546
San Franciso, CA 94120
415-421-4242

Specialty foods, gourmet cookware

ZABAR'S
2245 Broadway
New York, NY 10024
212-787-2000

*Specialty foods, gourmet cookware, small
appliances*

CREDITS

Photographer
BRENT LINDSTROM, *San Francisco*

Food and Prop Stylist
ERÉZ

Associate Photographer
J. MICHAEL TUCKER

Props
V. BREIER GALLERY, *San Francisco*
SUE FISHER KING, *San Francisco*
JASPER BYRON, *San Francisco*
F. DORIAN, INC., *San Francisco*
BEAVER BROS. ANTIQUES, *San Francisco*
BELLOCCHIO, *San Francisco, for their beautiful fabrics*
R. H., *San Francisco*
GUMP'S, *San Francisco*
OPUZEN DESIGN, *San Francisco, for Patza's most amazing hand-painted fabrics*
Special thanks to JOSEPHINE RIGG, *for her mother's silver collection*

Index

Hazelnut Mousse, 52–53
Italian Meringue, 39
Lemon Buttercream, 41–42
fruits, *see specific fruits*

G

garnish, *xx*
gelatin, *xxv*
ginger
Candied Fresh, 190
Spice Cookies, 207
Tiramisù, 71–72
Glaze, All-purpose Chocolate, 20
glazing, *xx*
grapefruit
Peel, Candied, 188–89
Sorbet with Vodka, 243
Grapes, Sorbet with Apples and, 239

H

hazelnut(s)
Chocolate Hazelnut Truffles, 182–83
Mousse frosting, 51–52
Pear Hazelnut Sour Cream Pie, 106–7
honey, *xxv–xxvi*
Honey Ice Cream, 251
Hot Fudge Sauce, 231

I

ice baths, *xx–xxi*
ice cream
Chocolate, 248
Milk Chocolate Malt, 254
Cinnamon, 249
Eggnog, 250
Honey, 251
Parfaits
Red, White, and Blue, 260–62
Vanilla, with Strawberry Sauce, 258–59

Peach, 252–53
Spago Banana Split, 230–31
Strawberry, 255
Sundaes, Blond Brownie, 159–60
Vanilla, 253
White Chocolate Mint, with White Chocolate Mint Truffles, 256–58
Individual Pear Tarts with Phyllo Layers, 130–31
Italian Meringue, 39

L

leavening agents, *xxvi*
lemon(s)
Buttermilk Cake, 40
with Lemon Buttercream, 41–42
Buttermilk Pound Cake, 176
Chiffon Cake, 43–44
Caramelized, with Fresh Berries and Crème Brûlée, 45–46
Curd, 119
Tart, 118–19
Linzer Torte, Strawberry, 110–11

M

macadamia nut(s)
Brittle, 61
Butter Cookies, 205
Cheesecake with Macadamia Brittle, 60–61
Tart with Chocolate Pâté Sucrée, 114–15
Macaroons, Apricot Coconut, 220
Marbled Brownies, 162–63
Mary's Cartoon Character Cake, 23–28
Cream Cheese Frosting, 26
Double Recipe Chocolate Chiffon Cake, 24–25
preparing and decorating, 27–28

About the Authors

MARY BERGIN started her culinary career in 1981 and became head pastry chef at Spago in 1987, where her duties included designing the desserts for the late Irving "Swifty" Lazar's annual Oscar night parties. In 1992, Mary moved to Las Vegas to open the new Spago restaurant in the Forum Shops at Caesars Palace. Since 1989, Mary has appeared several times on ABC's nationally syndicated *Home Show* to demonstrate her famous desserts. She has consulted on and contributed to various cookbooks, including Wolfgang Puck's *Adventures in the Kitchen*. Her recipes and desserts have been featured in *Bon Appétit*, the *Los Angeles Times*, and *The New York Times*, and on ABC's *Good Morning America*. She encourages her two children, Jackie and Anthony, to play an active role in tasting and experimenting in the kitchen.

JUDY GETHERS grew up in and around restaurants. Her family has owned Ratner's, a landmark restaurant in New York City, since 1905. Her first cookbook was *The World Famous Ratner's Meatless Cookbook*. Since then she has written *The Fabulous Gourmet Food Processor Cookbook, Italian Country Cooking,* and *The Sandwich Book.* She cofounded Ma Cuisine, a cooking school associated with Ma Maison restaurant. She worked with Mark Peel, chef and owner of Campanile Restaurant, on his latest cookbook. She collaborated with Wolfgang Puck on his most recent cookbook, *Adventures in the Kitchen,* and is now working with him on a new book.